Quantum Image Processing

Fei Yan • Salvador E. Venegas-Andraca

Quantum Image Processing

 Springer

Fei Yan
Changchun University of Science and
Technology
Changchun, China

Salvador E. Venegas-Andraca
Tecnologico de Monterrey
Escuela de Ingenieria y Ciencias
Monterrey, Mexico

ISBN 978-981-32-9333-5   ISBN 978-981-32-9331-1   (eBook)
https://doi.org/10.1007/978-981-32-9331-1

This Springer imprint is published by the registered company Springer Nature Singapore Pte Ltd.
The registered company address is: 152 Beach Road, #21-01/04 Gateway East, Singapore 189721, Singapore

Preface

Quantum information science is a deeply interdisciplinary field that involves physics, mathematics, and computer science. It is devoted to finding methods to exploit quantum mechanical effects in nature, notably superposition and entanglement, to perform information processing beyond the limits of conventional computation. Over the past several decades, various research groups around the world have strived to achieve the ambitious goal of building a quantum computer that could dramatically improve computational power for particular tasks.

Responding to the growing need to extract information from images and video, image processing is a fundamental task in many branches of science and engineering. Due to the restricted architecture of classical computers and the computational complexity of state-of-the-art classical algorithms in image processing and its applications, developing efficient algorithms to store and manipulate visual information has become an important and challenging research area.

Quantum image processing focuses on quantum algorithms for storing, processing, and retrieving visual information. Due to some of the astounding properties inherent to quantum information, for instance, computational parallelism, it is anticipated that quantum image processing technologies will offer capabilities and performance that are currently unrivaled by their traditional equivalents in areas such as computing speed, tamperproof security, and minimal storage requirements.

This book is divided into seven chapters. In Chap. 1, the key fundamentals of quantum computation and information are reviewed, and the history of quantum image processing is introduced. The widely used quantum image representations and their well-designed operations are presented in Chaps. 2 and 3. The outline of quantum image security technologies and a few quantum image understanding algorithms are suggested in Chaps. 4 and 5. The two emerging subtopics of quantum movies and quantum audio are elaborated in Chap. 6. Chapter 7 discusses open questions identified in the literature, along with future development trends in quantum image processing.

It is hoped that this book offers a rigorous introduction to quantum image processing and some thought-provoking snapshots of prospective developments. The completion of this book relied greatly on the research achievements published in the field and the two bibles: *Quantum Computation and Quantum Information* (Michael A. Nielsen et al.) and *Digital Image Processing* (Rafael C. Gonzalez et al.).

Immense gratitude is due to the emeritus professor of the Tokyo Institute of Technology, Kaoru Hirota, and Professor Zhengang Jiang at Changchun University of Science and Technology for their enlightenment and ongoing help that turned this book from an idea into reality. In addition, special commendation goes to Kehan Chen, Nianqiao Li, and Shan Zhao for their contributions to the timely and thorough organization of the figures and references in the book.

This work is supported by the National Natural Science Foundation of China (No. 61502053). SEVA gratefully acknowledges the financial support of CONACyT (SNI 41594) and Fronteras de la Ciencia (1007). Additionally, SEVA dedicates his work to his dearest wife Lourdes and beloved daughter Renata, his eternal gratitude for their love, support, and patience.

Being subject to the limits of the authors' ability and because quantum image processing is still in its primary stage, it is hard to avoid errors and omissions. The authors apologize for this and welcome criticism and suggestions.

Changchun, China   Fei Yan
Monterrey, Mexico   Salvador E. Venegas-Andraca

Contents

Chapter 1
Introduction and Overview

Quantum computation and quantum information comprise the study of information processing tasks that can be accomplished using quantum mechanical systems [3]. Goals include to study how information is represented and communicated using quantum states, and how to describe and handle the corruption of quantum and classical information [38]. Quantum computers, quantum cryptography, and quantum teleportation are among the most celebrated topics that have emerged from this field. These techniques rely distinctively on the quantum properties such as uncertainty, interference, and entanglement [4, 59].

The disciplines of computer science and computer engineering have transformed every aspect of human endeavors [50]. In these fields, exciting and cutting-edge research into new computational models, materials, and techniques for building computing hardware has been broached and/or realized [27]. Novel methods have been proposed to speed up certain tasks, and to build bridges between computer science and other scientific fields, allowing scientists to think of natural phenomena as computational procedures and simulate them [52, 56].

In its canonical form, theoretical computer science takes no account of the physical properties of the devices used to perform computational or information processing tasks [35]. This could be perceived as a drawback because the behavior of any physical device used for computation or information processing must ultimately be predicted within the ambit of the laws of physics [28].

In 1982, Feynman proposed a novel computational model [19], quantum computation, which was based on the principles of quantum physics. Quantum computation constitutes a truly innovative paradigm of computation, which offers new perspectives in many regards, among them future encouraging scenarios for high performance computing as well as novel algorithms that solve seemingly intractable problems in today's advanced classical computer models and technologies. The mathematical formulation and physical realization of quantum technology ensure improved miniaturization, massively accelerated performance of certain tasks, and new levels of secure communication, information processing, and ultra-precise

© Springer Nature Singapore Pte Ltd. 2020
F. Yan, S. E. Venegas-Andraca, *Quantum Image Processing*,
https://doi.org/10.1007/978-981-32-9331-1_1

measurement [10]. These are some of the theoretical discoveries and promising conjectures that have positioned quantum computation as a key element in modern science.

In addition, a growing number of quantum computing applications in several branches of science and technology have been suggested. One such emerging area is the field of quantum image processing (QIMP) [51]. In its early stage, the field is bedeviled with many questions [33]. To begin, what is the best way to represent images on quantum computers, and how one should prepare, process, and retrieve them? Then, to really say the field has matured, one should be capable of performing some basic image processing tasks and realizing some high-level applications using quantum computing hardware, before gradually accomplishing more advanced and robust image processing tasks. The advances highlighted in the following chapters indicate a promising role for QIMP in facilitating the acceleration, security, and integrity of traditional (digital) image processing tasks [60].

The discussion in this chapter is twofold. First, some fundamental concepts and theories of quantum computation and information are introduced. Further on, the birth and development of QIMP as a background are discussed.

1.1 Quantum Computation and Information

A recent study [37] echoed a longstanding claim that quantum computing technologies would usher in unprecedented accuracy and sophistication to solve numerous problems considered intractable using the best of today's classical (i.e., digital or nonquantum) computing resources. While acceptable large-scale quantum devices are still unavailable, the immense potential of quantum computing has attracted interest and investments aimed at the commercialization of its hardware and software. These make quantum computation and information become a cynosure among emerging computing paradigms [65].

1.1.1 Quantum Computers

An important law in the computer industry, Moore's law states that the number of transistors in a dense integrated circuit doubles roughly every 2 years [8]. This observation of Gordon Moore, co-founder of the Intel Corporation, proved to be accurate for several decades, and it has been used to guide long-term planning and to set targets for research and development in the semiconductor industry [15]. Advances in digital electronics are strongly tied to Moore's law, including quality-adjusted microprocessor prices, memory capacity, sensors, and even the number and size of pixels in digital cameras. Digital electronics have been consistent contributors to world economic growth in the late twentieth and early twenty-first centuries. Thus, Moore's law embodies a driver of technological and social change, productivity, and economic growth [30].

Moore's law comprises an observation and projection of an historical trend and is not a physical or natural law. Although the semiconductor industry's growth rate was steady from 1975 until approximately 2012, it was faster during the first decade of the new millennium. In general, it does not sound logic to extrapolate from an historical growth rate to an undefined future. For example, in the 2010 update to the International Technology Roadmap for Semiconductors it was predicted that growth would slow around 2013. Moreover, Gordon Moore himself, in 2015, foresaw that the rate of progress would reach saturation: "I see Moore's law dying here in the next decade or so" [11]. This is mainly because transistors are made of silicon. According to theoretical physicist Michio Kaku, when transistors are too closely packed (layers are 20 atoms across now, and this will likely decrease to five atoms), there will be two main problems [29]:

- The heat generated will be sufficient to melt the silicon.
- Quantum theory will dominate in the resultant small distance between atoms. From the Heisenberg uncertainty principle, it will be impossible to accurately locate electrons, which will result in leakage.

Therefore, while Moore's law gave good predictions, for further advancement, one should develop new technology and quantum computers are future candidates. A quantum computer is a device that performs quantum computing [31]. Such a computer is different from binary digital electronic computers based on transistors. Although common digital computing requires that the data be encoded into binary digits (bits), each of which is always in one of two definite states (0 or 1), quantum computation uses quantum bits or qubits, which can be in *superpositions* of states, i.e., linear combinations of their basis states.

As of 2019, quantum computer development is still in its infancy, but experiments are being performed in which quantum computational operations are executed on a very small number of quantum bits. Practical and theoretical research continues, and many governments and military agencies are funding quantum computing research in the hope of developing quantum computers for civilian, business, trade, environmental, and national security purposes.

Several significant advances have occurred in recent years. In January 2017, since its second-generation system (the 512-qubit D-Wave Two in May 2013) was bought by Google and NASA for research and practical use, D-Wave is reportedly selling a 2,000-qubit quantum computer (the D-Wave 2000Q [13], see Fig. 1.1), whose special-purpose processor was designed to implement quantum annealing, rather than operating as a universal-gate quantum computer [12]. In December 2017, Microsoft released a preview version of a Quantum Development Kit, including a programming language, *Q#*, which can be used to write programs for an emulated quantum computer [36]. In late 2017 and early 2018, IBM, Intel, and Google reported testing quantum processors containing 50, 49, and 72 qubits, respectively, all realized using superconducting circuits [41]. These circuits are approaching the number of qubits for which simulation of their quantum dynamics is expected to

Fig. 1.1 D-Wave 2000Q
quantum computer

become prohibitive on classical computers, although it has been argued that further improvements in error rates are required to put classical simulation out of reach. In February 2018, scientists reported the discovery of a new form of light, which possibly involves polaritons, which could be useful in the development of quantum computers [34]. In July 2018, a team led by the University of Sydney achieved the world's first multi-qubit demonstration of a quantum chemistry calculation performed on a system of trapped ions, one of the leading hardware platforms in the race to develop a universal quantum computer [26].

Large-scale quantum computers would theoretically be able to solve certain problems much more quickly than any classical computers that use even the best current algorithms, such as integer factorization using Shor's algorithm [48] and the simulation of quantum many-body systems [57]. There exist quantum algorithms, such as Simon's algorithm [49], that run faster than any possible probabilistic classical algorithm. A classical computer could in principle (with exponential resources) simulate a quantum algorithm, as quantum computation does not violate the Church–Turing thesis [66]. However, quantum computers may be able to efficiently solve problems that are not feasible on classical computers.

1.1.2 Quantum Bits and Quantum Registers

1.1.2.1 Quantum Bits

Analogous to the fundamental concept of classical computation and information, the bit, a quantum bit (or qubit) is the smallest unit of information in a quantum system [38]. The difference between bits and qubits is that a qubit can be in a superposition state, which can be described as a unit vector in two-dimensional Hilbert space (see appendix for more mathematical descriptions). As shown in Fig. 1.2, the vector can

Fig. 1.2 Diagram of a
qubit's superposition state

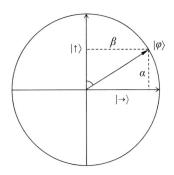

always be written as $|\varphi\rangle = \alpha|\uparrow\rangle + \beta|\rightarrow\rangle$, where $|\uparrow\rangle$ and $|\rightarrow\rangle$ are orthogonal
basis states and α and β are complex numbers for probability amplitudes. The
probabilities for $|\varphi\rangle$ to be in the $|\uparrow\rangle$ and $|\rightarrow\rangle$ states are, respectively, $|\alpha|^2$ and
$|\beta|^2$, where $|\alpha|^2 + |\beta|^2 = 1$. Geometrically, this can be interpreted as the condition
that the qubit's state is *normalized* to length 1 [38].

When $|\varphi\rangle$ is projected onto $|\uparrow\rangle$, $|\varphi\rangle$ becomes $|\varphi\rangle_\uparrow (= \alpha|\uparrow\rangle)$, which is equivalent
to measuring $|\varphi\rangle$ in the $|\uparrow\rangle$ direction. Similarly, when $|\varphi\rangle$ is projected onto $|\rightarrow\rangle$,
$|\varphi\rangle$ becomes $|\varphi\rangle_\rightarrow (= \beta|\rightarrow\rangle)$, which is equivalent to measuring $|\varphi\rangle$ in the $|\rightarrow\rangle$
direction. Therefore, when observing or measuring a qubit in a superposition state,
the state will be disturbed and changed; this phenomenon is called *collapse*. If one
lets $|\uparrow\rangle = |0\rangle$ and $|\rightarrow\rangle = |1\rangle$, then $|\varphi\rangle = \alpha|0\rangle + \beta|1\rangle$, so the states $|0\rangle$ and $|1\rangle$ are
known as computational basis states, and they form an orthonormal basis for this
vector space.

If one lets $u \in \{0, 1\}$, then $|u\rangle$ is a column vector (known as *ket*) with two
components in two-dimensional Hilbert space; that is, $|0\rangle = \begin{pmatrix} 1 \\ 0 \end{pmatrix}$ and $|1\rangle = \begin{pmatrix} 0 \\ 1 \end{pmatrix}$.
In addition, $\langle u|$ is the conjugate transpose of $|u\rangle$ and is a row vector (known as *bra*)
with two components: $\langle 0| = \begin{pmatrix} 1 & 0 \end{pmatrix}$ and $\langle 1| = \begin{pmatrix} 0 & 1 \end{pmatrix}$. If one lets $v \in \{0, 1\}$, then
$\langle u|v\rangle (= \langle u||v\rangle)$ is the inner product of $|u\rangle$ and $|v\rangle$. The inner product is a scalar,
for example, $\langle 0|0\rangle = \langle 1|1\rangle = 1$ and $\langle 0|1\rangle = \langle 1|0\rangle = 0$. It is interesting that *bra* and
ket constitute bra(c)ket, so that when "$\langle$" and "$\rangle$" match to form a complete bracket,
the bracket as a whole always represents a number [42].

In addition to the inner product, *bra* and *ket* may also be multiplied in reverse
order, and one can call $|u\rangle\langle v|$ the outer product of $|u\rangle$ and $|v\rangle$; it is an operator in
the matrix form. If $|0\rangle\langle 0|$ is operated on $|\varphi\rangle$, the result of $\alpha|0\rangle$ is obtained, which
indicates that $|0\rangle\langle 0|$ has extracted the $|0\rangle$ component from $|\varphi\rangle$, or that $|0\rangle\langle 0|$ projects
$|\varphi\rangle$ onto $|0\rangle$, and $|\varphi\rangle$ is measured in the $|0\rangle$ direction. Similarly, $|1\rangle\langle 1|$ has extracted
the $|1\rangle$ component from $|\varphi\rangle$, or that $|1\rangle\langle 1|$ projects $|\varphi\rangle$ onto $|1\rangle$, and $|\varphi\rangle$ is measured
in the $|1\rangle$ direction.

Even though a qubit can represent many states, when it is observed, the
measurement results can only be either 0 or 1, and each result exists with a certain
probability [38]. The measurement operation is represented by a "meter" symbol,
as shown in Fig. 1.3. As previously described, this operation converts a single-qubit

Fig. 1.3 Quantum circuit
symbol for measurement

state $|\varphi\rangle$ to a probabilistic classical bit M (distinguished from a qubit by drawing it as a double-line wire).

1.1.2.2 Quantum Registers

A quantum register is a system comprising multiple qubits [38]. It is the quantum analog of the classical processor register. Quantum computers perform calculations by manipulating qubits within a quantum register. While an n-size classical register can store a single value of the 2^n possibilities spanned by n bits, a quantum register can store all 2^n possibilities spanned by n qubits.

The state of a quantum register is the tensor product of n qubits' states. The tensor product is a way of combining vector spaces to form larger vector spaces [38]. This formation is crucial in understanding the quantum mechanics of multiparticle systems. The notation for the tensor product, $\otimes$, is used to express the composition of quantum systems. The short notation for the tensor product $|u\rangle \otimes |v\rangle$ of two vectors or two kets, $|u\rangle$ and $|v\rangle$, is $|uv\rangle$ or $|u\rangle|v\rangle$, and $A^{\otimes n} = A \otimes A \otimes \cdots \otimes A$ denotes the tensor product of a matrix A for n times.

Suppose there are two qubits in a quantum register. A two-qubit system has four computational basis states denoted as $|00\rangle, |01\rangle, |10\rangle$, and $|11\rangle$. A pair of qubits can also exist in superpositions of these four states, so the quantum state of two qubits involves associating a complex coefficient with each computational basis state, such that

$$|\varphi\rangle = \alpha_{00}|00\rangle + \alpha_{01}|01\rangle + \alpha_{10}|10\rangle + \alpha_{11}|11\rangle. \tag{1.1}$$

Similar to the case for a single qubit, the measurement result 00, 01, 10, and 11 occurs with probability $|\alpha_{00}|^2, |\alpha_{01}|^2, |\alpha_{10}|^2, |\alpha_{11}|^2$, and these probabilities sum to one. For a two-qubit system, one could measure just a subset of the qubits, say the first qubit. Measuring the first qubit alone gives 0 with probability $|a_{00}|^2 + |a_{01}|^2$, leaving the post-measurement state:

$$|\varphi'\rangle = \frac{\alpha_{00}|00\rangle + \alpha_{01}|01\rangle}{\sqrt{|a_{00}|^2 + |a_{01}|^2}}. \tag{1.2}$$

If the state of multiple qubits cannot be presented as a tensor product, then these qubits are in the *entangled* state [38]. For instance, $|\varphi\rangle_A = \frac{1}{\sqrt{2}}(|00\rangle + |11\rangle)$ and $|\varphi\rangle_B = \frac{1}{\sqrt{2}}(|01\rangle + |10\rangle)$ are in entangled states. In such a case, measurement of one qubit will affect the measurement of the other qubits. For example, when one measures the state of $|\varphi\rangle_A$, then the measurement of one qubit will make the state of the other qubit the same, while when one measures the state of $|\varphi\rangle_B$, the measurement of one qubit will make the state of the other qubit the opposite.

1.1.3   Quantum Circuits and Quantum Gates

1.1.3.1   Quantum Circuits

Changes to a quantum state can be described in the language of quantum computation. A quantum circuit is a quantum computation model in which a computation is a sequence of quantum logic gates (or simply quantum gates) [38]. Figure 1.4 shows a simple quantum circuit containing three quantum gates. The circuit is read from left to right, and each line represents a wire in the quantum circuit. While this may not correspond to a physical wire, it may instead correspond to the passage of time, or perhaps to a physical particle, e.g., a photon moving through space from one location to another [38]. It is conventionally assumed that the state input to the circuit is a computational basis state that is usually the state consisting of all $|0\rangle$s.

The state of qubits in quantum circuits evolves naturally over time, different combinations of quantum gates can implement specific quantum algorithms, and, finally, the results are presented with quantum measurements. In quantum computing, and specifically the quantum circuit model of computation, a quantum gate is a rudimentary quantum circuit operating on a small number of qubits [38]. Quantum gates are represented by *unitary* matrices. The number of qubits in the input and output of the gate must be equal; a gate which acts on n qubits is represented by a $2^n \times 2^n$ unitary matrix. It is noteworthy that it is impossible to make a copy of an unknown quantum state by using a circuit. This property, namely that qubits cannot be copied, is known as the *no-cloning* theorem [38], and is one of the primary differences between quantum and classical information.

1.1.3.2   Quantum Gates

Suppose an operator U_f on a quantum state is a unitary matrix, i.e.,

$$U_f U_f^{\dagger} = I, \tag{1.3}$$

Fig. 1.4 Quantum swapping gate

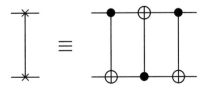

Gate	Equation	Matrix	Transform	Notation
Identity (I)	$I = \lvert 0\rangle\langle 0\rvert + \lvert 1\rangle\langle 1\rvert$	$\begin{pmatrix} 1 & 0 \\ 0 & 1 \end{pmatrix}$	$I\lvert 0\rangle = \lvert 0\rangle$ $I\lvert 1\rangle = \lvert 1\rangle$	—[I]—
Pauli-X (X or **NOT**)	$X = \lvert 0\rangle\langle 1\rvert + \lvert 1\rangle\langle 0\rvert$	$\begin{pmatrix} 0 & 1 \\ 1 & 0 \end{pmatrix}$	$X\lvert 0\rangle = \lvert 1\rangle$ $X\lvert 1\rangle = \lvert 0\rangle$	—[X]—
Hadamard (H)	$H = \dfrac{\lvert 0\rangle + \lvert 1\rangle}{\sqrt{2}}\langle 0\rvert + \dfrac{\lvert 0\rangle - \lvert 1\rangle}{\sqrt{2}}\langle 1\rvert$	$\dfrac{1}{\sqrt{2}}\begin{pmatrix} 1 & 1 \\ 1 & -1 \end{pmatrix}$	$H\lvert 0\rangle = \dfrac{1}{\sqrt{2}}(\lvert 0\rangle + \lvert 1\rangle)$ $H\lvert 1\rangle = \dfrac{1}{\sqrt{2}}(\lvert 0\rangle - \lvert 1\rangle)$	—[H]—
Controlled -NOT (**CNOT**)	$\mathbf{CNOT} = \lvert 0\rangle\langle 0\rvert \otimes I + \lvert 1\rangle\langle 1\rvert \otimes X$	$\begin{pmatrix} 1 & 0 & 0 & 0 \\ 0 & 1 & 0 & 0 \\ 0 & 0 & 0 & 1 \\ 0 & 0 & 1 & 0 \end{pmatrix}$	$\mathbf{CNOT}\lvert 00\rangle = \lvert 00\rangle$ $\mathbf{CNOT}\lvert 01\rangle = \lvert 01\rangle$ $\mathbf{CNOT}\lvert 10\rangle = \lvert 11\rangle$ $\mathbf{CNOT}\lvert 11\rangle = \lvert 10\rangle$	
Toffoli (T or **CCNOT**)	$\mathbf{T} = \lvert 0\rangle\langle 0\rvert \otimes I \otimes I$ $+ \lvert 1\rangle\langle 1\rvert \otimes \mathbf{CNOT}$	$\begin{pmatrix} 1&0&0&0&0&0&0&0 \\ 0&1&0&0&0&0&0&0 \\ 0&0&1&0&0&0&0&0 \\ 0&0&0&1&0&0&0&0 \\ 0&0&0&0&1&0&0&0 \\ 0&0&0&0&0&1&0&0 \\ 0&0&0&0&0&0&0&1 \\ 0&0&0&0&0&0&1&0 \end{pmatrix}$	$\mathbf{T}\lvert 000\rangle = \lvert 000\rangle, \mathbf{T}\lvert 001\rangle = \lvert 001\rangle$ $\mathbf{T}\lvert 010\rangle = \lvert 010\rangle, \mathbf{T}\lvert 011\rangle = \lvert 011\rangle$ $\mathbf{T}\lvert 100\rangle = \lvert 100\rangle, \mathbf{T}\lvert 101\rangle = \lvert 101\rangle$ $\mathbf{T}\lvert 110\rangle = \lvert 111\rangle, \mathbf{T}\lvert 111\rangle = \lvert 110\rangle$	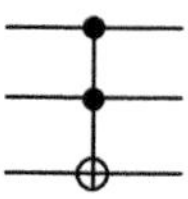

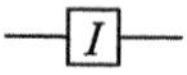

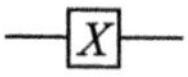

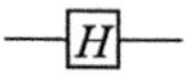

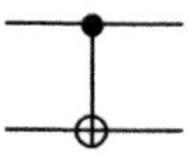

Fig. 1.5 Commonly used quantum gates

where $U_f^{\dagger}$ is the conjugate-transpose matrix of U_f and I is an identity matrix as shown in Fig. 1.5 when it is in the two-dimensional format.

The unitary transform uses the unitary matrix as the operator. The qubit is still in its normalized state after the unitary transform. Since the unitary transform is reversible, so is the quantum gate, i.e., the input state is turned into the output state by using the quantum gate (composed of the U_f transform), and the quantum gate (composed of the $U_f^{\dagger}$ transform), can turn the output state into the input state, i.e.,

$$U_f\lvert x\rangle = \lvert f(x)\rangle, \tag{1.4}$$

and

$$U_f^{\dagger}\lvert f(x)\rangle = \lvert x\rangle. \tag{1.5}$$

It is noteworthy that quantum *parallelism* allows quantum computers to simultaneously evaluate a function $f(x)$ for many values of x [38].

Fig. 1.6 Quantum
controlled-U gate

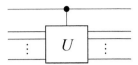

Let us recall Fig. 1.4 to find that this circuit completes the swap operation, noting that these gates have the following sequence of effects on a computational basis state $|a, b\rangle$:

$$|a, b\rangle \xrightarrow{CNOT} |a, a \oplus b\rangle$$

$$\xrightarrow{CNOT} |a \oplus (a \oplus b), (a \oplus b)\rangle = |b, a \oplus b\rangle \qquad (1.6)$$

$$\xrightarrow{CNOT} |b, (a \oplus b) \oplus b\rangle = |b, a\rangle,$$

where all additions are of modulo 2. The circuit's effect, therefore, is interchanging the states of the two qubits.

Figure 1.5 presents some commonly used quantum gates, their matrix representations, and their circuits. In addition, supposing U is any unitary matrix acting on some number n of qubits (in Fig. 1.6), U can be considered a quantum gate on these qubits. One can then define a controlled-U gate, which is a natural extension of the CNOT gate. This type of gate has a single control qubit, indicated by the line with the solid black circle, and n target qubits, indicated by the boxed U. Setting the control qubit to 0 has no effect on the target qubits. Setting it to 1, however, the gate U is applied to the target qubits.

1.2   Background of Quantum Image Processing

Quantum computation and information are transitioning from emerging branches of physics to mature research fields in science and engineering. Besides advancing their mathematical and physical foundations, a growing number of scientists and engineers are identifying and developing cross-fertilizing initiatives in quantum information processing in fields, such as artificial intelligence, pattern recognition, machine learning, neural network, cognition, and image processing [53].

1.2.1   Quantum Interdisciplinary Research

Several areas of quantum interdisciplinary research are now introduced and some studies on these efforts are noted.

1.2.1.1 Quantum Machine Learning

Quantum machine learning is an emerging interdisciplinary research area where quantum physics and machine learning meet. It is most commonly used in machine learning algorithms for analyzing classical data on quantum computers. It is known that machine learning algorithms can process immense amounts of data, but quantum machine learning intelligently increases such capabilities through the creation of opportunities to analyze quantum states and systems, including hybrid methods that involve both classical and quantum processing, in which computationally difficult subroutines are outsourced to a quantum device. Since these routines can be more complex, they can be executed more quickly assisted by quantum devices [6, 44].

1.2.1.2 Quantum Neural Networks

Quantum neural networks are neural network models based on quantum mechanical principles. Two approaches exist in quantum neural network research: one exploits quantum information processing to improve existing neural network models (and sometimes vice versa), while the other searches for potential quantum effects in the human brain. Quantum neural network research is still a nascent field, with several ideas of varying scope and mathematical rigor proposed, with most based on the idea of replacing classical binary or McCulloch–Pitts neurons with a qubit (which can be called a "quron"), resulting in neural units that can superpose the "firing" and "resting" states [18, 40].

1.2.1.3 Quantum Cognition

Quantum cognition is an emerging area of study in which the mathematical formalism of quantum theory is applied to model cognitive phenomena, such as information processing by the human brain, language, decision-making, human memory, conceptual reasoning, human judgment, and perception. Quantum cognition is based on a quantum-like paradigm or a generalized quantum paradigm, in which information processing by complex systems, such as the human brain, accounts for the contextual dependence of information and probabilistic reasoning, and which, in turn, can be mathematically described in the framework of quantum information and quantum probability theory [9, 20].

Such thoughts have reinvigorated interest in answering questions about which areas of classical computing—its components, devices, or technologies—quantum computing could best replace, interact with, or simply coalesce with to produce the envisioned supercomputing devices. Much like the transition from analog devices (such as phones and computers) to their digital equivalents, as well as the current use of mechanical and hybrid vehicles, it is envisaged that quantum and digital components, devices, and technologies will function seamlessly, whether independently or as units of a hybrid system [65].

Considering the ubiquity and primacy of image and video processing in modern life, a subdiscipline focused on ensuring a smooth transition from digital to quantum image processing has emerged.

1.2.2 Quantum-Based Image Processing Techniques

Given the need to extract information from the three-dimensional world, the storage, processing, and retrieval of visual information are first-order tasks for research of image processing and related areas, such as pattern recognition and artificial intelligence. However, the restricted architecture of classical computers and the often overwhelming computational complexity of state-of-the-art classical algorithms make it necessary to find better (i.e., more efficient) ways to manipulate visual information [61].

With the rapid development of quantum computation and information, notably Feynman's quantum computation model [19], Deutsch's quantum parallelism assertion [14], Shor's integer factoring algorithm [48], and Grover's database searching algorithm [25], the analysis of previously mentioned problems through the lens of quantum computation and information may result in new ways of understanding the nature of visual information [55].

1.2.2.1 Classifications of Quantum-Related Image Areas

Technically, efforts in quantum-related image processing can be classified into three main groups [63], the first two being outside the scope of this book.

1. Quantum-assisted digital image processing (QDIP): These applications aim to improve some well-known digital or classical image processing tasks and applications by exploiting some useful properties of quantum computing algorithms [28, 62].

    The first published material relating quantum mechanics to image processing can be traced to Vlasov's work [58] in 1997, which focused on the use of a quantum system to recognize orthogonal images. Years later, a signal processing framework [16] that was aimed at developing new or modifying existing signal processing algorithms was proposed by borrowing from the principles of quantum mechanics. By means of a simple example, Schützhold demonstrated that the task of finding and identifying certain patterns in an otherwise unstructured picture dataset can be accomplished efficiently by a quantum computer [45]. This was followed by the conclusion that quantum algorithms (such as Grover's algorithm) can be used in image processing in [2]. In that paper, they described a method which used a quantum algorithm to detect the posture of certain targets and perform the image template matching.

2. Optics-based quantum imaging (OQI): These applications focus on techniques for optical imaging and parallel information processing at the quantum level by exploiting the quantum nature of light and the intrinsic parallelism of optical signals [7, 23].

    A primary technique in OQI, ghost imaging is used to retrieve an object from the cross-correlation function of two separate beams, neither of which obtains the information from the object [1]. One beam interrogates a target and illuminates a single-pixel detector that provides no spatial resolution, while the other does not interact with the target, but it impinges on a high-resolution camera, hence affording a multiple-pixel output [17]. The timeline for this subdiscipline's development shows its modest beginning in 1995, when the two beams of ghost imaging were formed from a stream of entangled photons [39]. The reconstruction of the image was attributed to the nonlocal quantum correlations between the photon pairs. For several years, ghost imaging was considered an effect of quantum nonlocality due to the earlier experiments. Challenging this interpretation, Bennink et al. demonstrated ghost imaging using two classically correlated beams [5], following which it was found that many of the features obtained with entangled photons could be reproduced with a classical pseudothermal light source. However, the nature of the spatial correlations exhibited with a pseudothermal source, and whether they can be interpreted as classical intensity correlations or are fundamentally nonlocal quantum correlations, is still uncertain [22, 43, 46, 47].

3. Classically inspired quantum image processing (QIMP): Inspired by the impending realization of quantum computing hardware, these applications focus on extending classical image processing tasks and applications to a quantum computing framework [28, 62].

    The pioneering research that led to what is now called QIMP should be attributed to Venegas-Andraca and Bose's qubit lattice description for quantum images in 2003 [55]. Lattore then proposed another kind of representation, the real ket [32], whose purpose was to encode quantum images as a basis for further applications in QIMP. Recently, an integrated method of OQI and QIMP was proposed to implement the ghost imaging experiment by utilizing the quantum image circuit [64]. A complete ghost imaging circuit was established, including the creation of quantum speckle patterns, the interaction between the patterns and the quantum phase mask, and quantum computation of the cross-correlation. The proposed protocol provided a platform to circumvent the need for computing overhead in quantum ghost imaging.

The emerging subdiscipline of QIMP focuses on extending conventional image processing operations to the quantum computing framework [28]. Because of some of the powerful properties of quantum computation, notably entanglement and parallelism, QIMP is already living up to its promise to herald the realization of technologies with unrivalled competition in terms of computing speed, security, and storage requirements [62].

1.2.2.2 Storing an Image in a Quantum System

Image processing is a branch of computer science and engineering in which information coming from the perception of electromagnetic waves is captured, stored, and manipulated [24]. It is of interest to the scientific community for two main reasons: improvement and availability of visual information for human interpretation, and processing of scene data for autonomous machine perception and artificial intelligence processes [54]. The raw material for image processing is grayscale and/or color images (video can ultimately be converted to sets of frames). In particular, the use of color is motivated by two principal factors: (1) color is a powerful descriptor for object recognition, identification, and delimitation; and (2) the human vision system is excellent at detecting thousands of color shades and intensities, compared to only about two dozen shades of gray [51].

Human color perception is a physiopsychological phenomenon whose origin is in the fact that the human eye can detect electromagnetic waves within a certain frequency range (roughly 400–700 nm) [55]. Due to the structure of the human eye, almost all colors are seen as combinations of the three so-called primary colors: red, green, and blue (RGB). Several models have been developed to standardize the specification of colors (some are hardware-oriented, while others are oriented toward manipulation and hardcopy printing). Two color models are extensively used in image processing, i.e., RGB and HSI (hue, saturation, and intensity) [24].

Color models are used to specify colors in a standard way that makes sense under the theoretical and technological assumptions of classical computers and/or printing systems. In the case of quantum computers, the continuous nature of the parameters of a qubit allows to store information without preprocessing. This approach has a clear advantage over color models: every color can be studied and analyzed using actual values of its physical parameter (i.e., frequency), rather than a representation (e.g., a linear combination of RGB) [55].

When Venegas-Andraca and Bose proposed the qubit lattice representation [55] in 2003, they defined a machine A capable of detecting electromagnetic waves and, depending on the frequency of the detected wave, outputting an initialized qubit (note that a necessary property of A is to initialize qubits in different quantum states for different detected frequencies). A acts like an injective function: $F \mapsto \psi$, where F is the set of monochromatic electromagnetic waves whose frequencies can be detected by A, and ψ is the set of quantum states of the form:

$$|\psi\rangle = \cos\frac{\theta}{2}|0\rangle + e^{i\gamma}\sin\frac{\theta}{2}|1\rangle, \tag{1.7}$$

where $\theta \in [0, \pi]$. Thus for each frequency value of a particular monochromatic electromagnetic wave, it is always possible to find a value for θ in Eq. (1.7) such

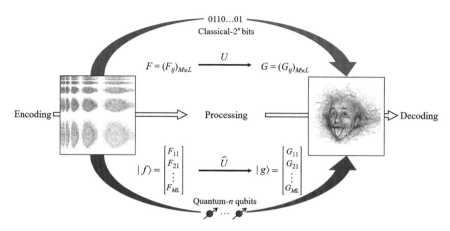

Fig. 1.7 Comparison of image processing by classical and quantum computers (figure and descriptions adapted from [67])

that A can initialize qubits in different states when different waves are detected. Parameter γ is left uninitialized for the moment, as the focus of the study is on how to store, process, and retrieve information using a single quantum parameter [55].

An example of a realization of machine A is given here. First, build an apparatus for frequency detection and recording; then, apply a magnetic field proportional to the stored frequency to a spin-half particle originally prepared in either the spin-up or spin-down state. In that way, it is possible to produce a quantum state whose real parameter θ is proportional to the recorded frequency [21]. Because of the continuous nature of θ, it is easy to accommodate the recording of a new color whose frequency lies anywhere in a given domain without readjusting the storage protocol. With digital storage protocols, the number of bits required to record color must be adjusted once the storage capacity limit is reached [51].

In addition, image processing by classical and quantum computers is briefly compared, as shown in Fig. 1.7, where F and G are the input and output images, respectively. On a classic computer, an $M \times L$ image can be represented as a matrix, encoded with at least 2^n bits $\left(n = \lceil log_2(ML) \rceil\right)$. Classical image transformation is conducted by matrix computation U. Alternatively, the same image can be represented as a quantum state and encoded in n qubits. Quantum image transformation is carried out by unitary evolution $\hat{U}$ under a suitable Hamiltonian [67].

In this chapter, some essentials of quantum computation and information are reviewed to help readers outside of quantum physics (e.g., computer scientists) to understand the kernel of the QIMP area. Also introduced are several similar concepts originated from both quantum computation and information and computer science and engineering, such as quantum machine learning and quantum neural networks. The background of QIMP and its radical difference from digital image processing on classical computers are suggested as the cornerstone of the discussions in this book.

In the rest of the book, the popular quantum image representations and their operations and applications are introduced. In fact, these pioneering representations and the ensuing developments provide the essential proof that image processing in the quantum computing domain can accelerate processing tasks, reduce computational requirements, and facilitate secure transmission. These benefits are attributed to the characteristics of quantum computation and information, e.g., entanglement and parallelism.

References

1. Basano, L., Ottonello, P.: A conceptual experiment on single-beam coincidence detection with pseudothermal light. Opt. Express **15**(19), 12386–12394 (2007)
2. Beach, G., Lomont, C., Cohen, C.: Quantum image processing (quip). In: Proceedings of the 32nd Applied Imagery Pattern Recognition Workshop, pp. 39–44 (2003)
3. Bennett, C., Divincenzo, D.: Quantum information and computation. Nature **404**(6775), 247–255 (2000)
4. Bennett, C., Shor, P.: Quantum information theory. IEEE Trans. Inf. Theory **44**(6), 2724–2742 (1998)
5. Bennink, R., Bentley, S., Boyd, R.: "two-photon" coincidence imaging with a classical source. Phys. Rev. Lett. **89**(11), 113601 (2002)
6. Biamonte, J., Wittek, P., Pancotti, N., Rebentrost, P., Wiebe, N., Lloyd, S.: Quantum machine learning. Nature **549**, 195–202 (2017)
7. Boyd, R., Reynolds, P.: Introduction to the special issue on quantum imaging. Quantum Inf. Process **11**(4), 887–889 (2012)
8. Brock, D.: Understanding Moore's Law: Four Decades of Innovation. Chemical Heritage Press, Philadelphia (2006)
9. Bruza, P., Wang, Z., Busemeyer, J.: Quantum cognition: a new theoretical approach to psychology. Trends Cogn. Sci. **19**(7), 383–393 (2015)
10. Caraiman, S., Manta, V.: New applications of quantum algorithm to computer graphics the quantum random sample consensus algorithm. In: Proceedings of the 6th ACM Conference on Computing Frontiers, pp. 81–88 (2009)
11. Courtland, R.: The visionary engineer reflects on 50 years of Moore's law (2015). https://spectrum.ieee.org/computing/hardware/gordon-moore-the-man-whose-name-means-progress
12. Cruz-Santos, W., Venegas-Andraca, S., Lanzagorta, M.: A QUBO formulation of the stereo matching problem for d-wave quantum annealers. Entropy **20**(10), 786 (2018)
13. D-Wave: D-Wave announces D-Wave 2000Q quantum computer and first system order (2017). https://www.dwavesys.com/press-releases/d-wave%C2%A0announces%C2%A0d-wave-2000q-quantum-computer-and-first-system-order
14. Deutsch, D.: Quantum theory, the Church-Turing principle and the universal quantum computer. In: Proceedings of the Royal Society of London A, vol. 400, pp. 97–117 (1985)
15. Disco, C., Meulen, B.: Getting New Technologies Together: Studies in Making Sociotechnical Order. Walter de Gruyter, Berlin (1998)
16. Eldar, Y., Oppenheim, A.: Quantum signal processing. IEEE Signal Process. Mag. **19**(6), 12–32 (2002)
17. Erkmen, B., Shapiro, J.: Ghost imaging: from quantum to classical to computational. Adv. Opt. Photon. **2**(4), 405–450 (2010)
18. Ezhov, A., Ventura, D.: Quantum Neural Networks. Future Directions for Intelligent Systems and Information Sciences. Springer, Berlin (2000)

19. Feynman, R.: Simulating physics with computers. Int. J. Theor. Phys. **21**(6–7), 467–488 (1982)
20. Fisher, M.: Quantum cognition: the possibility of processing with nuclear spins in the brain. Ann. Phys. **362**, 593–602 (2015)
21. Galvão, E., Hardy, L.: Substituting a qubit for an arbitrarily large number of classical bits. Phys. Rev. Lett. **90**(8), 087902 (2003)
22. Gatti, A., Bondani, M., Lugiato, L., Paris, M., Fabre, C.: Comment on "can two-photon correlation of chaotic light be considered as correlation of intensity fluctuations?". Phys. Rev. Lett. **98**(3), 039301 (2007)
23. Gatti, A., Brambilla, E., Lugiato, L.: Quantum imaging. Prog. Opt. **51**(7), 251–348 (2008)
24. Gonzalez, R., Woods, R.: Digital Image Processing, 3rd edn. Pearson Education, London (2008)
25. Grover, L.: A fast quantum mechanical algorithm for database search. In: Proceedings of the 28th Annual ACM Symposium on Theory of Computing, pp. 212–219 (1996)
26. Hempel, C., Maier, C., Romero, J., McClean, J., Monz, T., Shen, H., Jurcevic, P., Lanyon, B., Love, P., Babbush, R., Aspuru-Guzik, A., Blatt, R., Roos, C.: Quantum chemistry calculations on a trapped-ion quantum simulator. Phys. Rev. X **8**(3), 031022 (2018)
27. Iliyasu, A.: Algorithmic frameworks to support the realisation of secure and efficient image-video processing applications on quantum computers. Ph.D Thesis, Tokyo Institute of Technology, Tokyo (2012)
28. Iliyasu, A.: Towards realising secure and efficient image and video processing applications on quantum computers. Entropy **15**, 2874–2974 (2013)
29. Kaku, M.: Tweaking Moore's law and the computers of the post-silicon era (2012). https://www.youtube.com/watch?v=bm6ScvNygUU
30. Keyes, R.: The impact of Moore's law. IEEE Solid-State Circuits Soc. Newsl. **11**(3), 25–27 (2006)
31. Ladd, T., Jelezko, F., Laflamme, R., Nakamura, Y., Monroe, C., O'Brien J.L.: Quantum computers. Nature **464**, 45–53 (2010)
32. Latorre, J.: Image compression and entanglement. arXiv: quant-ph/0510031 (2005)
33. Le, P.: Flexible representation and processing transformations for quantum images, and their applications. Ph.D Thesis, Tokyo Institute of Technology, Tokyo (2012)
34. Liang, Q., Venkatramani, A., Cantu, S., Nicholson, T., Gullans, M., Gorshkov, A., Thompson, J., Chin, C., Lukin, M., Vuletić, V.: Observation of three-photon bound states in a quantum nonlinear medium. Science **359**(6377), 783–786 (2018)
35. Mermin, N.: Quantum Computer Science: An Introduction. Cambridge University Press, Cambridge (2007)
36. Microsoft: the Q# programming language (2019). https://docs.microsoft.com/en-us/quantum/language/?view=qsharp-preview
37. National, Q.: UK Quantum technology landscape 2016 (2017). http://uknqt.epsrc.ac.uk/files/ukquantumtechnologylandscape2016
38. Nielsen, M., Chuang, I.: Quantum Computation and Quantum Information. Cambridge University Press, Cambridge (2000)
39. Pittman, T., Shih, Y., Strekalov, D., Sergienko, A.: Optical imaging by means of two-photon quantum entanglement. Phys. Rev. A **52**(5), R3429–R3432 (1995)
40. Purushothaman, G., Karayiannis, N.: Quantum neural networks (QNNs): inherently fuzzy feedforward neural networks. IEEE Trans. Neural Netw. **8**(3), 679–693 (1997)
41. Ray, A.: Roadmap for 1000 qubits fault-tolerant quantum computers (2018). https://amitray.com/roadmap-for-1000-qubits-fault-tolerant-quantum-computers/
42. Rieffel, E., Polak, W.: An introduction to quantum computing for non-physicists. ACM Comput. Surv. **32**(3), 300–335 (2000)
43. Scarcelli, G., Berardi, V., Shih, Y.: Scarcelli, Berardi, and Shih reply. Phys. Rev. Lett. **98**, 039302 (2007)
44. Schuld, M., Sinayskiy, I., Petruccione, F.: An introduction to quantum machine learning. Contemp. Phys. **56**(2), 172–185 (2015)
45. Schützhold, R.: Pattern recognition on a quantum computer. Phys. Rev. A **67**(6), 062311 (2003)

46. Shapiro, J., Boyd, R.: Response to "the physics of ghost imaging: nonlocal interference or local intensity fluctuation correlation?". Quantum Inf. Process. **11**(4), 1003–1011 (2012)
47. Shih, Y.: The physics of ghost imaging: nonlocal interference or local intensity fluctuation correlation? Quantum Inf. Process. **11**(4), 995–1001 (2012)
48. Shor, P.: Algorithms for quantum computation: discrete logarithms and factoring. In: Proceedings of the 35th Annual Symposium on Foundations of Computer Science, pp. 124–134 (1994)
49. Simon, D.: On the power of quantum computation. SIAM J. Comput. **26**(5), 1474–1483 (1997)
50. Tucker, A.: Computer Science Handbook. CRC Press, Boca Raton (2004)
51. Venegas-Andraca, S.: Discrete quantum walks and quantum image processing. Ph.D Thesis, the University of Oxford, Oxford (2005)
52. Venegas-Andraca, S.: Quantum Walks for Computer Scientists. Morgan and Claypool, San Rafael (2008)
53. Venegas-Andraca, S.: Introductory words: special issue on quantum image processing published by quantum information processing. Quantum Inf. Process. **14**(5), 1535–1537 (2015)
54. Venegas-Andraca, S., Bose, S.: Quantum computation and image processing: new trends in artificial intelligence. In: Proceedings of International Joint Conferences on Artificial Intelligence, pp. 1563–1566 (2003)
55. Venegas-Andraca, S., Bose, S.: Storing, processing, and retrieving an image using quantum mechanics. In: Proceedings of SPIE Conference of Quantum Information and Computation, vol. 5105, pp. 137–147 (2003)
56. Venegas-Andraca, S., Cruz-Santos, W., Mcgeoch, C., Lanzagorta, M.: A cross-disciplinary introduction to quantum annealing-based algorithms. Contemp. Phys. **59**(2), 174–197 (2018)
57. Vidal, G.: Efficient simulation of one-dimensional quantum many-body systems. Phys. Rev. Lett. **93**, 040502 (2004)
58. Vlasov, A.: Quantum computations and images recognition. arXiv:quant-ph/9703010 (1997)
59. Weedbrook, C., Pirandola, S., García-Patrón, R., Cerf, N., Ralph, T., Shapiro, J., Lloyd, S.: Gaussian quantum information. Rev. Mod. Phys. **84**(2), 621–669 (2012)
60. Yan, F.: Quantum computation based image data searching, image watermarking, and representation of emotion space. Ph.D Thesis, Tokyo Institute of Technology, Tokyo (2014)
61. Yan, F., Iliyasu, A., Jiang, Z.: Quantum computation-based image representation, processing operations and their applications. Entropy **16**(10), 5290–5338 (2014)
62. Yan, F., Iliyasu, A., Venegas-Andraca, S.: A survey of quantum image representations. Quantum Inf. Process. **15**(1), 1–35 (2016)
63. Yan, F., Iliyasu, A., Le, P.: Quantum image processing: a review of advances in its security technologies. Int. J. Quant. Inf. **15**(3), 1730001 (2017)
64. Yan, F., Chen, K., Iliyasu, A., Zhao, J.: Circuit-based modular implementation of quantum ghost imaging. arXiv:1806.06702 (2018)
65. Yan, F., Jiao, S., Iliyasu, A., Jiang, Z.: Chromatic framework for quantum movies and applications in creating montages. Front. Comp. Sci. **12**(4), 736–748 (2018)
66. Yao, A.: Classical physics and the Church-Turing thesis. J. ACM **50**(1), 100–105 (2003)
67. Yao, X., Wang, H., Liao, Z., Chen, M., Pan, J., Li, J., Zhang, K., Lin, X., Wang, Z., Luo, Z., Zheng, W., Li, J., Zhao, M., Peng, X., Suter, D.: Quantum image processing and its application to edge detection: theory and experiment. Phys. Rev. X **7**, 031041 (2017)

Chapter 2
Quantum Image Representations

QIMP is devoted to utilizing quantum computing technologies to capture, manipulate, and recover quantum images in different formats for various purposes [28]. This requires the encoding of images based on the quantum mechanical composition of any potential quantum computing hardware to be developed [5]. This chapter discusses several current mainstream quantum image representations (QIRs) and their basic transformations.

2.1 Quantum Image Models

Available QIRs can be classified under various categories based on the requirements defined to store the content of an image in a quantum system, i.e., image color model, image coordinate model, and image color information encoding model [28]. In the following lines, each group is discussed.

2.1.1 Image Color Model

All of the QIRs in this group utilize the color model/visual difference to encode the content of an image. In their qubit lattice QIR, Venegas-Andraca et al. averred that the frequency of the physical nature of color could represent a color instead of the traditional color models, e.g., RGB or HSI, so a color could be represented by one qubit in a quantum computing system [27]. Similarly, all of the other QIRs using

---

© Portions of this chapter are reprinted from ref. [28], with permission of Springer.

© Springer Nature Singapore Pte Ltd. 2020
F. Yan, S. E. Venegas-Andraca, *Quantum Image Processing*,
https://doi.org/10.1007/978-981-32-9331-1_2

this model are built on the chromatic content of the image. Typically, the QIRs in this model can be further grouped as follows:

- Binary-based
- Grayscale-based
- RGB-based

In [26], a method for storing and retrieving geometrical patterns using maximally entangled states on binary images was presented. It harnesses entangled states so that object shapes can be reconstructed without the use of auxiliary information. The binary-based QIR in [26] can be used as a basis for more sophisticated QIMP algorithms like segmentation, thresholding, and dithering. Furthermore, advanced methods for storing and retrieving patterns using quantum entangled systems should include more color details.

Along these lines, a flexible representation for quantum images (FRQI) was proposed to integrate the grayscale color and position information of an image in a normalized state that facilitates geometric and color transformations on the image [10]. A single qubit is dedicated to encoding color information, thereby ensuring that transformations on the image content can target the color only, or both the color and position simultaneously. Specified quantum gates applied on predetermined areas of the image can transform the color information as desired [15].

To effectively mimic human perception of visual effects, a true color image with the three primary colors R, G, and B is a natural extension in the QIMP area. Color image representations either utilize two sets of quantum states to, respectively, represent M colors and N pixels in an image [16], or use different levels of angles for RGB information and the tensor product with location information (Y- and X-axis) to represent an image [23, 29]. Different from the simple color operations that can be performed on a quantum image encoded in the FRQI representation, RGB-based QIRs can separate an image into more than just its R, G, and B components. They have an additional α channel to facilitate operations on the image's content, as in multi-channel quantum images (MCQI) [24], that can operate on the color of interest (COI), color swapping (CS), and α blending transformations, which will be reviewed in Sect. 2.3. In color image representation utilizing two sets of quantum states for M colors and N coordinates, respectively (QSMC&QSNC) [16], it uses two sets of quantum states for M colors and N coordinates, respectively, which can both represent grayscale and color information of an image. In addition, it can provide lossless compression with acceptable compression ratios and a quantum search-based image segmentation method that is universal for grayscale and color images.

2.1.2 Image Coordinate Model

QIRs that utilize different coordinate systems to capture information about an image are now addressed. QIRs that conform to this model include:

- Cartesian coordinate system-based
- Log-polar coordinate system-based
- Multi-dimension-based

A typical example of a coordinate system is the Cartesian coordinate system. Pioneer QIRs include the qubit lattice, which maps every pixel to a single qubit and stores images in two-dimensional arrays of qubits without preprocessing [27], and the real ket, which utilizes the coefficients of a basis state of a qubit sequence to represent the grayscale value of every pixel and stores an image in a quantum superposition [9]. These could be described as QIRs processed on the basis of intuitive, two-dimensional Cartesian coordinate systems, and most importantly, they facilitate the basic geometric transformations on an image due to their special coordinate structures. The third pioneering QIR, the FRQI representation [12], also falls under the Cartesian coordinate system, and the flip, coordinate swapping, orthogonal rotation, and their variants for quantum images have been fully studied [11, 15].

Image representations on various coordinate systems often yield different operations and applications. Many complex affine transformations, such as rotation and scaling, are not easily performed on QIRs based on the image coordinate model because many irreversible interpolations are needed. Log-polar coordinates are widely employed in sampling in classical image processing, where the sampling resolutions of the log-radius and angular orientations are assumed to be 2^m and 2^n, respectively, in a $2^m \times 2^n$ log-polar image. A quantum log-polar image (QUALPI) has been proposed [31] for storing and processing images sampled in log-polar coordinates. Complex geometric transformations can be performed based on QUALPI images. For example, symmetry transformations, including quantum centrosymmetry and quantum axisymmetry, can be efficiently performed, and the rotation transformation by shifting the angular directions is lossless and reversible because there is no interpolation. A fast rotation-invariant quantum image registration algorithm was designed for QUALPI images, through which the exact rotation difference between two quantum images can be found. The relationship between these two kinds of two-dimensional image sampling methods (the coordinate transformation between Cartesian coordinate system-based and log-polar coordinate system-based images) is discussed in [31].

Three-dimensional descriptions of objects are useful because they rely on human intuition and experience with the physical world. Furthermore, in science and engineering, expressing problems within the frame of multi-dimensional Cartesian systems using n-dimensional Euclidean spaces is common practice [18]. A multi-dimensional image representation using a normal arbitrary quantum superposition state (NAQSS) [17] expands the position information of an image to k binary arrays in k coordinates in the k-dimensional space. NAQSS requires $n+1$ qubits, where n qubits represent colors and coordinates of 2^n pixels, one qubit represents information to improve the accuracy of image segmentation, and $n+1$ qubits describe only the image (not including additional segmentation information) in FRQI representation. In addition, due to a bijective function between color and angle built in this quantum image model, it has no constraints in terms of the color representation (it can represent both grayscale and RGB images by adjusting the bijective function) [3].

2.1.3 Image Color Information Encoding Model

Finally, similar to the different classical image file formats, e.g., BMP, TIFF, and JPEG, an image's two fundamental items of information, i.e., color and position, can be encoded in various ways. Considering this, QIRs under the color information encoding model are divided into two categories:

- Encoded using one qubit through its angle parameter
- Encoded in the basis states of a sequence of qubits

In the first category are some of the pioneer QIRs. Representation models encode the color information in the state of one qubit by establishing a bijective relationship between the frequency of the monochromatic electromagnetic wave that determines the color, and the angle parameter of a qubit, such as a qubit lattice [27], FRQI [12], or QSMC&QSNC [16]. While their pixel position encoding varies—e.g., the qubit lattice model uses no explicit quantum encoding of position information—the position information of every pixel can be stored in a basis state of a $2n$-qubit sequence in the FRQI representation, and the position information can be encoded in the angle parameter of a qubit by creating a bijection between the set of pixel coordinates and a set of angles in the QSMC&QSNC method. It should be noted that in this classification, the original classical image cannot be accurately retrieved, notwithstanding a finite number of measurements. This is because the quantum measurements only provide probabilistic results of the color angle [19]. Therefore, multiple copies of the same quantum image must be prepared, followed by a statistical procedure to estimate the probability amplitudes of the quantum states encoding the colors of each pixel with a given accuracy [14].

Furthermore, Caraiman's QIR approach (CQIR) in [1] and the novel enhanced quantum representation (NEQR) model [30] were simultaneously and independently proposed. In both QIRs, color information is encoded in the basis states of a sequence of qubits so that the whole image is stored in two qubit sequences. This is the second category identified above. Assume m qubits are used to encode all of the possible gray levels presented in the image, which means the color model is an m-qubit register. Both the color and position of a pixel are encoded in the basic quantum states (instead of the superposition state with complex numbers as coefficients); therefore, both the color and position information can be possibly retrieved deterministically through a finite number of projective measurements. In addition, the number of representable colors and positions in an image does not depend on the actual physical implementation of the quantum system, and a larger class of more complex image processing operations can be applied using this model because the color is represented using a computational basis state that can act as a control for applying value-dependent color transforms and for computing statistics in the image, as addressed in [2]. However, additional qubits are required to encode the color information of images in this complex representation.

2.2 Flexible Representation for Quantum Images

The FRQI representation has shown widespread appeal in recent QIMP literature. This representation is now introduced and some of its properties, as well as related transformations, are highlighted [12].

2.2.1 FRQI Representation and Initialization

FRQI is similar to pixel representation of images on traditional computers. It captures the essential information about the colors and the position of every point in an image, and integrates them into a quantum state with the formula:

$$|I\rangle = \frac{1}{2^n} \sum_{i=0}^{2^{2n}-1} |c_i\rangle \otimes |i\rangle, \tag{2.1}$$

where

$$|c_i\rangle = \cos\theta_i |0\rangle + \sin\theta_i |1\rangle, \tag{2.2}$$

where $|0\rangle$ and $|1\rangle$ are two-dimensional computational basis states; $|i\rangle$, $i = 0, 1,\ldots, 2^{2n} - 1$, are 2^{2n}-dimensional computational basis states; and $\theta = (\theta_0, \theta_1, \ldots, \theta_{2^{2n}-1})$, $\theta_i \in [0, \frac{\pi}{2}]$, is the vector of angles encoding colors. The two parts in the FRQI representation of an image, $|c_i\rangle$ and $|i\rangle$, respectively encode information about the colors and corresponding positions in the image. An example of a 2×2 FRQI image with its quantum state is shown in Fig. 2.1.

In quantum computation, computers are usually initialized in well-prepared states [19]. Hence, a preparation process is necessary to transform quantum computers from the initialized state to the desired quantum image state. The polynomial preparation theorem (PPT), which follows from Theorem 2.1, demonstrates an efficient preparation process [12].

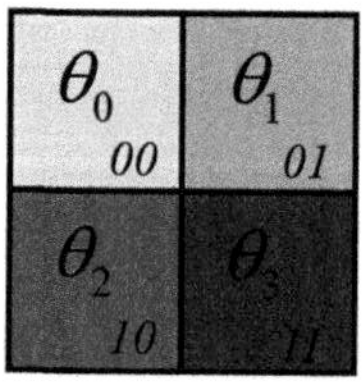

$$|I\rangle = \frac{1}{2}[(\cos\theta_0\,|0\rangle + \sin\theta_0\,|1\rangle)\otimes|00\rangle + (\cos\theta_1\,|0\rangle + \sin\theta_1\,|1\rangle)\otimes|01\rangle$$
$$+ (\cos\theta_2\,|0\rangle + \sin\theta_2\,|1\rangle)\otimes|10\rangle + (\cos\theta_3\,|0\rangle + \sin\theta_3\,|1\rangle)\otimes|11\rangle]$$

Fig. 2.1   A 2×2 FRQI image and its quantum state

Theorem 2.1 *Given a vector $\theta = (\theta_0, \theta_1, \cdots, \theta_{2^{2n}-1})$ of angles ($\theta_i \in [0, \frac{\pi}{2}]$, $i = 0, 1, \cdots, 2^{2n} - 1$), there is a unitary transform $\mathcal{P}$ that turns quantum computers from the initialized state, $|0\rangle^{\otimes 2n+1}$, to the FRQI state in Eq. (2.1), composed of a polynomial number of simple gates.*

Proof There are two steps to achieve the unitary transform $\mathcal{P}$, where Hadamard transforms are first used to change $|0\rangle^{\otimes 2n+1}$ to $|H\rangle$, followed by controlled-rotation transforms from $|H\rangle$ to $|I\rangle$.

Considering the two-dimensional identity matrix I and the $2n$ Hadamard matrices $H^{\otimes 2n}$, applying the transform $\mathcal{H} = I \otimes H^{\otimes 2n}$ on $|0\rangle^{\otimes 2n+1}$ produces the state $|H\rangle$:

$$\mathcal{H}(|0\rangle^{\otimes 2n+1}) = \frac{1}{2^n}|0\rangle \otimes \sum_{i=0}^{2^{2n}-1} |i\rangle = |H\rangle. \tag{2.3}$$

In addition, the rotation matrices $R_y(2\theta_i)$ and controlled-rotation matrices R_i with $i = 0, 1, \cdots, 2^{2n} - 1$ are considered, i.e.,

$$R_y(2\theta_i) = \begin{pmatrix} \cos\theta_i & -\sin\theta_i \\ \sin\theta_i & \cos\theta_i \end{pmatrix}, \tag{2.4}$$

$$R_i = \left(I \otimes \sum_{j=0, j\neq i}^{2^{2n}-1} |j\rangle\langle j|\right) + R_y(2\theta_i) \otimes |i\rangle\langle i|. \tag{2.5}$$

The controlled-rotation R_i is a unitary matrix, since $R_i R_i^\dagger = I^{\otimes 2n+1}$. Applying R_k and $R_l R_k$ on $|H\rangle$ gives:

$$R_k(|H\rangle) = R_k\left(\frac{1}{2^n}|0\rangle \otimes \sum_{i=0}^{2^{2n}-1} |i\rangle\right)$$

$$= \frac{1}{2^n}\left[I|0\rangle \otimes \left(\sum_{i=0, i\neq k}^{2^{2n}-1} |i\rangle\langle i|\right)\left(\sum_{i=0}^{2^{2n}-1} |i\rangle\right)\right.$$

$$+ R_y(2\theta_k)|0\rangle \otimes |k\rangle\langle k| \left(\sum_{i=0}^{2^{2n}-1} |i\rangle \right) \Bigg] \tag{2.6}$$

$$= \frac{1}{2^n} \left[|0\rangle \otimes \left(\sum_{i=0,i\neq k}^{2^{2n}-1} |i\rangle \right) + (\cos\theta_k|0\rangle + \sin\theta_k|1\rangle) \otimes |k\rangle \right],$$

and

$$R_l R_k |H\rangle = R_l(R_k|H\rangle)$$

$$= \frac{1}{2^n} \Bigg[|0\rangle \otimes \left(\sum_{i=0,i\neq k,l}^{2^{2n}-1} |i\rangle \right) + (\cos\theta_k|0\rangle + \sin\theta_k|1\rangle) \otimes |k\rangle$$

$$+ (\cos\theta_l|0\rangle + \sin\theta_l|1\rangle) \otimes |l\rangle \Bigg] . \tag{2.7}$$

It is obvious from Eq. (2.7) that

$$\mathscr{R}|H\rangle = \left(\prod_{i=0}^{2^{2n}-1} R_i \right) |H\rangle = |I\rangle. \tag{2.8}$$

Therefore, the unitary transform $\mathscr{P} = \mathscr{R}\mathscr{H}$ turns quantum computers from the initialized state $|0\rangle^{\otimes 2n+1}$ to the FRQI state $|I\rangle$. The computational complexity of the preparation for FRQI image can be calculated as $O(2^{4n})$ [12].

The essential requirements to represent a classical or quantum image are simplicity and efficiency in the storage and retrieval of the image [14]. The storage of an FRQI image is achieved by the preparation process using the PPT as discussed earlier. The measurement of the quantum image state produces a probability distribution that is used for the retrieval of the image. As presented in Sect. 1.1.2, measuring a quantum state produces an outcome and a post-measurement quantum state, which is a projection of the state vector onto the basis vector that corresponds to the outcome obtained. Therefore, to extract the angles encoding the gray levels and the corresponding positions from the image, many identical FRQI states are required. Multiple measurement operations on these identical quantum states give information about the quantum state in the form of a probability distribution [12].

It is noteworthy that with general quantum states, the probability distributions are not enough to clearly understand the states because their coefficients are complex numbers. The FRQI, however, contains only real-valued coefficients that enable retrieval of all of the information about the state [14].

2.2.2   Geometric Transformations on FRQI Images

Having the basic model to represent images on a quantum computer, a discussion of transformations used to change information on quantum images can begin. Fast geometric transformations on quantum images (GTQI) [11] are operations performed based on the geometric information of images, i.e., information about the position of every point in the image. The flips, coordinate swapping, orthogonal rotations, and their variants for FRQI images are introduced using basic NOT, CNOT, and Toffoli gates (refer to Fig. 1.5 for a reminder of those gates).

2.2.2.1   Flip and Coordinate Swap Operations

Flip and coordinate swaps are fundamental operations in classical image processing, hence both operations must be defined within the quantum computing realm. The flipping operation on FRQI images is defined as follows [11].

Definition 2.1 The flipping operations on FRQI images along the X- and Y-axis are the operations F_I^X and F_I^Y, which, when applied on $|I\rangle$ in Eq. (2.1), produce outputs of the form:

$$F_I^X(|I\rangle) = \frac{1}{2^n} \sum_{k=0}^{2^{2n}-1} |c_k\rangle \otimes F^X(|k\rangle),\tag{2.9}$$

$$F_I^Y(|I\rangle) = \frac{1}{2^n} \sum_{k=0}^{2^{2n}-1} |c_k\rangle \otimes F^Y(|k\rangle),\tag{2.10}$$

where $|k\rangle = |y\rangle|x\rangle$ and

$$F^X(|y\rangle|x\rangle) = |\bar{y}\rangle|x\rangle,\tag{2.11}$$

$$F^Y(|y\rangle|x\rangle) = |y\rangle|\bar{x}\rangle,\tag{2.12}$$

$$|x\rangle = |x_{n-1}x_{n-2}\ldots x_0\rangle, |y\rangle = |y_{n-1}y_{n-2}\ldots y_0\rangle,\tag{2.13}$$

$$|\bar{x}\rangle = |\bar{x}_{n-1}\bar{x}_{n-2}\ldots\bar{x}_0\rangle, |\bar{y}\rangle = |\bar{y}_{n-1}\bar{y}_{n-2}\ldots\bar{y}_0\rangle,\tag{2.14}$$

where

$$\bar{x}_i = 1 - x_i, \bar{y}_i = 1 - y_i, i = 0, 1, \ldots, n-1.\tag{2.15}$$

It is found that F^X and F^Y operations can be built using NOT gates and the complexity of flipping operations, as in Eqs. (2.11) and (2.12), is $O(n)$ on $2n$-qubit

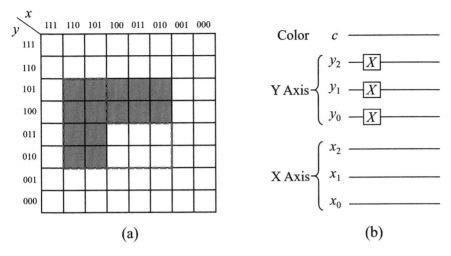

Fig. 2.2 (**a**) Image flipping along X-axis and (**b**) its circuit

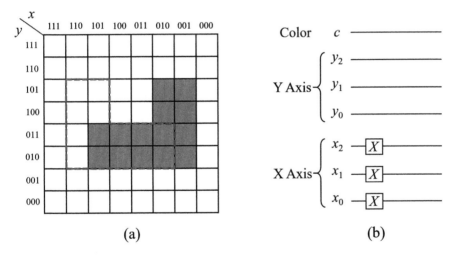

Fig. 2.3 (**a**) Image flipping along Y-axis and (**b**) its circuit

FRQI images [12]. Figures 2.2 and 2.3 show examples of image flipping along the X- and Y-axis, respectively, where the original position of the block is depicted by red dotted lines for comparison.

These flipping operations can be naturally extended to coordinate-swapping operations, which are defined as follows [11].

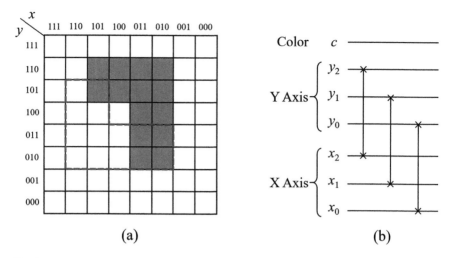

(a)   (b)

Fig. 2.4 (**a**) An example of a coordinate-swapping operation and (**b**) its circuit

Definition 2.2 The coordinate-swapping operation C_I, when applied on $|I\rangle$ in Eq. (2.1), produces outputs of the form:

$$C_I\left(|I\rangle\right) = \frac{1}{2^n} \sum_{k=0}^{2^{2n}-1} |c_k\rangle \otimes C\left(|k\rangle\right), \qquad (2.16)$$

where $|k\rangle = |yx\rangle$ and

$$C\left(|yx\rangle\right) = |xy\rangle. \qquad (2.17)$$

The complexity of the coordinate-swapping operation C_I, as in Eq. (2.16), on $2n$-qubit FRQI images is $O(n)$ [12]. Figure 2.4 shows an example of a coordinate-swapping operation and its circuit, in which the swap gate can be built from three CNOT gates, as shown in Fig. 1.4 in Sect. 1.1.3.1.

2.2.2.2 Orthogonal Rotation Operations

Image orthogonal rotations are image rotations with the angles 90°, 180°, and 270°. Mathematical results show that orthogonal rotations can be achieved by flipping and coordinate swapping [11].

Definition 2.3 The orthogonal rotation operations on FRQI images are the operations R_I^{90}, R_I^{180}, and R_I^{270}, which, when applied on $|I\rangle$ in Eq. (2.1), produce outputs of the form:

$$R_I^a\left(|I\rangle\right) = \frac{1}{2^n} \sum_{k=0}^{2^{2n}-1} \left(\cos\theta_k |0\rangle + \sin\theta_k |1\rangle\right) \otimes R^a\left(|k\rangle\right), \tag{2.18}$$

where $a \in \{90, 180, 270\}$, $|k\rangle = |yx\rangle$, and

$$R^{90}\left(|yx\rangle\right) = |x\bar{y}\rangle,$$
$$R^{180}\left(|yx\rangle\right) = |\bar{y}\bar{x}\rangle, \tag{2.19}$$
$$R^{270}\left(|yx\rangle\right) = |\bar{x}y\rangle.$$

Proof The rotations can be built from flipping and coordinate-swapping operations as

$$R^{90} = CF^X,$$
$$R^{180} = F^Y F^X, \tag{2.20}$$
$$R^{270} = CF^Y.$$

The complexity of the orthogonal rotations R^{90}, R^{180}, and R^{270} on $2n$-qubit FRQI images is $O(n)$ [12]. Figures 2.5 show examples of image orthogonal rotations and their corresponding circuits.

2.2.2.3 Restricted Geometric Transformations

Once geometric transformations became well understood, quantum programmers thought of designing smaller versions of geometric transformations as the main components to realize other more complex operations [6]. By imposing additional restrictions to indicate specific locations, the transformations described earlier can be confined to small subareas within a larger image. Operations restricted to smaller subareas of an image are referred to as restricted geometric transformations on quantum images [7].

In the FRQI representation, the realization of these kinds of transformations becomes simple by exercising more control over the original transformation. Figure 2.6 shows the example of a 90° rotation of the lower-left quarter of an image. To clarify the circuit's complexity when the additional control conditions are added to the GTQI operations, Le et al. discussed regarding the relationship between the number of control conditions and the size of the affected area in an FRQI image [15]. The more controls a transformation has, the smaller the size of the affected

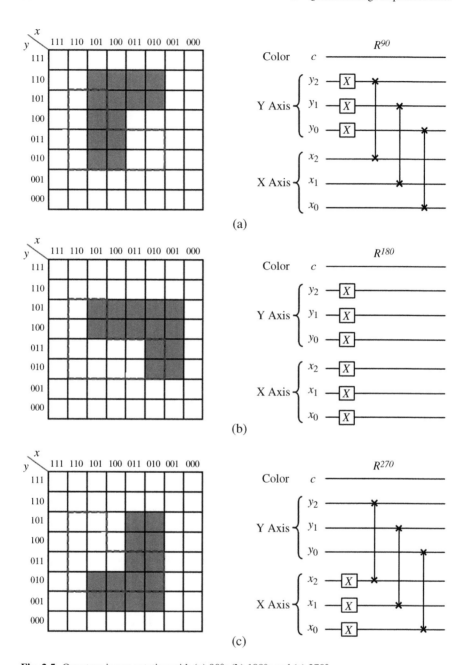

Fig. 2.5 Quantum image rotation with (**a**) 90°; (**b**) 180°; and (**c**) 270°

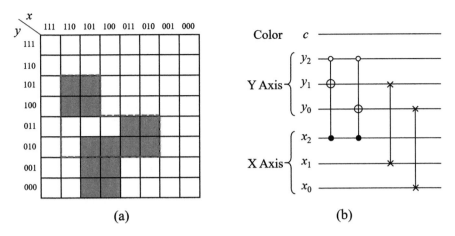

Fig. 2.6 (**a**) 90° image rotation (lower-left quarter) and (**b**) its circuit

area. Specifying the area in which the transformation will be applied increases the complexity of the new transformation in terms of the depth and the number of basic gates in the corresponding circuit.

2.2.3 Color Transformations on FRQI Images

Color transformation on quantum images (CTQI) [13] is an operation used to process the color information of FRQI images (either an area of an image or the whole image). FRQI utilizes a single qubit to store the color information of the image, which ensures that the transformation of the image content can focus on only the color of the pixels, or both their color and position. When a single-qubit gate is applied on the color wire in FRQI representation, the color of every position in the entire image is changed. The basic single-qubit gates and their performance on FRQI images are discussed below.

2.2.3.1 Color Transformation Based on NOT Gate

The first single-qubit gate is a NOT gate or X gate. Its function is defined as

$$X = \begin{pmatrix} 0 & 1 \\ 1 & 0 \end{pmatrix},$$
(2.21)

$$X|0\rangle = |1\rangle, X|1\rangle = |0\rangle.$$
(2.22)

When the X gate is applied on a color wire, its performance is

$$X(|c(\theta_k)\rangle) = |c\left(\frac{\pi}{2} - \theta_k\right)\rangle, \forall k \in \left\{0, 1, \ldots, 2^{2n} - 1\right\}, \tag{2.23}$$

where $|c(\theta_k)\rangle$ is the color information, as defined in Eq. (2.2).

The function of the X gate is like a color-inversion operation. It inverts the color of an entire image, from black to white and vice versa.

2.2.3.2   Color Transformation Based on Pauli-Z Gate

The second single-qubit gate is the Pauli-Z gate (or Z gate), whose function is defined as

$$Z = \begin{pmatrix} 1 & 0 \\ 0 & -1 \end{pmatrix}, \tag{2.24}$$

$$Z|0\rangle = |0\rangle, Z|1\rangle = -|1\rangle. \tag{2.25}$$

When applied on a color wire, the Z gate performs the transformation:

$$Z(|c(\theta_k)\rangle) = |c(-\theta_k)\rangle, \forall k \in \{0, 1, \ldots, 2^{2n} - 1\}. \tag{2.26}$$

Its function is to change the sign of the angle that encodes the color information, which is useful when combined with other gates.

2.2.3.3   Color Transformation Based on Hadamard Gate

The third single-qubit gate is the Hadamard gate, or H gate, whose function is

$$H = \frac{1}{\sqrt{2}} \begin{pmatrix} 1 & 1 \\ 1 & -1 \end{pmatrix}, \tag{2.27}$$

$$H|0\rangle = \frac{1}{\sqrt{2}}(|0\rangle + |1\rangle), H|1\rangle = \frac{1}{\sqrt{2}}(|0\rangle - |1\rangle). \tag{2.28}$$

When the H gate is applied on a color wire, its performance is

$$H(|c(\theta_k)\rangle) = |c\left(\frac{\pi}{4} - \theta_k\right)\rangle, \forall k \in \left\{0, 1, \ldots, 2^{2n} - 1\right\}, \tag{2.29}$$

whose function is to neutralize the color of every position in the image.

2.2.3.4   General Form of Color Transformations

The general form of the above transformations, X, Z, and H, can be expressed as the unitary matrix:

$$C(2\theta) = \begin{pmatrix} \cos\theta & \sin\theta \\ \sin\theta & -\cos\theta \end{pmatrix}, \qquad (2.30)$$

where $\theta \in \left[0, \frac{\pi}{2}\right]$. When applied on the color wire of an image, the $C(2\theta)$ operator transforms the color information as

$$C(2\theta)(|c(\theta_k)\rangle) = |c(\theta - \theta_k)\rangle, \forall k \in \left\{0, 1, \ldots, 2^{2n} - 1\right\}. \qquad (2.31)$$

This operation changes the original color, encoded by θ_k, to a new color, encoded by $\theta - \theta_k$. Combining this operation with the Z gate, one can obtain a new color represented by $\theta + \theta_k$. The transformations X, H, and Z are special cases of $C(\theta)$, where θ equals π, $\frac{\pi}{2}$, and 0, respectively.

Finally, an example of color transformation on a quantum image is shown in Fig. 2.7, where (a) is the original 8×8 FRQI image that includes four gray levels (black, dark gray, light gray, and white). Applying the NOT gate on the color wire of the circuit in (b), the color-transformed image shown in (c) can be obtained. The function of the NOT gate is analogous to inverting all the color information of the image. In fact, by specifying the subareas and imposing the necessary constraints as discussed in Sect. 2.2.2.3, multiple color transformations can be run on a single FRQI image.

To summarize, FRQI is a normalized quantum state which captures the color and position information of each pixel in the image. Based on its flexible model, basic geometric and color transformations similar to classical image processing can be easily constructed. Other FRQI-based operations as well as related applications will be introduced in the following chapters.

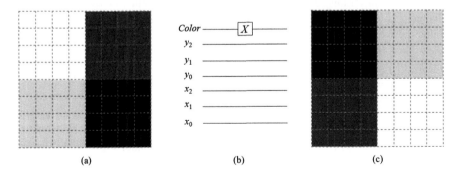

Fig. 2.7   (a) A synthetic 8×8 FRQI image; (b) the quantum circuit; and (c) the transformed image

2.3 Multi-Channel Representation for Quantum Images

By extending the grayscale information encoded in an FRQI image to a color representation, a multi-channel representation for quantum images (MCQI), which uses R, G, and B channels to represent color information about the image while retaining its normalized state, was proposed in [23]. MCQI allows to design some low-complexity color information operators. These can be realized by applying quantum gates on the R, G, and/or B wires of the circuits, which implies that the computational complexities of these operators are independent of the image size. Moreover, MCQI and related operations provide efficient tools for quantum watermarking algorithms, etc. based on color images by hiding secret information in the design of quantum circuits [24].

2.3.1 RGBα Color Space

The RGB color model [21], one of the best-known multi-channel color models, specifies colors in three primary channels or components, i.e., red (R), green (G), and blue (B). It is an additive color model in which red, green, and blue light are combined in various ways to reproduce a broad array of colors. The amount of each component gives an image intensity. If all components have the highest intensity, then the resulting color is white. In the RGB color model, one original color image can be constructed from three grayscale images (channels or components). As the most widely used color spaces for sensing, representation, and display of images in electronic systems, the RGB color model plays an important role in image processing [21].

The RGBα color space is actually a use of the RGB color model with extra information. The color belongs to the RGB color space, as discussed earlier, and α represents the α channel, which is normally used as an opacity channel [4].

Specifically, if a pixel has a value of 0 in its alpha channel (i.e., $T_\alpha = 0$), then this pixel is fully transparent (thus invisible), whereas a value of 255 in the alpha channel ($T_\alpha = 255$) gives a fully opaque pixel (i.e., traditional digital images). Values between 0 and 255 make it possible for pixels to show through a background like a glass (i.e., translucency). For example, given two images A and B (assuming images of the same size), A is the original image and B is the background image, and after α blending, the obtained image D can be defined as

$$D_X(i, j) = \left[T_\alpha A_X(i, j) + (255 - T_\alpha) B_X(i, j) \right]/255, \tag{2.32}$$

where $A_X(i, j)$, $B_X(i, j)$, and $D_X(i, j)$ are the X channel's grayscale values of pixels of images A, B, and D, respectively, and $X \in \{R, G, B\}$. T_α is the transparency parameter of the α channel. Examples of α blending images are shown in Fig. 2.8.

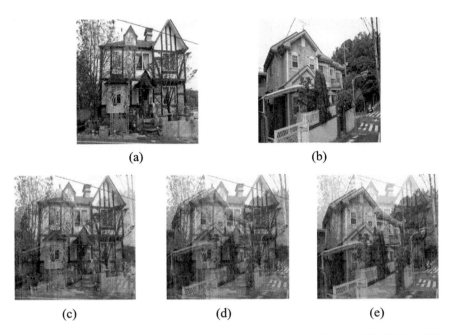

Fig. 2.8 Example of α blending operation: (**a**) Image A; (**b**) Image B; (**c**) $T_\alpha = 178$; (**d**) $T_\alpha = 128$; and (**e**) $T_\alpha = 77$

2.3.2   MCQI Representation and Initialization

To process color images on quantum computers, a new representation encoding information from the R, G, and B channels should be established, and this multi-channel information should be stored in quantum states simultaneously. Based on FRQI representation, multi-channel representation of quantum images (MCQI) was proposed to capture RGB channel information [24]. This is accomplished by assigning three qubits to encode color information about images. The mathematical expression is

$$|I\rangle = \frac{1}{2^{n+1}} \sum_{i=0}^{2^{2n}-1} |C_{RGB}^i\rangle \otimes |i\rangle, \tag{2.33}$$

where $|C_{RGB}^i\rangle$ encodes R, G, and B channel information and is defined as

$$
\begin{aligned}
|C_{RGB}^i\rangle = {} & \cos\theta_R^i |000\rangle + \cos\theta_G^i |001\rangle + \cos\theta_B^i |010\rangle \\
& + \sin\theta_R^i |100\rangle + \sin\theta_G^i |101\rangle + \sin\theta_B^i |110\rangle \\
& + \cos\theta_\alpha |011\rangle + \sin\theta_\alpha |111\rangle,
\end{aligned}
\tag{2.34}
$$

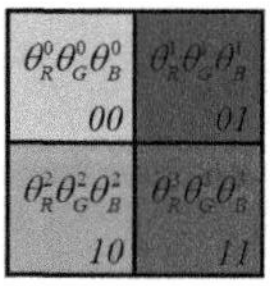

$\theta_R^0\theta_G^0\theta_B^0$	$\theta_R^1\theta_G^1\theta_B^1$
00	01
$\theta_R^2\theta_G^2\theta_B^2$	$\theta_R^3\theta_G^3\theta_B^3$
10	11

$$|I\rangle = \frac{1}{4}[(\cos\theta_R^0|000\rangle + \cos\theta_G^0|001\rangle + \cos\theta_B^0|010\rangle + \sin\theta_R^0|100\rangle + \sin\theta_G^0|101\rangle + \sin\theta_B^0|110\rangle)\otimes|00\rangle$$
$$+ (\cos\theta_R^1|000\rangle + \cos\theta_G^1|001\rangle + \cos\theta_B^1|010\rangle + \sin\theta_R^1|100\rangle + \sin\theta_G^1|101\rangle + \sin\theta_B^1|110\rangle)\otimes|01\rangle$$
$$+ (\cos\theta_R^2|000\rangle + \cos\theta_G^2|001\rangle + \cos\theta_B^2|010\rangle + \sin\theta_R^2|100\rangle + \sin\theta_G^2|101\rangle + \sin\theta_B^2|110\rangle)\otimes|10\rangle$$
$$+ (\cos\theta_R^3|000\rangle + \cos\theta_G^3|001\rangle + \cos\theta_B^3|010\rangle + \sin\theta_R^3|100\rangle + \sin\theta_G^3|101\rangle + \sin\theta_B^3|110\rangle)\otimes|11\rangle]$$

Fig. 2.9 A 2×2 MCQI image and its quantum state

where $|000\rangle, |001\rangle, \ldots, |111\rangle$ are eight-dimensional computational basis states; $\{\theta_R^i, \theta_G^i, \theta_B^i\} \in [0, \pi/2]$ are three angles encoding colors of the R, G, and B channels, respectively, of the i-th pixel; and $|i\rangle$, $i = 0, 1, \ldots, 2^{2n} - 1$, are 2^{2n}-dimensional computational basis states. Only three channels (i.e., six coefficients) are enough to encode the RGB information of the MCQI image. Hence, the coefficients of $|011\rangle$ and $|111\rangle$ (i.e., $\cos\theta_\alpha$ and $\sin\theta_\alpha$) are set to be constant ($\theta_\alpha = 0$) to carry no information [23]. An example of a 2×2 MCQI image with its quantum state is presented in Fig. 2.9. The computational complexity of preparing the MCQI image is the same as for FRQI, i.e., $O(2^{4n})$ [24].

An MCQI image is stored in the preparation process using the MC-PPT that extends the vector in Theorem 2.1 to three vectors of angles [24]. MC-PPT steers an MCQI image from its initialized state to the desired quantum image state, which captures all of the information about the image. In addition, to retrieve the quantum image, the R, G, and B states must be measured separately. To illustrate this point, Eq. (2.34) is rewritten as

$$|C_{RGB}^i\rangle = |C_R\rangle|00\rangle + |C_G\rangle|01\rangle + |C_B\rangle|10\rangle + |C_\alpha\rangle|11\rangle, \tag{2.35}$$

where

$$\begin{aligned} |C_R\rangle &= \cos\theta_R^i|0\rangle + \sin\theta_R^i|1\rangle, \\ |C_G\rangle &= \cos\theta_G^i|0\rangle + \sin\theta_G^i|1\rangle, \\ |C_B\rangle &= \cos\theta_B^i|0\rangle + \sin\theta_B^i|1\rangle, \\ |C_\alpha\rangle &= \cos\theta_\alpha|0\rangle + \sin\theta_\alpha|1\rangle. \end{aligned} \tag{2.36}$$

From Eqs. (2.35) and (2.36), the measurement operation is applied separately to $|C_R\rangle$, $|C_G\rangle$, and $|C_B\rangle$, encoding the grayscale values of the R, G, and B channels using two control operations from c_2 and c_3 qubits, as shown in Fig. 2.10. Each measurement on $|C_X\rangle$ (where $X \in \{R, G, B\}$) gives either 0 or 1 as a result. Many measurements reveal either 0 with probability $\cos^2\theta_X^i$ or 1 with probability $\sin^2\theta_X^i$. The grayscale value of the X channel can be retrieved from this probability.

An improved version of MCQI representation, color quantum image based on phase transform (CQIPT) [22], was proposed, where the color information is prepared by controlled-phase gates. This is especially flexible for many image processing and security algorithms based on phase encoding.

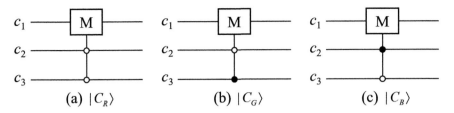

Fig. 2.10 General quantum circuit for measurement operations on $|C_X\rangle$

2.3.3 Color Transformations on MCQI Images

FRQI and MCQI representations use the same method for position information encoding, e.g., the same arrangement for position qubits. They differ in their use of color qubits; FRQI uses one qubit to encode an image color, whereas MCQI uses three qubits to carry multi-channel color information. Consequently, MCQI representation exhibits two features:

- All of the FRQI-based geometric operations, such as flipping and coordinate swapping, are directly extended to MCQI images.
- Since multi-channel information is stored in three color qubits, more color information-based image operations can be developed.

Color transformations on MCQI images [25] are now introduced. These are executed using the basic quantum gates, including NOT, CNOT, and swap gates. None of these transformations can be executed on FRQI images.

2.3.3.1 Channel of Interest Operation

The channel of interest (COI) operator shifts the grayscale value of a color channel (R, G, B, or α) [25], and is defined as

$$COI_X = U_X \otimes I^{\otimes 2n}, \quad X \in \{R, G, B, \alpha\}. \tag{2.37}$$

The COI_X operator is realized by using a $U_X = C^2(R_y(2\theta))$ gate, where θ is the shifting parameter. The calculation produces the result $|I_X\rangle$ from the application of COI_X on $|I\rangle$, given as

$$|I_X\rangle = COI_X|I\rangle$$

$$= \left(U_X \otimes I^{\otimes 2n}\right)\left(\frac{1}{2^{n+1}}\sum_{i=0}^{2^{2n}-1}|C_{RGB\alpha}^i\rangle \otimes |i\rangle\right) \tag{2.38}$$

$$= \frac{1}{2^{n+1}}\sum_{i=0}^{2^{2n}-1}|C_{RGB\alpha}^{X_i}\rangle \otimes |i\rangle,$$

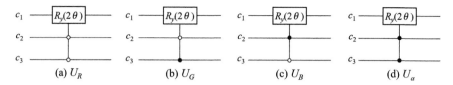

Fig. 2.11 General quantum circuit for U_X operations

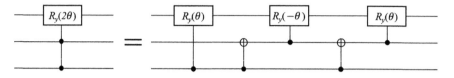

Fig. 2.12 A $C^2(R_y(2\theta))$ gate can be built from $C(R_y(\theta))$, $C(R_y(-\theta))$, and CNOT gates

where the $|C^i_{RGB\alpha}\rangle$ state carries the RGB color information defined in Eq. (2.34), and $|C^{X_i}_{RGB\alpha}\rangle$ is the new color state after applying the COI_X operator, shown as

$$|C^{R_i}_{RGB\alpha}\rangle = \cos(\theta^i_R - \theta)|000\rangle + \cos\theta^i_G|001\rangle + \cos\theta^i_B|010\rangle + \cos\theta^i_\alpha|011\rangle$$
$$+ \sin(\theta^i_R - \theta)|100\rangle + \sin\theta^i_G|101\rangle + \sin\theta^i_B|110\rangle + \sin\theta^i_\alpha|111\rangle,$$
$$(2.39)$$

$$|C^{G_i}_{RGB\alpha}\rangle = \cos\theta^i_R|000\rangle + \cos(\theta^i_G - \theta)|001\rangle + \cos\theta^i_B|010\rangle + \cos\theta^i_\alpha|011\rangle$$
$$+ \sin\theta^i_R|100\rangle + \sin(\theta^i_G - \theta)|101\rangle + \sin\theta^i_B|110\rangle + \sin\theta^i_\alpha|111\rangle,$$
$$(2.40)$$

$$|C^{B_i}_{RGB\alpha}\rangle = \cos\theta^i_R|000\rangle + \cos\theta^i_G|001\rangle + \cos(\theta^i_B - \theta)|010\rangle + \cos\theta^i_\alpha|011\rangle$$
$$+ \sin\theta^i_R|100\rangle + \sin\theta^i_G|101\rangle + \sin(\theta^i_B - \theta)|110\rangle + \sin\theta^i_\alpha|111\rangle,$$
$$(2.41)$$

$$|C^{\alpha_i}_{RGB\alpha}\rangle = \cos\theta^i_R|000\rangle + \cos\theta^i_G|001\rangle + \cos\theta^i_B|010\rangle + \cos(\theta^i_\alpha - \theta)|011\rangle$$
$$+ \sin\theta^i_R|100\rangle + \sin\theta^i_G|101\rangle + \sin\theta^i_B|110\rangle + \sin(\theta^i_\alpha - \theta)|111\rangle.$$
$$(2.42)$$

All of the colors in the quantum image $|I_X\rangle$ come from the original image $|I\rangle$ by shifting the angle θ on the R, G, B, or α channel. The quantum circuits of U_X (U_R, U_G, U_B, and U_α) are $C^2(R_y(2\theta))$ gates, as shown in Fig. 2.11, and the $C^2(R_y(2\theta))$ can be constructed from elementary gates (controlled-rotation and CNOT gates), as shown in Fig. 2.12.

Specifically, the rotation operation is applied to the c_1 qubit, and control operations are from the c_2 and c_3 qubits. No operation is applied to position qubits, so the complexity of the COI operation on a quantum computer is independent of image size, and is $O(1)$ [25].

2.3.3.2   Channel-Swapping Operation

The channel-swapping (CS) operator is used to swap the grayscale values between two channels (R and G, R and B, or G and B) [25], and is defined as

$$CS_Y = I \otimes U_Y \otimes I^{\otimes 2n}, \quad Y \in \{RG, RB, GB\}. \tag{2.43}$$

The CS_Y operator uses a CNOT gate or swap gate on c_2 and c_3 color qubits. The application of CS_Y on $|I\rangle$ produces the result $|I_Y\rangle$, given as

$$
\begin{aligned}
|I_Y\rangle &= CS_Y|I\rangle \\
&= \left(I \otimes U_Y \otimes I^{\otimes 2n}\right)\left(\frac{1}{2^{n+1}}\sum_{i=0}^{2^{2n}-1}|C^i_{RGB\alpha}\rangle \otimes |i\rangle\right) \\
&= \frac{1}{2^{n+1}}\sum_{i=0}^{2^{2n}-1}|C^{Y_i}_{RGB\alpha}\rangle \otimes |i\rangle,
\end{aligned}
\tag{2.44}
$$

where $|C^{Y_i}_{RGB\alpha}\rangle$ is the new color state after applying the CS_Y operator, shown as

$$
\begin{aligned}
|C^{RG_i}_{RGB\alpha}\rangle &= \cos\theta^i_G|000\rangle + \cos\theta^i_R|001\rangle + \cos\theta^i_B|010\rangle + \cos\theta^i_\alpha|011\rangle \\
&\quad + \sin\theta^i_G|100\rangle + \sin\theta^i_R|101\rangle + \sin\theta^i_B|110\rangle + \sin\theta^i_\alpha|111\rangle,
\end{aligned}
\tag{2.45}
$$

$$
\begin{aligned}
|C^{RB_i}_{RGB\alpha}\rangle &= \cos\theta^i_B|000\rangle + \cos\theta^i_G|001\rangle + \cos\theta^i_R|010\rangle + \cos\theta^i_\alpha|011\rangle \\
&\quad + \sin\theta^i_B|100\rangle + \sin\theta^i_G|101\rangle + \sin\theta^i_R|110\rangle + \sin\theta^i_\alpha|111\rangle,
\end{aligned}
\tag{2.46}
$$

$$
\begin{aligned}
|C^{GB_i}_{RGB\alpha}\rangle &= \cos\theta^i_R|000\rangle + \cos\theta^i_B|001\rangle + \cos\theta^i_G|010\rangle + \cos\theta^i_\alpha|011\rangle \\
&\quad + \sin\theta^i_R|100\rangle + \sin\theta^i_B|101\rangle + \sin\theta^i_G|110\rangle + \sin\theta^i_\alpha|111\rangle.
\end{aligned}
\tag{2.47}
$$

Quantum image $|I_Y\rangle$ is obtained from the original image $|I\rangle$ by applying the CS_Y operation. The quantum circuits of U_Y (U_{RG}, U_{RB}, and U_{GB}) are shown in Fig. 2.13. Since unitary operations (U_{RG}, U_{RB}, and U_{GB}) are constructed using two CNOT gates (Fig. 2.13a, b) and one swap gate (Fig. 2.13c), the complexity of the channel-swapping operation is $O(1)$ [25].

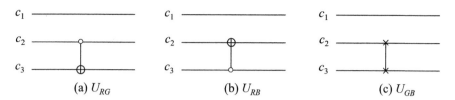

Fig. 2.13 General quantum circuit for U_Y operations

2.3.3.3 α Blending Operation

The α blending (αB) operator is used to blend an image A with a background image B to create the appearance of partial or full transparency [25], and is defined as

$$\alpha B_{AB} = U_{AB} \otimes I^{\otimes 2n}. \tag{2.48}$$

Assume that images A and B are MCQI images of the same size with four components (R, G, B, and α), where A is the image to be blended and B is the background image. To encode the two images in MCQI states, one ancilla qubit is used with the MCQI qubits (three color qubits and $2n$ position qubits for a $2^n \times 2^n$ image), shown as

$$|I_{AB}\rangle = \frac{1}{2^{n+\frac{3}{2}}} \sum_{i=0}^{2^n-1} \left(|0\rangle \otimes |C_A^i\rangle + |1\rangle \otimes |C_B^i\rangle \right) \otimes |i\rangle, \tag{2.49}$$

where $|C_A^i\rangle$ and $|C_B^i\rangle$ are the color states of images A and B, respectively, and are defined as

$$|C_A^i\rangle = \cos\theta_{AR}^i |000\rangle + \cos\theta_{AG}^i |001\rangle + \cos\theta_{AB}^i |010\rangle + \cos\theta_{A\alpha}^i |011\rangle$$
$$+ \sin\theta_{AR}^i |100\rangle + \sin\theta_{AG}^i |101\rangle + \sin\theta_{AB}^i |110\rangle + \sin\theta_{A\alpha}^i |111\rangle, \tag{2.50}$$

$$|C_B^i\rangle = \cos\theta_{BR}^i |000\rangle + \cos\theta_{BG}^i |001\rangle + \cos\theta_{BB}^i |010\rangle + \cos\theta_{B\alpha}^i |011\rangle$$
$$+ \sin\theta_{BR}^i |100\rangle + \sin\theta_{BG}^i |101\rangle + \sin\theta_{BB}^i |110\rangle + \sin\theta_{B\alpha}^i |111\rangle, \tag{2.51}$$

where θ_{AX} and θ_{BX} ($X \in \{R, G, B, \alpha\}$) are angles encoding the color information of images A and B, respectively. Since the two images are totally opaque before blending, the initial values of $\theta_{A\alpha}^i$ and $\theta_{B\alpha}^i$ are 0. After storing the two images concurrently, two controlled-rotation gates are applied on the a_1 and color (c_1, c_2, c_3) qubits, where the control operations are on a_1, c_2, and c_3 and the rotations are

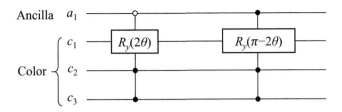

Fig. 2.14 General quantum circuit for U_{AB} operations

on the c_1 qubits (as shown in Fig. 2.14). The computational procedure is

$$|I_{\alpha B}\rangle = \alpha B_{AB}|I_{AB}\rangle$$

$$= \frac{1}{2^{n+\frac{3}{2}}} \sum_{i=0}^{2^n-1} U_{AB}\big(|0\rangle \otimes |C_A^i\rangle + |1\rangle \otimes |C_B^i\rangle\big) \otimes I^{\otimes 2n}|i\rangle \tag{2.52}$$

$$= \frac{1}{2^{n+\frac{3}{2}}} \sum_{i=0}^{2^n-1} \big(|0\rangle \otimes |C_A'^i\rangle + |1\rangle \otimes |C_B'^i\rangle\big) \otimes |i\rangle,$$

where

$$|C_A'^i\rangle = \cos\theta_{AR}^i|000\rangle + \cos\theta_{AG}^i|001\rangle + \cos\theta_{AB}^i|010\rangle + \cos(\theta_{A\alpha}^i - \theta)|011\rangle$$

$$+ \sin\theta_{AR}^i|100\rangle + \sin\theta_{AG}^i|101\rangle + \sin\theta_{AB}^i|110\rangle + \sin(\theta_{A\alpha}^i - \theta)|111\rangle, \tag{2.53}$$

$$|C_B'^i\rangle = \cos\theta_{BR}^i|000\rangle + \cos\theta_{BG}^i|001\rangle + \cos\theta_{BB}^i|010\rangle + \cos\left(\theta_{B\alpha}^i + \theta - \frac{\pi}{2}\right)|011\rangle$$

$$+ \sin\theta_{BR}^i|100\rangle + \sin\theta_{BG}^i|101\rangle + \sin\theta_{BB}^i|110\rangle + \sin\left(\theta_{B\alpha}^i + \theta - \frac{\pi}{2}\right)|111\rangle. \tag{2.54}$$

Generally, αB operations can be used in image matte, image rendering, and watermarking. In addition, by utilizing the restricted geometric transformations in Sect. 2.2.2.3, the color transformations above can realize a restricted color transformation, which is a color transformation on just the part of the image of interest.

To summarize, MCQI representation is an extension of FRQI representation that facilitates more advanced color image processing by applying different operations on the R, G, and B channels. Related applications will be discussed in later chapters.

2.4 Novel Enhanced Representation for Quantum Images

In the FRQI and MCQI representations, the color information is encoded by the superposition of one and three qubits, separately. Therefore, these quantum images will probably be retrieved based on multiple measurements. A novel enhanced quantum representation for digital images (NEQR) [30] that improves on the earlier models is now introduced. The new model uses the basis state of a qubit sequence to store the grayscale value of every pixel. Therefore, two qubit sequences, representing the grayscale and positional information of all of the pixels, are used in NEQR representation to store the whole image.

2.4.1 NEQR Representation and Initialization

NEQR representation uses the basis state of a qubit sequence to store the grayscale value of every pixel, instead of an angle encoded in a qubit, as in FRQI representation [30]. The representation of a $2^n \times 2^n$ NEQR image is defined as

$$|I\rangle = \frac{1}{2^n} \sum_{y=0}^{2^n-1} \sum_{x=0}^{2^n-1} |f(y,x)\rangle|yx\rangle = \frac{1}{2^n} \sum_{y=0}^{2^n-1} \sum_{x=0}^{2^n-1} \bigotimes_{i=0}^{q-1} |C_{yx}^i\rangle|yx\rangle. \qquad (2.55)$$

where $f(y,x)$ is the grayscale value, defined as

$$f(y,x) = C_{yx}^{q-1} C_{yx}^{q-2} \dots C_{yx}^1 C_{yx}^0, \qquad (2.56)$$

where $C_{yx}^i \in \{0,1\}$ and $f(y,x) \in [0, 2^q - 1]$. An example of a 2×2 NEQR image and its quantum state is shown in Fig. 2.15.

The computational complexity of preparing an NEQR image exhibits an approximately quadratic decrease, i.e., $O(qn \cdot 2^{2n})$, compared to FRQI and MCQI images [30]. However, it should be stressed that NEQR representation uses more qubits to encode a quantum image. From its representation, $q+2n$ qubits are needed to construct the quantum image model for a $2^n \times 2^n$ image with gray range 2^q. The $2n$ qubits for position information is the same as for FRQI and MCQI representation. NEQR uses q qubits for color information, while FRQI and MCQI use one qubit

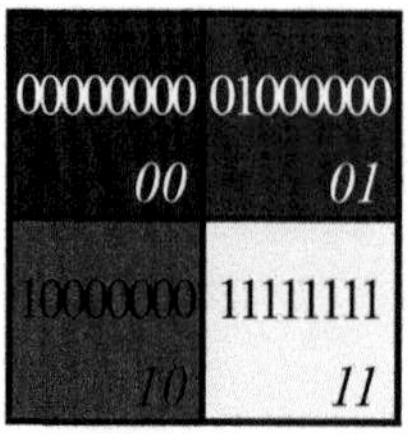

$$|I\rangle = \frac{1}{2}(|0\rangle \otimes |00\rangle + |64\rangle \otimes |01\rangle + |128\rangle \otimes |10\rangle + |255\rangle \otimes |11\rangle)$$

$$= \frac{1}{2}(|00000000\rangle \otimes |00\rangle + |01000000\rangle \otimes |01\rangle$$

$$+ |10000000\rangle \otimes |10\rangle + |11111111\rangle \otimes |11\rangle)$$

Fig. 2.15 A 2×2 NEQR image and its quantum state

and three qubits, respectively. Researchers have devised improved NEQR (INEQR) and generalized QIR (GQIR) by resizing the quantum image to an arbitrary size for wider applications [8].

The first step in preparing an NEQR image is similar to that for an FRQI image, as presented in Sect. 2.2.1, hence, it is not repeated here. In the second step, the grayscale value for every pixel is set. This step is divided into 2^{2n} sub-operations to store the grayscale information for every pixel. During image retrieval from the quantum image, every pixel should be recovered individually by quantum measurements over the computational basis. After all pixels are recovered, the accurate classical image will be retrieved from the NEQR image model [30].

2.4.2   Color Transformations on NEQR Images

This section will discuss how to use the NEQR representation for QIMP, including complement color transformation as well as color transformation on the quantum image [30].

2.4.2.1   Complement Color Transformation

Complement color transformation changes all the grayscales of the pixels in an NEQR image to the complement values on 2^q [30]. The complement color transformation U_C is defined as

$$U_C = X^{\otimes q} \otimes I^{\otimes 2n}, \qquad (2.57)$$

where X denotes the NOT gate and I represents the identity gate, as presented in Fig. 1.5.

For a quantum image $|I\rangle$, U_C takes q NOT gates for each color qubit and $2n$ identity gates for others. Therefore, this operation inverts all the color qubits in the NEQR model and changes the grayscale value of every pixel in the image to its opposite value. Equation (2.58) produces the result of the U_C operation on the quantum image $|I\rangle$ as

$$
\begin{aligned}
U_C(|I\rangle) &= U_C \left(\frac{1}{2^n} \sum_{y=0}^{2^n-1} \sum_{x=0}^{2^n-1} |f(y,x)\rangle |y\rangle |x\rangle \right) \\
&= \frac{1}{2^n} \sum_{y=0}^{2^n-1} \sum_{x=0}^{2^n-1} \left(\bigotimes_{i=0}^{q-1} \left(X |C_{yx}^i\rangle \right) |y\rangle |x\rangle \right) \\
&= \frac{1}{2^n} \sum_{y=0}^{2^n-1} \sum_{x=0}^{2^n-1} |2^q - 1 - f(y,x)\rangle |y\rangle |x\rangle.
\end{aligned}
\qquad (2.58)
$$

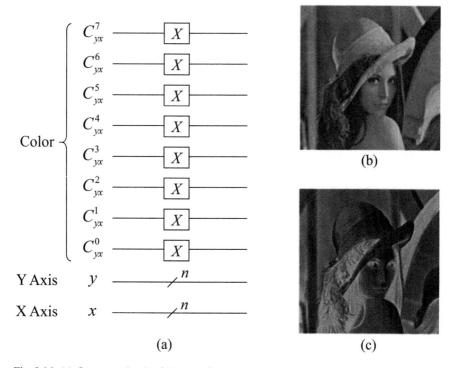

(a)   (c)

Fig. 2.16 (**a**) Quantum circuit of U_C transformation; (**b**) Lena image; and (**c**) the transformed image (reprinted from ref. [30], with permission of Springer)

Figure 2.16 shows the quantum circuit of U_C on the NEQR model, with the Lena image used as an example. This complement color transformation makes the target in the image (notably medical images) easier to be found [30].

In the NEQR image, all of the pixels are stored in a $2n + q$ qubit sequence. This means that all of the color transformations for all of the pixels can be performed simultaneously. Hence, complement color transformations have a computational complexity of no more than $O(2n + q)$ [30].

2.4.2.2 And/or Color Transformation

Digital and/or binary gates, as traditionally defined in computer science, are irreversible operations. Since unitary operators are reversible and all operations in quantum computation are required to be physically realizable, then and/or operators must be reformulated in quantum computation. Luckily, any irreversible operation can be expressed as a reversible operation (usually at the expense of some ancilla information).

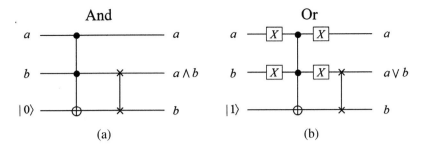

Fig. 2.17 (**a**) Quantum $\cap$ gate and (**b**) quantum $\cup$ gate

Two common quantum gates (the Toffoli gate and swap gate, introduced in Sect. 1.1.3) and an ancillary qubit are utilized to construct quantum and/or gates [30]. The following notations are used: symbols $\wedge$ and $\vee$ are used to refer to and/or operations over binary variables, respectively, while the symbols $\cap$ and $\cup$ are used to refer to and/or operations over qubits.

An ancillary qubit initialized as $|0\rangle$ is employed to construct the quantum circuit of the quantum $\cap$ gate, shown in Fig. 2.17a. The quantum transform is

$$\cap : |a\rangle|b\rangle|0\rangle \rightarrow |a\rangle|a \cap b\rangle|b\rangle. \tag{2.59}$$

Similarly, a quantum $\cup$ gate is constructed with an ancillary qubit initialized as $|1\rangle$ as in Fig. 2.17b. The transformation of a quantum $\cup$ gate is given by

$$\cup : |a\rangle|b\rangle|1\rangle \rightarrow |a\rangle|a \cup b\rangle|b\rangle. \tag{2.60}$$

The quantum $\cap$ gate is utilized to design the operation U_S [30], defined as

$$U_S : |C_{yx}^{q-1}\rangle|C_{yx}^{0}\rangle|0\rangle \rightarrow |C_{yx}^{q-1}\rangle|C_{yx}^{q-1} \cap C_{yx}^{0}\rangle|C_{yx}^{0}\rangle, \tag{2.61}$$

whose input is the highest qubit $|C_{yx}^{q-1}\rangle$ and lowest qubit $|C_{yx}^{0}\rangle$ in the color qubit sequence, and whose output will be stored in the qubit $|C_{yx}^{0}\rangle$. The U_S transformation on a quantum image $|I\rangle$ is

$$
\begin{aligned}
U_S : |I\rangle|0\rangle &\rightarrow \frac{1}{2^n} \sum_{y=0}^{2^n-1} \sum_{x=0}^{2^n-1} \left(\bigotimes_{i=0}^{q-1} |C_{yx}^{i}\rangle \right) |C_{yx}^{q-1} \cap C_{yx}^{0}\rangle|y\rangle|x\rangle|C_{yx}^{0}\rangle \\
&= \frac{1}{2^n} \sum_{y=0}^{2^n-1} \sum_{x=0, C_{yx}^{q-1}=1}^{2^n-1} |1\rangle \left(\bigotimes_{i=0}^{q-2} |C_{yx}^{i}\rangle \right) |C_{yx}^{0}\rangle|y\rangle|x\rangle|C_{yx}^{0}\rangle \\
&\quad + \frac{1}{2^n} \sum_{y=0}^{2^n-1} \sum_{x=0, C_{yx}^{q-1}=0}^{2^n-1} |0\rangle \left(\bigotimes_{i=0}^{q-2} |C_{yx}^{i}\rangle \right) |0\rangle|y\rangle|x\rangle|C_{yx}^{0}\rangle.
\end{aligned}
\tag{2.62}
$$

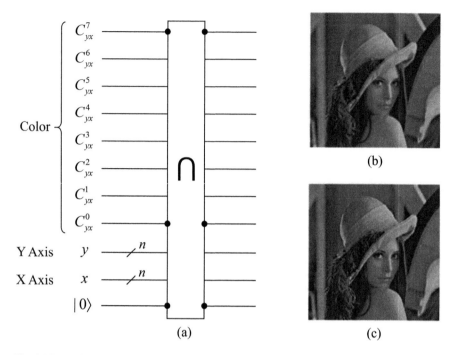

Fig. 2.18 (**a**) Quantum circuit of U_S transformation; (**b**) Lena image; and (**c**) the transformed image (reprinted from ref. [30], with permission of Springer)

Figure 2.18 shows the quantum circuit of the U_S transformation and the comparative results, where a quantum ∩ gate is taken on $|C_{yx}^7\rangle$, $|C_{yx}^0\rangle$, and an ancillary qubit $|0\rangle$. This kind of transformation can be applied in image-adaptive quantization [20].

To summarize, the NEQR representation utilizes the basis state of a qubit sequence to represent the grayscale of pixels, instead of the probability amplitude of a single qubit used in the FRQI representation. In this manner, it reduces the computational complexity of image preparation and provides more accurate information retrieval. In the following chapters, some NEQR-based quantum image applications will be introduced.

In this chapter, mainstream QIRs are reviewed and classified into three models based on different requirements to capture the content of a quantum image. They are thoroughly compared in terms of their color information encoding strategies, computational complexities of preparation, and measurement-based retrievals. The preparation, compression, and retrieval of FRQI, MCQI, and NEQR representations are fully introduced. While designing the position and color transformations of these QIRs, some definitions and theorems are given, which will guide in part the subsequent QIMP studies.

References

1. Caraiman, S., Manta, V.: Image processing using quantum computing. In: 16th International Conference on System Theory, Control and Computing (ICSTCC), pp. 1–6 (2012)
2. Caraiman, S., Manta, V.: Image segmentation on a quantum computer. Quantum Inf. Process. 14(5), 1693–1715 (2015)
3. Fan, P., Zhou, R., Jing, N., Li, H.: Geometric transformations of multidimensional color images based on NASS. Inf. Sci. 340–341, 191–208 (2016)
4. Hillman, P., Hannah, J., Renshaw, D.: Alpha channel estimation in high resolution images and image sequences. In: IEEE Computer Society Conference on Computer Vision and Pattern Recognition (CVPR), pp. 1063–1068 (2001)
5. Iliyasu, A.: Algorithmic frameworks to support the realisation of secure and efficient image-video processing applications on quantum computers. Ph.D Thesis, Tokyo Institute of Technology, Tokyo (2012)
6. Iliyasu, A., Le, P., Dong, F., Hirota, K.: Watermarking and authentication of quantum images based on restricted geometric transformations. Inf. Sci. 186(1), 126–149 (2012)
7. Iliyasu, A., Le, P., Fangyan, D., Hirota, K.: Restricted geometric transformations and their applications for quantum image watermarking and authentication. In: Proceeding of the 10th Asian Conference on Quantum Information Sciences (AQIS 2010), pp. 96–97 (2010)
8. Jiang, N., Lu, X., Hu, H., Dang, Y., Cai, Y.: A novel quantum image compression method based on JPEG. Int. J. Theor. Phys. 57(3), 611–636 (2018)
9. Latorre, J.: Image compression and entanglement. arXiv: quant-ph/0510031 (2005)
10. Le, P., Dong, F., Hirota, K.: Flexible representation of quantum images and its computational complexity analysis. In: Proceedings of the 10th Symposium on Advanced Intelligent Systems (ISIS 2009), pp. 146–149 (2009)
11. Le, P., Iliyasu, A., Dong, F., Hirota, K.: Fast geometric transformations on quantum images. IAENG Int. J. Appl. Math. 40(3), 113–123 (2010)
12. Le, P., Dong, F., Hirota, K.: A flexible representation of quantum images for polynomial preparation, image compression, and processing operations. Quantum Inf. Process. 10(1), 63–84 (2011)
13. Le, P., Iliyasu, A., Dong, F., Hirota, K.: Efficient colour transformations on quantum image. J. Adv. Comput. Intell. Intell. Inf. 15(6), 698–706 (2011)
14. Le, P., Iliyasu, A., Dong, F., Hirota, K.: A flexible representation and invertible transformations for images on quantum computers. New Adv. Intell. Signal Process. Stud. Comput. Intell. 372, 179–202 (2011)
15. Le, P., Iliyasu, A., Dong, F., Hirota, K.: Strategies for designing geometric transformations on quantum images. Theor. Comput. Sci. 412(15), 1406–1418 (2011)
16. Li, H., Zhu, Q., Lan, S., Shen, C., Zhou, R., Mo, J.: Image storage, retrieval, compression and segmentation in a quantum system. Quantum Inf. Process. 12(6), 2269–2290 (2013)
17. Li, H., Zhu, Q., Zhou, R., Song, L., Yang, X.: Multi-dimensional color image storage and retrieval for a normal arbitrary quantum superposition state. Quantum Inf. Process. 13(4), 991–1011 (2014)
18. Li, H., Fan, P., Xia, H., Song, S., He, X.: The multi-level and multi-dimensional quantum wavelet packet transforms. Sci. Rep. 8, 13884 (2018)
19. Nielsen, M., Chuang, I.: Quantum Computation and Quantum Information. Cambridge University Press, Cambridge (2000)
20. Pang, C., Zhou, Z., Guo, G.: A hybrid quantum encoding algorithm of vector quantization for image compression. arXiv:cs/0605002v3[cs.MM] (2006)
21. Plataniotis, K., Venetsanopoulos, A.: Color Image Processing and Applications. Springer, Berlin (2000)
22. Song, X., Wang, S., Niu, X.: Multi-channel quantum image representation based on phase transform and elementary transformations. J. Inf. Hiding Multimedia Signal Process. 5(4), 574–585 (2014)

23. Sun, B., Le, P., Iliyasu, A., Yan, F., Garcia, J., Dong, F., Hirota, K.: A multi-channel representation for images on quantum computers using the RGBα color space. In: IEEE 7th International Symposium on Intelligent Signal Processing (WISP), pp. 1–6 (2011)
24. Sun, B., Iliyasu, A., Yan, F., Dong, F., Hirota, K.: An RGB multi-channel representation for images on quantum computers. J. Adv. Comput. Intell. Intell. Inf. **17**(3), 404–417 (2013)
25. Sun, B., Iliyasu, A., Yan, F., Garcia, J., Dong, F., Al-Asmari, A., Hirota, K.: Multi-channel information operations on quantum images. J. Adv. Comput. Intell. Intell. Inf. **18**(2), 140–149 (2014)
26. Venegas-Andraca, S., Ball, J.: Processing images in entangled quantum systems. Quantum Inf. Process. **9**(1), 1–11 (2010)
27. Venegas-Andraca, S., Bose, S.: Storing, processing, and retrieving an image using quantum mechanics. In: Proceedings of SPIE Conference of Quantum Information and Computation, vol. 5105, pp. 137–147 (2003)
28. Yan, F., Iliyasu, A., Venegas-Andraca, S.: A survey of quantum image representations. Quantum Inf. Process. **15**(1), 1–35 (2016)
29. Yang, Y., Jia, X., Sun, S., Pan, Q.: Quantum cryptographic algorithm for color images using quantum Fourier transform and double random-phase encoding. Inf. Sci. **277**, 445–457 (2014)
30. Zhang, Y., Lu, K., Gao, Y., Wang, M.: NEQR: a novel enhanced quantum representation of digital images. Quantum Inf. Process. **12**(8), 2833–2860 (2013)
31. Zhang, Y., Lu, K., Gao, Y., Xu, K.: A novel quantum representation for log-polar images. Quantum Inf. Process. **12**(9), 3103–3126 (2013)

Chapter 3
Quantum Image Operations

A crucial feature in image processing consists of developing and providing access to a toolbox of mathematical operations to transform image contents. Quantum operations can be applied to a quantum image to transform an input image to an output image (or another representation). In these operations, what kind of results one might expect to achieve with a given type of operation, and what might be the computational burden associated with a given operation, should be understood. Currently available quantum image operations include interpolation [8, 16, 27, 28], translation [22], compression [7], and restoration [9]. In this chapter, the operations of quantum image comparison [25], scaling [6], and rotation [26] are introduced.

3.1 Parallel Comparison of Multiple Pairs of Quantum Images

Image searching can be defined as a computational process in which an image is provided as input and the corresponding output is a set of images that are related to the input image. Inspired by the paramount importance of image searching and its achievements on conventional computers [3], image searching appears to be an indispensable operation in QIMP [1].

It is envisaged that quantum image searching will likely become faster than classical searching because of the inherent parallelism of quantum computation [11]. A first step on the development of quantum image searching algorithms would be to propose a scheme to evaluate the extent to which two or more images are

---

© Springer Nature Singapore Pte Ltd. 2020
F. Yan, S. E. Venegas-Andraca, *Quantum Image Processing*,
https://doi.org/10.1007/978-981-32-9331-1_3

similar [25]. The main content of this section is tailored toward achieving this essential step of quantum image searching.

3.1.1   Representation of Strip Using Multiple Quantum Images

The strip representation is a method to encode 2^m FRQI images as a single array. Thanks to quantum parallelism, the strip representation can be used to transform multiple images using a limited amount of quantum resources. The definition and main properties of strip representation are now introduced.

Definition 3.1   A strip $|S(m)\rangle$ is an array comprising 2^m FRQI images, which is defined by

$$|S(m)\rangle = \frac{1}{2^{m/2}} \sum_{s=0}^{2^{2m}-1} |I_s\rangle \otimes |s\rangle, \tag{3.1}$$

where

$$|I_s\rangle = \frac{1}{2^n} \sum_{i=0}^{2^{2n}-1} |c_{s,i}\rangle \otimes |i\rangle, \tag{3.2}$$

$$|c_{s,i}\rangle = \cos\theta_{s,i}|0\rangle + \sin\theta_{s,i}|1\rangle, \tag{3.3}$$

$$\theta_{s,i} \in \left[0, \frac{\pi}{2}\right], i = 0, 1, \ldots, 2^{2n}-1, s = 0, 1, \ldots, 2^m - 1, \tag{3.4}$$

where $|s\rangle$ is the position of each image in the strip, m is the number of qubits required to encode the images being compared, $|I_s\rangle$ is an FRQI image as defined in Eq. (2.1) at position $|s\rangle$, and $|c_{s,i}\rangle$ and $|i\rangle$ encode the information about the colors and their corresponding positions in the image $|I_s\rangle$. Furthermore, the state $|S(m)\rangle$ is normalized, confirmed by

$$\||S(m)\rangle\| = \frac{1}{2^{m/2}} \sqrt{\sum_{s=0}^{2^m-1} \||I_s\rangle\|^2}$$

$$= \frac{1}{2^{m/2+n}} \sqrt{\sum_{s=0}^{2^m-1} \sum_{i=0}^{2^{2n}-1} (\cos^2\theta_{s,i} + \sin^2\theta_{s,i})} = 1. \tag{3.5}$$

The size of a strip in the representation captures the input state of the strip comprising 2^m quantum images. Each image in the strip is an FRQI state, while the combination of such states in the strip is best represented as a multiple FRQI, or simply an *m*FRQI state. The *m*FRQI state can represent 2^m quantum images using only $m + 2n + 1$ qubits, since all of the images in this strip have the same size. The mathematical structure of a strip and FRQI images allow us to have full access to each and every image as well as all pixels in a given image.

3.1.2 Scheme to Compare Quantum Images in Parallel

A scheme to compare quantum images, together with several definitions, which will form the basis of further discussion, is presented. First, two arbitrary FRQI images $|I_k\rangle$ and $|I_t\rangle$ are defined as

$$|I_k\rangle = \frac{1}{2^n} \sum_{i=0}^{2^{2n}-1} (\cos\theta_{k,i}|0\rangle + \sin\theta_{k,i}|1\rangle) \otimes |i\rangle, \tag{3.6}$$

and

$$|I_t\rangle = \frac{1}{2^n} \sum_{i=0}^{2^{2n}-1} (\cos\theta_{t,i}|0\rangle + \sin\theta_{t,i}|1\rangle) \otimes |i\rangle. \tag{3.7}$$

In the following lines, a definition of similarity between two FRQI images is presented, which consists of a function whose domain is the set of FRQI image pairs and corresponding range is the set $[0, 1]$. In addition, given a strip comprising 2^m quantum images, parallel comparison of quantum images allows us to retrieve the similarities between 2^{m-1} pairs of images in the strip simultaneously.

Definition 3.2 The difference between the i-th pixels of two FRQI images $|I_k\rangle$ and $|I_t\rangle$, as defined in Eqs. (3.6) and (3.7), is given by

$$\sigma_{k,t}^i = |\theta_{k,i} - \theta_{t,i}|, \sigma_{k,t}^i \in [0, \pi/2], \tag{3.8}$$

where $\theta_{k,i}$ and $\theta_{t,i}$ represent the respective color information at position i of the two images.

Definition 3.3 The similarity between two FRQI images $|I_k\rangle$ and $|I_t\rangle$, as defined in Eqs. (3.6) and (3.7), is a function of the pixel difference $\sigma_{k,t}$ at every position of the images, given by

$$\text{sim}(|I_k\rangle, |I_t\rangle) = f\left(\sigma_{k,t}^0, \sigma_{k,t}^1, \ldots, \sigma_{k,t}^{2^{2n}-1}\right), \tag{3.9}$$

where $\text{sim}(|I_k\rangle, |I_t\rangle) \in [0, 1]$.

Two special cases of the similarity between two quantum images are as follows:

- if $\forall i, \sigma^i_{k,t} = \pi/2$, then $\text{sim}(|I_k\rangle, |I_t\rangle) = 0$ and the two images are totally different;
- if $\forall i, \sigma^i_{k,t} = 0$, then $\text{sim}(|I_k\rangle, |I_t\rangle) = 1$ and the two images are exactly the same,

where $i = 0, 1, \ldots, 2^{2n} - 1$, and $\sigma^i_{k,t}$ is the pixel difference at position i as defined in Definition 3.2.

The strip representation introduced in Definition 3.1 is used to compare quantum images of equal size and it provides an efficient way to compare multiple pairs of quantum images in parallel. The comparison of quantum images in parallel consists of the following three steps [25]:

Step 1:   Preparation of the strip comprising 2^m quantum images

The color information and corresponding positions of every point in the classical version are integrated into the quantum state, and 2^m quantum images to be compared are combined to form a strip. The routine involved in preparing FRQI images and its extension to encode multiple FRQI images as a strip are discussed thoroughly in Sect. 2.2.1 and [4]. Availability of a classical version of each image from which their quantum versions are prepared is assumed.

Step 2:   Comparison of quantum images through quantum operations

The strip is transformed using a gate array comprising geometric transformation (in Sect. 2.2.2) and color transformation (in Sect. 2.2.3) on all images contained in it. For this step, transformations are built in order to compute the function of pixel difference as defined in Eq. (3.8). This transformation step is followed by a measurement strategy designed to obtain a probability distribution. Since measurements are known to destroy the superposition state in quantum systems (as discussed in Sect. 1.1.2), the strip must be prepared $n > 1$ times.

Step 3:   Observation of readouts from quantum measurements

The readouts from the n quantum measurements are used to generate probability distributions. Extracting and analyzing these distributions give information about the similarity values between the quantum images being compared. The strip preparation will continue until $\min(P(|s_{m-1}, \ldots, s_0\rangle)) \geq \delta$, where $\min(P(|s_{m-1}, \ldots, s_0\rangle))$ is the minimum of the probabilities of the readouts from the experiments, and $\delta \in [0, 1]$ is a preset threshold, which can be read as a reasonable estimate of the similarity between the two quantum images being compared.

The comparison of quantum images in this scheme is further specified below, where the evaluation of the similarity between two images and parallel comparison of multiple pairs of images are discussed.

3.1.3   Evaluation of Similarity Between Two Quantum Images

As the basis of parallel quantum image comparison, the comparison between two quantum images [24] is discussed first. According to Eqs. (3.1), (3.6), and (3.7), the state of the strip comprising two images ($m = 1, k = 0, t = 1, s = 0, 1$) becomes

$$|S(1)\rangle = \frac{1}{\sqrt{2}}(|I_0\rangle \otimes |0\rangle + |I_1\rangle \otimes |1\rangle), \tag{3.10}$$

where

$$|I_0\rangle = \frac{1}{2^n} \sum_{i=0}^{2^{2n}-1} (\cos\theta_{0,i}|0\rangle + \sin\theta_{0,i}|1\rangle) \otimes |i\rangle, \tag{3.11}$$

and

$$|I_1\rangle = \frac{1}{2^n} \sum_{i=0}^{2^{2n}-1} (\cos\theta_{1,i}|0\rangle + \sin\theta_{1,i}|1\rangle) \otimes |i\rangle, \tag{3.12}$$

are the two FRQI images being compared, which are, respectively, located in the upper and lower part of the strip.

The structure of the circuit employed to compare two FRQI images is shown in Fig. 3.1. A Hadamard gate, which maps the basis state $|0\rangle$ to $(|0\rangle + |1\rangle)/\sqrt{2}$ and $|1\rangle$ to $(|0\rangle - |1\rangle)/\sqrt{2}$, is applied on the strip wire s_0 to obtain the recombination of $|I_0\rangle$ and $|I_1\rangle$. This is followed by a measurement operation M_0.

Corresponding to the circuit shown in Fig. 3.1, the new state of the quantum system after applying the Hadamard gate on the strip wire s_0 (denoted by $H_0|S(1)\rangle$)

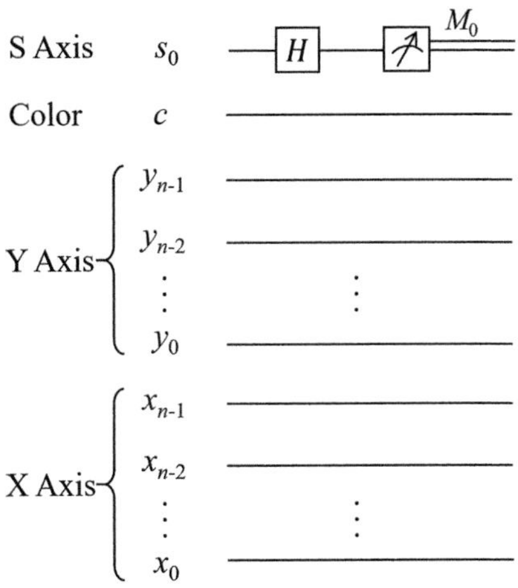

Fig. 3.1 Generalized circuit for comparing two FRQI images

is given by

$$H_0|S(1)\rangle = \frac{1}{\sqrt{2}}(|I_0\rangle \otimes H|0\rangle + |I_1\rangle \otimes H|1\rangle)$$

$$= \frac{1}{2}\Big[|I_0\rangle \otimes (|0\rangle + |1\rangle) + |I_1\rangle \otimes (|0\rangle - |1\rangle)\Big] \qquad (3.13)$$

$$= \frac{1}{2}\Big[(|I_0\rangle + |I_1\rangle) \otimes |0\rangle + (|I_0\rangle - |I_1\rangle) \otimes |1\rangle\Big],$$

where

$$|I_0\rangle \pm |I_1\rangle = \frac{1}{2^n} \sum_{i=0}^{2^{2n}-1} \Big[(\cos\theta_{0,i} \pm \cos\theta_{1,i})|0\rangle + (\sin\theta_{0,i} \pm \sin\theta_{1,i})|1\rangle\Big]|i\rangle.$$

$$(3.14)$$

The result of the measurement M_0 obviously depends on the disparities between $|I_0\rangle$ and $|I_1\rangle$. In accordance with the measurement postulate in [12], the probability of state $|1\rangle$ on strip wire s_0 is

$$P_{s_0}(|1\rangle) = \left(\frac{1}{2^{n+1}}\right)^2 \sum_{i=0}^{2^{2n}-1} \Big[(\cos\theta_{0,i} - \cos\theta_{1,i})^2 + (\sin\theta_{0,i} - \sin\theta_{1,i})^2\Big]$$

$$= \frac{1}{2^{2n+1}} \sum_{i=0}^{2^{2n}-1} \Big[1 - \cos(\theta_{0,i} - \theta_{1,i})\Big] \qquad (3.15)$$

$$= \frac{1}{2} - \frac{1}{2^{2n+1}} \sum_{i=0}^{2^{2n}-1} \cos\sigma_{0,1}^i.$$

It is apparent from Eq. (3.15) that the pixel difference $\sigma_{0,1}^i$ is related to the probability $P_{s_0}(|1\rangle)$ of getting a readout of 1 from strip wire s_0 in the measurement, and $P_{s_0}(|1\rangle)$ will increase with the pixel difference. Furthermore, the similarity between $|I_0\rangle$ and $|I_1\rangle$, which is a function of the pixel differences at every position, depends on $P_{s_0}(|1\rangle)$, as given by

$$\mathrm{sim}(|I_0\rangle, |I_1\rangle) = 1 - 2P_{s_0}(|1\rangle)$$

$$= \frac{1}{2^{2n}} \sum_{i=0}^{2^{2n}-1} \cos\sigma_{0,1}^i, \qquad (3.16)$$

which is in line with the definition of similarity between two FRQI images in Eq. (3.9). Extension to compare many pairs of quantum images in parallel will be discussed and exemplified in the next subsection.

3.1.4 Parallel Comparison of Multiple Quantum Images in a Strip

Operations on a strip (in Definition 3.1) facilitate simultaneously transforming the information in every image contained in the strip. The generalized circuit structure to compare 2^{m-1} pairs of quantum images in parallel is presented in Fig. 3.2.

Let $|I_k\rangle$ and $|I_{k+2^r}\rangle$ (r is the index of s_r in the circuit) denote the k-th and $(k+2^r)$-th images, respectively, in a strip. Then, the mFRQI state of the strip is given by

$$
|S(m)\rangle = \frac{1}{2^{m/2}} \sum_{s=0}^{2^m-1} |I_s\rangle \otimes |s\rangle
$$

$$
= \frac{1}{2^{m/2}} \sum_{z=1}^{2^{m-r-1}} \sum_{k=g(z)}^{\frac{1}{2}g(2z)-1} \left(|I_k\rangle \otimes |k\rangle + |I_{k+2^r}\rangle \otimes |k+2^r\rangle \right),
$$

(3.17)

where

$$
g(z) = (z-1)2^{r+1},
$$

(3.18)

where $m \geq 2$, $|s\rangle = |s_{m-1}, \ldots, s_{r+1}, s_r, s_{r-1}, \ldots, s_0\rangle$, and $s_r \in \{0, 1\}$.

Fig. 3.2 Generalized circuit for comparing multiple FRQI images in parallel

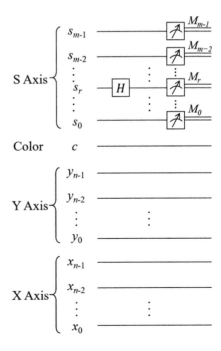

Applying the Hadamard gate on the strip wire s_r (indicated by $H_r|S(m)\rangle$) transforms the state of the strip to

$$
H_r|S(m)\rangle = \frac{1}{2^{m/2}} \sum_{s=0}^{2^m-1} |I_s \otimes |s_{m-1}, \ldots, s_{r+1}\rangle \otimes H|s_r\rangle \otimes |s_{r-1}, \ldots, s_0\rangle
$$

$$
= \frac{1}{2^{m/2}} \sum_{z=1}^{2^{m-r-1}\frac{1}{2}g(2z)-1} \sum_{k=g(z)} |I_k\rangle \otimes |s_{m-1}, \ldots, s_{r+1}\rangle \otimes H|0\rangle \otimes |s_{r-1}, \ldots, s_0\rangle
$$

$$
+ \frac{1}{2^{m/2}} \sum_{z=1}^{2^{m-r-1}\frac{1}{2}g(2z)-1} \sum_{k=g(z)} |I_{k+2^r}\rangle \otimes |s_{m-1}, \ldots, s_{r+1}\rangle \otimes H|1\rangle \otimes |s_{r-1}, \ldots, s_0\rangle
$$

$$
= \frac{1}{2^{(m+1)/2}} \sum_{z=1}^{2^{m-r-1}\frac{1}{2}g(2z)-1} \sum_{k=g(z)} (|I_k\rangle + |I_{k+2^r}\rangle) \otimes |s_{m-1}, \ldots, s_{r+1}, 0, s_{r-1}, \ldots, s_0\rangle
$$

$$
+ \frac{1}{2^{(m+1)/2}} \sum_{z=1}^{2^{m-r-1}\frac{1}{2}g(2z)-1} \sum_{k=g(z)} (|I_k\rangle - |I_{k+2^r}\rangle) \otimes |s_{m-1}, \ldots, s_{r+1}, 1, s_{r-1}, \ldots, s_0\rangle,
$$

$$\tag{3.19}$$

where

$$
|I_k\rangle \pm |I_{k+2^r}\rangle = \frac{1}{2^n} \sum_{i=0}^{2^{2n}-1} (|c_{k,i}\rangle \pm |c_{k+2^r,i}\rangle) \otimes |i\rangle
$$

$$
= \frac{1}{2^n} \sum_{i=0}^{2^{2n}-1} \Big[(\cos\theta_{k,i} \pm \cos\theta_{k+2^r,i})|0\rangle
$$

$$
+ (\sin\theta_{k,i} \pm \sin\theta_{k+2^r,i})|1\rangle \Big] \otimes |i\rangle. \tag{3.20}
$$

The probabilities of the readouts from the m measurements are given by

$$
P_{s_r}(|s_{m-1}, \ldots, s_{r+1}, 1, s_{r-1}, \ldots, s_0\rangle)
$$

$$
= \frac{1}{2^{m+2n}} \sum_{z=1}^{2^{m-r-1}\frac{1}{2}g(2z)-1} \sum_{k=g(z)}^{2^{2n}-1} \sum_{i=0} 1 - \cos(\theta_k - \theta_{k+2^r})
$$

$$\tag{3.21}$$

$$
= \frac{1}{2} - \frac{1}{2^{m+2n}} \sum_{z=1}^{2^{m-r-1}\frac{1}{2}g(2z)-1} \sum_{k=g(z)}^{2^{2n}-1} \sum_{i=0} \cos\sigma_{k,k+2^r}^i.
$$

The states $|s_{m-1}, \ldots, s_{r+1}, 0, s_{r-1}, \ldots, s_0\rangle$ and $|s_{m-1}, \ldots, s_{r+1}, 1, s_{r-1}, \ldots, s_0\rangle$ represent a pair of images that are, respectively, at the k-th and $(k + 2^r)$-th positions of the strip. To determine the similarity of every pair of images, the generalized representation of the probability of $|I_{k+2^r}\rangle$ in the strip is given by

$$P_{s_r}(|k + 2^r\rangle) = \frac{1}{2^{m+2n}} \sum_{i=0}^{2^{2n}-1} 1 - \cos(\theta_k - \theta_{k+2^r})$$

$$= \frac{1}{2^m} - \frac{1}{2^{m+2n}} \sum_{i=0}^{2^{2n}-1} \cos \sigma_{k+2^r}^i. \tag{3.22}$$

In addition, the similarity between $|I_k\rangle$ and $|I_{k+2^r}\rangle$, which are encoded in the strip comprising 2^m images, is

$$\text{sim}(|I_k\rangle, |I_{k+2^r}\rangle) = 1 - 2^m P_{s_r}(|k + 2^r\rangle)$$

$$= \frac{1}{2^{2n}} \sum_{i=0}^{2^{2n}-1} \cos \sigma_{k,k+2^r}^i, \tag{3.23}$$

which is also determined in accordance with Eq. (3.9).

An example to demonstrate how two pairs of images can be compared and the implication of applying the Hadamard gate on different strip wires [25] is presented in Fig. 3.3. A strip comprising four images $|I_0\rangle$, $|I_1\rangle$, $|I_2\rangle$, and $|I_3\rangle$, with the differences between their content captured by their varying color angles, is presented in Fig. 3.3a. The circuit in Fig. 3.3b is used to compare $|I_0\rangle$ with $|I_2\rangle$ and $|I_1\rangle$ with $|I_3\rangle$ by applying a Hadamard gate on the strip wire s_1, while the circuit in Fig. 3.3c is used to compare $|I_0\rangle$ with $|I_1\rangle$ and $|I_2\rangle$ with $|I_3\rangle$ by applying a Hadamard gate on the strip wire s_0.

According to Eq. (3.1), the mFRQI state of this strip ($m = 2$) is given by

$$|S(2)\rangle = \frac{1}{2}(|I_0\rangle \otimes |00\rangle + |I_1\rangle \otimes |01\rangle + |I_2\rangle \otimes |10\rangle + |I_3\rangle \otimes |11\rangle). \tag{3.24}$$

The difference between applying the Hadamard gate on strip wire s_1 and s_0 is elaborated in Table 3.1. The table also shows the transformed state, the probability of the state on strip wires, and the similarity between the images being compared. The probability and similarity are calculated using Eqs. (3.22) and (3.23), where $m = 2$, $n = 1$, and $r = 0$ or 1, respectively.

From Fig. 3.3 and Table 3.1, it is evident that different pairs of images can be compared by simply moving the Hadamard operation from one wire on the S-axis to another. However, comparing several pairs of images, such as $|I_0\rangle$ with $|I_3\rangle$ and $|I_1\rangle$ with $|I_2\rangle$ in Fig. 3.3, is difficult to accomplish in this manner because they do not satisfy the relationship defined earlier in Eq. (3.23). To compare two

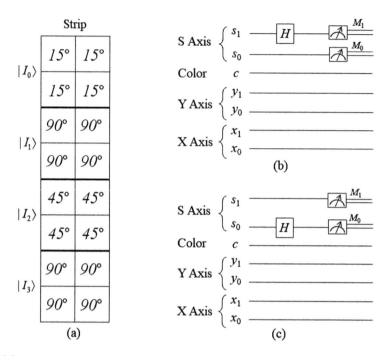

Fig. 3.3 An example to realize the simultaneous comparison of two pairs of images

Table 3.1 Image comparison by applying Hadamard operation on different strip wires

Image comparison	Circuit	Transformed state	Probability	Similarity
$\lvert I_0\rangle, \lvert I_2\rangle$	Fig. 3.3b	$\frac{1}{2\sqrt{2}}[(\lvert I_0\rangle + \lvert I_2\rangle)\lvert 00\rangle$ $+(\lvert I_1\rangle + \lvert I_3\rangle)\lvert 01\rangle$ $+(\lvert I_0\rangle - \lvert I_2\rangle)\lvert 10\rangle$ $+(\lvert I_1\rangle - \lvert I_3\rangle)\lvert 11\rangle]$	$P_{s_1}(\lvert 10\rangle) = 0.033$	$\mathrm{sim}(\lvert I_0\rangle, \lvert I_2\rangle) = 0.866$
$\lvert I_1\rangle, \lvert I_3\rangle$			$P_{s_1}(\lvert 11\rangle) = 0$	$\mathrm{sim}(\lvert I_1\rangle, \lvert I_3\rangle) = 1$
$\lvert I_0\rangle, \lvert I_1\rangle$	Fig. 3.3c	$\frac{1}{2\sqrt{2}}[(\lvert I_0\rangle + \lvert I_1\rangle)\lvert 00\rangle$ $+(\lvert I_0\rangle - \lvert I_1\rangle)\lvert 01\rangle$ $+(\lvert I_2\rangle + \lvert I_3\rangle)\lvert 10\rangle$ $+(\lvert I_2\rangle - \lvert I_3\rangle)\lvert 11\rangle]$	$P_{s_0}(\lvert 01\rangle) = 0.185$	$\mathrm{sim}(\lvert I_0\rangle, \lvert I_1\rangle) = 0.259$
$\lvert I_2\rangle, \lvert I_3\rangle$			$P_{s_0}(\lvert 11\rangle) = 0.073$	$\mathrm{sim}(\lvert I_2\rangle, \lvert I_3\rangle) = 0.707$

arbitrary quantum images and/or contents of their sub-blocks from a strip, additional geometric transformations (in Sect. 2.2.2) and control conditions are required in the current quantum system [25].

To summarize, a method to compare multiple pairs of quantum images, whose similarities are estimated according to the probability distributions of the readouts from quantum measurements, has been introduced. The method offers a first step toward an image database search on quantum computers, whereby an image could be retrieved as a search result from a database based on the extent of its similarity to a reference image. Exploiting the parallelism of quantum computation, it is envisaged that quantum image database searches could be significantly faster than those on classical computers [23].

3.2 Quantum Image Up-Scaling Based on Nearest-Neighbor Interpolation

Image scaling, which has been extensively studied and widely used as a basic image processing method, aims to resize a digital image, where interpolation methods are necessary to produce new pixels (when up-scaling) or delete redundant pixels (when down-scaling). In [5], Jiang et al. proposed a quantum image scaling method, including up-scaling and down-scaling with a $2^{r_y} \times 2^{r_x}$ scaling ratio on a $2^{n_1} \times 2^{n_2}$ quantum image, while later in [6], they improved the method with an $r_y \times r_x$ scaling ratio on a quantum image of arbitrary size $H \times W$, where $r_y \times r_x \in \mathbb{N}$. The latter method is now introduced.

3.2.1 Generalized Quantum Image Representation

Developed from NEQR representation, a generalized quantum image representation (GQIR) was proposed [6] to store a quantum image of arbitrary size $H \times W$. GQIR uses $h = \lceil \log_2 H \rceil$ qubits for the Y-axis and $w = \lceil \log_2 W \rceil$ qubits for the X-axis to represent an $H \times W$ image, which is defined as

$$|I\rangle = \frac{1}{\sqrt{2}^{h+w}} \left(\sum_{y=0}^{H-1} \sum_{x=0}^{W-1} \bigotimes_{i=0}^{q-1} |C_{yx}^i\rangle |yx\rangle \right), \qquad (3.25)$$

where

$$|yx\rangle = |y\rangle|x\rangle = |y_0 y_1 \ldots y_{h-1}\rangle |x_0 x_1 \ldots x_{w-1}\rangle, \ y_i, x_i \in \{0, 1\}, \qquad (3.26)$$

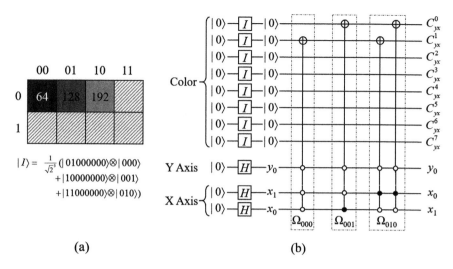

Fig. 3.4 (a) A 1×3 GQIR image and its quantum state and (b) its circuit initialization

is the location information and

$$|C_{yx}\rangle = |C_{yx}^0 C_{yx}^1 \ldots C_{yx}^{q-1}\rangle, \ C_{yx}^i \in \{0, 1\}, \tag{3.27}$$

is the color information. GQIR requires $h + w + q$ qubits to represent an $H \times W$ quantum image with gray range 2^q. However, it will generate a $(2^h - H)$-row and $(2^w - W)$-column redundancy, which is caused by an intrinsic property of the binary computation.

Figure 3.4 shows a 1×3 GQIR image, its quantum state, and its circuit initialization. The image is put into a $2^1 \times 2^2 = 2 \times 4$ box, where only three effective pixels, $|yx\rangle = |000\rangle, |001\rangle, |010\rangle$, are set to the desired value, while others are redundant (i.e., they remain the initial state $|0\rangle$).

3.2.2 Scheme of Quantum Image Up-Scaling Operation

Regardless of the interpolation used, image scaling can be decomposed in two directions, e.g., first in the horizontal direction, and then in the vertical direction [3]. The function of image scaling can be presented as

$$I' = S(I, r_x, r_y) = S_y\big(S_x(I, r_x), r_y\big) = S_x\big(S_y(I, r_y), r_x\big), \tag{3.28}$$

where I is the original image, I' is the scaled image, and r_x and r_y are, respectively, the horizontal and vertical scaling ratios. S can be decomposed into S_x and S_y,

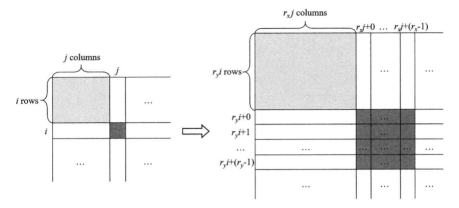

Fig. 3.5 Essence of up-scaling based on nearest-neighbor interpolation

which are the horizontal and vertical scaling functions, respectively [6]. For brevity, this section only discusses up-scaling, i.e., $r > 1$; down-scaling can be implemented following the discussion in [5].

Nearest-neighbor interpolation [3], which is technically the repetition of pixels within an image, is used here for image up-scaling. As shown in Fig. 3.5, if the scaling ratio is $r_y \times r_x$, then the pixel (i, j) in the original image is enlarged to an $r_y \times r_x$ image block in the up-scaled image. Because i rows and j columns are before pixel (i, j) in the original image, there are $r_y i$ rows and $r_x j$ columns before the corresponding image block in the up-scaled image [6].

3.2.3   Circuit Implementation of Up-Scaling Operation

Assume that an $H \times W$ quantum image $|I\rangle$ is up-scaled to an $H' \times W'$ quantum image $|I'\rangle$ based on nearest-neighbor interpolation. The scale ratio is $r_y \times r_x$, i.e., $H' = r_y H$ and $W' = r_x W$, where $r_x, r_y \in \mathbb{N}$. According to Fig. 3.5, the quantum up-scaling scheme is as follows [6].

First, an operation is defined as

$$U_{(r_y i+k),(r_x j+l)} = \bigotimes_{t=0}^{q-1} U^t_{(r_y i+k),(r_x j+l)}, \tag{3.29}$$

where $U^t_{(r_y i+k),(r_x j+l)}$ is an $(h + w + h' + w' + 1)$-CONT gate that transforms $|C'^t_{(r_y i+k),(r_x j+l)}\rangle$ (which is initialized as $|0\rangle$) to the state $|C^t_{ij}\rangle$. Therefore, the color information $|C'_{(r_y i+k),(r_x j+l)}\rangle$ of a pixel in the up-scaled image $|I'\rangle$ can be set to its

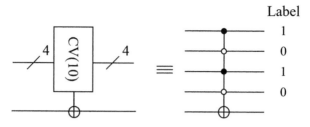

Fig. 3.6 Quantum module $CV(10)$ with a NOT gate as its target

desired color information $|C_{ij}\rangle$,

$$U_{(r_y i+k),(r_x j+l)}|C'_{(r_y i+k),(r_x j+l)}\rangle = \bigotimes_{t=0}^{q-1} U^t_{(r_y i+k),(r_x j+l)}|C'^t_{(r_y i+k),(r_x j+l)}\rangle \qquad (3.30)$$

$$= |C^0_{ij}C^1_{ij}\dots C^{q-1}_{ij}\rangle = |C_{ij}\rangle.$$

Considering that an $(h+w+h'+w'+1)$-CONT gate includes multiple control qubits, a circuit module $CV(v)$ has been defined [6]. $CV(v)$ is a control unit with an n-qubit binary sequence as its input, where $0 \le v \le 2^n - 1$. A simple example of the $CV(v)$ module is given in Fig. 3.6, where the target is a NOT gate, so it is a 4-CONT gate. Since the control value is $(1010)_2 = (10)_{10}$, the module is represented as $CV(10)$.

The circuit to implement the $U^t_{(r_y i+k),(r_x j+l)}$ operation is shown in Fig. 3.7a, and it includes four CV control units. When $y = i$, $x = j$, $y' = r_y i + k$, and $x' = r_x j + l$, $|C''_{(r_y i+k),(r_x j+l)}\rangle$ is set to the value of $|C^t_{ij}\rangle$. Figure 3.7b shows the circuit of $U_{(r_y i+k),(r_x j+l)} = \bigotimes_{t=0}^{q-1} U^t_{(r_y i+k),(r_x j+l)}$, where $U_{(r_y i+k),(r_x j+l)}$ is simply denoted as U for the ensuing computations.

As discussed earlier, the module U with four control units sets the color information $|C_{ij}\rangle$ of a pixel in the up-scaled image. Next, it should be repeated $r_y r_x HW$ times to realize the initialization of all of the color information in the up-scaled image [6]. The repetition is accompanied by updating the parameters, i.e., $CV(i)$ $(0 \le i \le H-1)$, $CV(j)$ $(0 \le j \le W-1)$, $CV(r_y i + k)$ $(0 \le k \le r_y - 1)$, and $CV(r_x j + l)$ $(0 \le l \le r_x - 1)$.

The circuit implementation of quantum image up-scaling is presented in Fig. 3.8. In its first part, $h' + w'$ Hadamard gates are used to obtain the position information $y'_0, y'_1, \dots, y'_{h'-1}$ and $x'_0, x'_1, \dots, x'_{w'-1}$ of the up-scaled image (i.e., an $H' \times W'$ blank box). The latter part realizes the color initialization of these pixels in the blank box to build up a complete up-scaled image [6].

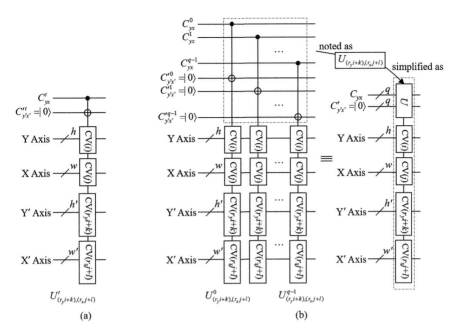

Fig. 3.7 Circuit modules of (**a**) $U^t_{(r_y i+k),(r_x j+l)}$ and (**b**) $U_{(r_y i+k),(r_x j+l)}$ (reprinted from ref. [6], with permission of Springer)

3.2.4 Example of Quantum Image Up-Scaling

An example to illustrate the up-scaling circuit [6] is given. Suppose the gray range of a 1×2 GQIR image is 2^1, i.e., $H = 1$, $W = 2$, and $q = 1$, as shown in Fig. 3.9a. It is worth noting that when $H = 1$ or $W = 1$ in Eq. (3.25), one has $h = 1$ or $w = 1$. If the scaling ratio is $r_y \times r_x = 5 \times 3$, then the size of the up-scaled image should be 5×6, and then $h' = \lceil \log_2 5 \rceil = 3$ and $w' = \lceil \log_2 6 \rceil = 3$.

Figure 3.10 shows the quantum circuit of the example, where seven $|0\rangle$ qubits are used to initialize the color and position information of the up-scaled image. The circuit includes 30 layers, where the first 15 layers (in the dark-gray background) enlarge pixel $(0, 0)$ and the others (in the light-gray background) enlarge pixel $(0, 1)$ in the original image, respectively, to two 5×3 blocks in the up-scaled image, as seen in Fig. 3.9b. The simplification of the up-scaling circuit is fully discussed in [6].

To summarize, to encode a quantum image of arbitrary size, a generalized quantum image representation (GQIR) was introduced. Based on this, a quantum image up-scaling algorithm using nearest-neighbor interpolation with an integer scaling ratio was discussed. The presented method encourages research such as improving the scaling ratio from integers to real numbers, and realizing quantum scaling circuits based on other interpolation methods, e.g., bilinear and bicubic.

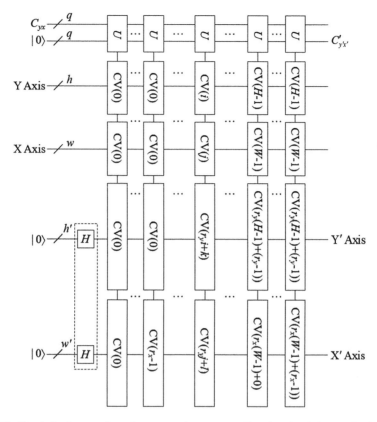

Fig. 3.8 Circuit implementation of quantum image up-scaling (reprinted from ref. [6], with permission of Springer)

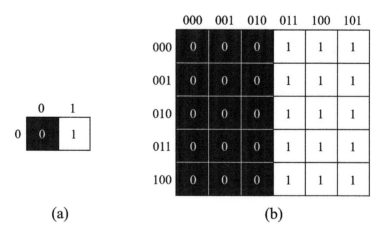

Fig. 3.9 (a) A 1×2 GQIR image and (b) the 5×6 up-scaled image

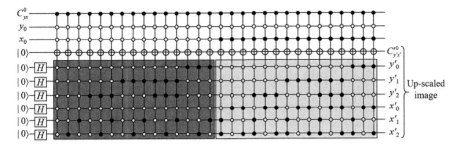

Fig. 3.10 Quantum image up-scaling circuit for the example in Fig. 3.9 (reprinted from ref. [6], with permission of Springer)

3.3 Quantum Image Rotation by an Arbitrary Angle

In classical image processing and related fields, such as computer vision and pattern recognition, image rotation is regarded as a key tool for activities, such as image registration, fusion, and mosaicing. Nonetheless, image rotation has not been sufficiently studied as it relates to quantum computing. This section introduces a quantum algorithm for image rotation consisting of a sequence of three shear mappings (horizontal, vertical, then horizontal again) onto NEQR images [26].

3.3.1 Three Shear Transformations

In digital image processing, it is known that an arbitrary two-dimensional rotation can be performed by a series of three shear transformations [14, 19],

$$\begin{pmatrix} \cos\theta & \sin\theta \\ -\sin\theta & \cos\theta \end{pmatrix} = \begin{pmatrix} 1 & \alpha \\ 0 & 1 \end{pmatrix} \begin{pmatrix} 1 & 0 \\ \beta & 1 \end{pmatrix} \begin{pmatrix} 1 & \alpha \\ 0 & 1 \end{pmatrix}, \tag{3.31}$$

where $\begin{pmatrix} 1 & \alpha \\ 0 & 1 \end{pmatrix}$ and $\begin{pmatrix} 1 & 0 \\ \beta & 1 \end{pmatrix}$ are, respectively, horizontal and vertical shearing transformations. A shear transformation can be defined as a transformation in which all of the points along a given line $\mathscr{L}$ remain fixed, while other points are shifted parallel to $\mathscr{L}$ by a distance proportional to their perpendicular distance from $\mathscr{L}$ [17]. Moreover, the shear factor is defined as the proportionality constant, which is the distance a point P moves divided by the perpendicular distance of P from $\mathscr{L}$ [10].

The ideas of quantum image rotation are provided by using the three shear transformations. In such case, quantum images are partitioned into halves by a reference line to obtain top-bottom or left-right sub-images, and shear transformations are computed on both halves. As a result, the computation of each shear transformation displaces quantum pixels in different halves in opposite directions (which is also the expected behavior of shear transformations on classical pixels).

The shear factor is always presented by a trigonometric function of an angle, and consequently, pixel displacements produced by shear transformations are usually expressed as floating point numbers. This is in accordance with Eq. (3.31), as rotations generally produce pixel positions described by vectors $y_i \in \mathbb{R}^2$. Similar with the problem in classical image processing [18], since the positions of quantum pixels are described by vectors $x_i \in \mathbb{Z}^2$, one must define a quantum procedure to accommodate y_i in x_i.

A quantum computer system can be viewed as a quantum network consisting of quantum logic gates, each performing an elementary unitary operation on one or more two-state quantum systems [21]. As Eq. (3.31) shows, shear transformations are not unitary operations, but it is known that any classical irreversible circuit can be substituted by a reversible circuit that uses Toffoli gates [13]. Moreover, a Toffoli gate can be implemented both as a classical and quantum logic gate. Following that rationale, the quantum circuits that compute shear transformations and subsequent rotations on quantum images are presented in the following subsections.

3.3.2   Quantum Modules for Shear Transformations

To achieve the quantum rotation method, some quantum computing units and modules of shear mapping operations should be understood.

3.3.2.1   Quantum Adder

In this subsection, a quantum adder circuit, as originally introduced in [20], is presented. The aim is to perform the following computation:

$$|a, b\rangle \rightarrow |a, a + b\rangle, \tag{3.32}$$

where $|a\rangle$ and $|b\rangle$ are two input quantum kets, and the two output kets are $|a\rangle$ and $|d\rangle$, where $|d\rangle = |a\rangle + |b\rangle$. As presented in Fig. 3.11, a quantum adder consists of $2n - 1$ carry modules and $2n$ sum modules. In addition, the carry module can be decomposed to two Toffoli gates and one CNOT gate, while the sum module can be executed by two CNOT gates, as presented in Fig. 3.11b and c. Moreover, as discussed in [2] and [20], quantum subtraction can be implemented by the quantum adder(s) because quantum gates are reversible. The subtraction is illustrated by locating the black bar at the left side of the module from the original right within the adder.

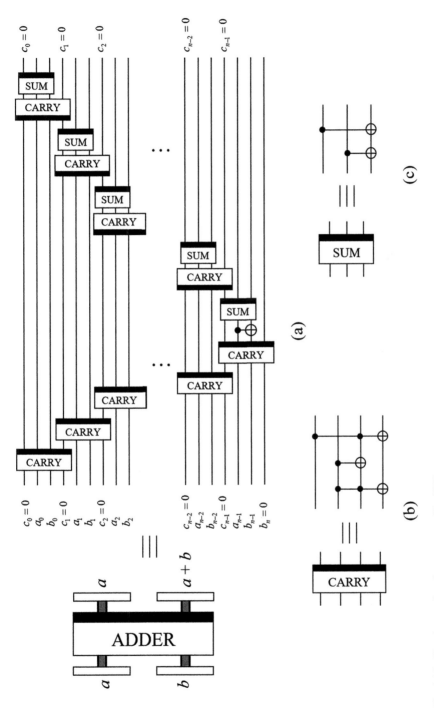

Fig. 3.11 Circuit to realize the quantum adder [20]

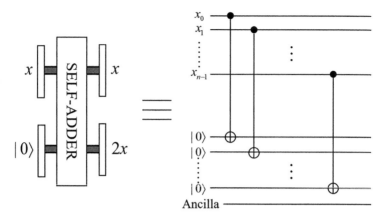

Fig. 3.12 Circuit to realize the quantum self-adder [26]

3.3.2.2   Quantum Self-Adder

Let x be a binary number, then the binary representation of $2x$ can be achieved simply by concatenating x with a zero at the least significant position. Formally,

$$x = \sum_{i=0}^{n-1} \alpha_i 2^i \Rightarrow 2x = \sum_{j=0}^{n} \beta_j 2^j, \tag{3.33}$$

where $\beta_0 = 0$ and $\beta_j = \alpha_{i-1}$ for $j \in \{1, \ldots, n\}$. Inspired by this procedure, the following computation is presented:

$$(U_{n-1} \otimes U_{n-2} \otimes \cdots \otimes U_0 \otimes I)|x\rangle \otimes |0\rangle^{\otimes n+1} = |x\rangle \otimes |x_{n-1}x_{n-2} \ldots x_0 0\rangle$$
$$= |x\rangle \otimes |2x\rangle, \tag{3.34}$$

where unitary operators $U_{n-1}U_{n-2} \ldots U_0$ are CNOT quantum gates [26]. For instance, let $|x\rangle = |x_2 x_1 x_0\rangle = |110\rangle$, then $|2x\rangle = |1100\rangle$, through which $U_2 =$ NOT, $U_1 =$ NOT, and $U_0 = I$. The quantum circuit of a self-adder (sometimes labeled "S-A") in Fig. 3.12 implements Eq. (3.34).

3.3.2.3   Quantum Controlled-Multiplier

Let a and x be binary numbers, where $x = \sum_{i=0}^{n-1} 2^i x_i$, then the multiplication ax can be expressed as

$$ax = a\sum_{i=0}^{n-1} 2^i x_i = \sum_{i=0}^{n-1} (2^i a)x_i. \tag{3.35}$$

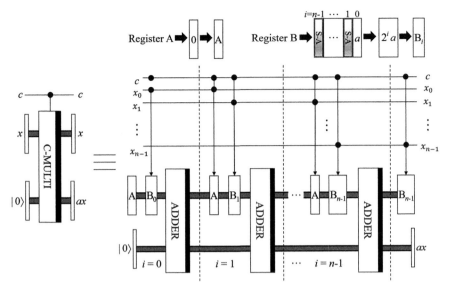

Fig. 3.13 Circuit to realize the quantum controlled-multiplier [26]

A quantum controlled-multiplier (C-MULTI) is provided that, based on the self-adder circuit presented above and Eq. (3.35), performs the following operation:

$$\text{C-MULTI}|a\rangle|b\rangle|0\rangle = |a\rangle|b\rangle|ab\rangle. \tag{3.36}$$

The circuit to implement C-MULTI module is presented in Fig. 3.13, and it is realized by n stages of quantum adders. During each stage, it must be considered whether $2^i a$ should be added according to the state of the qubit $|x_i\rangle$, $i = 0, 1, \ldots n-1$.

As presented in Sect. 1.1.2.2, inputs that are encoded in binary form for the computational basis of the selected qubits are called a quantum register, or simply a register. For instance, if the number 5 is loaded into a quantum register, one must prepare three qubits in the state of $|1\rangle \otimes |0\rangle \otimes |1\rangle$. Given one quantum control multiplier [26], two registers (denoted as Registers A and B) are required during the three steps that follow Fig. 3.13.

Step 1: Initializing Registers A and B as $|0\rangle^{\otimes n}$ and $|a\rangle$, respectively. A Toffoli gate controlled by ancilla qubit "c" and x_0 is responsible for manipulating Register A or B and is taken as an input of the quantum adder in the step when $i = 0$. The other input is temporarily set to $|0\rangle$.

Step 2: Updating Register B to $2a$ by executing the S-A module in the step when $i = 1$. Similarly, the Toffoli gate that is controlled by the ancilla qubit "c" and x_1 (in this turn) takes Register A or B as an input of the quantum adder. During the addition, the other input is the temporary addition outcome through the previous step, i.e., $i = 0$.

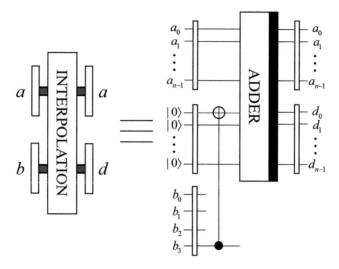

Fig. 3.14 Circuit to realize the quantum interpolation [26]

Step 3:   Following the rationale described in Steps 1 and 2, go through the circuit
           stages defined for $i \in \{2, \ldots, n-1\}$. The output of the last quantum adder
           is ax.

3.3.2.4   Quantum Interpolation

As stated earlier, the shear factor, which is essentially a trigonometric function of
a rotation angle, is seldom an integer. To locate a sheared pixel in the coordinate
system, the nearest-neighbor value (NNV) interpolation [15] according to the
smallest absolute difference to the four known adjacent position values is employed
to determine a proper pixel position.

Given the NNV interpolation in a quantum computing framework, the circuit
design is shown in Fig. 3.14, in which $|a\rangle = |a_{n-1} \ldots a_0\rangle$ is the integer part of
a decimal and $|b\rangle = |b_3 b_2 b_1 b_0\rangle$ is the fractional part with four effective decimal
places. $|b_3\rangle$ is the most critical bit when converting a decimal to an integer. If it
is 1, then the integer part should be increased by 1; otherwise, the integer part is
left as it was. The operation is executed by the CNOT gate and the adder module,
and its output $|d\rangle = |d_{n-1} \ldots d_0\rangle$ is the result of the quantum interpolation [26].
The quantum interpolation operation is referred to as the IP module in the following
discussions.

3.3.3   Scheme of Quantum Image Rotation Operation

Image rotation is a process of generating another image, whose pixels are all rotated
by a certain angle about a specified point. In this section, the strategy to realize

quantum image rotation will be introduced based on three-phase shear mappings, i.e., horizontal shear, vertical shear, and a second horizontal shear.

3.3.3.1   Quantum Image Rotation Based on Three-Phase Shear Mappings

As introduced earlier, image rotation can be formulated as

$$\begin{pmatrix} y_t \\ x_t \end{pmatrix} = R \begin{pmatrix} y_0 \\ x_0 \end{pmatrix}, \tag{3.37}$$

where y_0 and x_0 represent the pixel position within the original image, while y_t and x_t represent the corresponding position within the rotated image [3]. R denotes the rotation matrix:

$$R = \begin{pmatrix} \cos\theta & \sin\theta \\ -\sin\theta & \cos\theta \end{pmatrix}, \tag{3.38}$$

where θ represents the rotation angle and its sign indicates the rotation direction, i.e., clockwise $(-)$ or counterclockwise $(+)$. To realize the quantum image rotation operation using shear mappings, the matrix R can be rewritten as

$$
\begin{aligned}
R &= \begin{pmatrix} 1 & 0 \\ \tan(\theta/2) & 1 \end{pmatrix}^{-1} \begin{pmatrix} 1 & 0 \\ \tan(\theta/2) & 1 \end{pmatrix} \begin{pmatrix} \cos\theta & \sin\theta \\ -\sin\theta & \cos\theta \end{pmatrix} \\
&= \begin{pmatrix} 1 & 0 \\ \tan(\theta/2) & 1 \end{pmatrix}^{-1} \begin{pmatrix} \cos\theta & \sin\theta \\ -\tan(\theta/2) & 1 \end{pmatrix} \\
&= \begin{pmatrix} 1 & 0 \\ \tan(\theta/2) & 1 \end{pmatrix}^{-1} \begin{pmatrix} \cos\theta & \sin\theta \\ -\tan(\theta/2) & 1 \end{pmatrix} \begin{pmatrix} 1 & 0 \\ \tan(\theta/2) & 1 \end{pmatrix} \begin{pmatrix} 1 & 0 \\ \tan(\theta/2) & 1 \end{pmatrix}^{-1} \\
&= \begin{pmatrix} 1 & 0 \\ \tan(\theta/2) & 1 \end{pmatrix}^{-1} \begin{pmatrix} 1 & \sin\theta \\ 0 & 1 \end{pmatrix} \begin{pmatrix} 1 & 0 \\ \tan(\theta/2) & 1 \end{pmatrix}^{-1}.
\end{aligned} \tag{3.39}
$$

The multiple output values obtained through the above process must be distributed to the corresponding output pixels to prevent more than one pixel being located at the same position [3]. Therefore, the matrix R^{-1} (the inverse of R) is used and Eq. (3.37) is transformed to:

$$R^{-1} \begin{pmatrix} y_t \\ x_t \end{pmatrix} = \begin{pmatrix} y_0 \\ x_0 \end{pmatrix} = \begin{pmatrix} 1 & 0 \\ \tan(\theta/2) & 1 \end{pmatrix} \begin{pmatrix} 1 & -\sin\theta \\ 0 & 1 \end{pmatrix} \begin{pmatrix} 1 & 0 \\ \tan(\theta/2) & 1 \end{pmatrix} \begin{pmatrix} y_t \\ x_t \end{pmatrix}. \tag{3.40}$$

It has been shown how the operation of quantum image rotation is decomposed into three phases (two horizontal shears and one vertical shear). During the three-phase shear mappings, the pixels in each row or column are translated by the same distance (i.e., the relative positions of these pixels remain unchanged), which results in a favorable anti-aliasing property. The realization of horizontal and vertical shears as unitary circuits is now discussed.

3.3.3.2 Shear Mapping Operations

Shear mapping can be either horizontal (shear parallel to the X-axis) or vertical (shear parallel to the Y-axis). Horizontal shear is a function that shifts an original point with coordinates (x, y) to another point at $(x + y \tan(\theta/2), y)$, while vertical shear is a movement from a point (x, y) to another one, $(x, y - x \sin \theta)$. In the following, the function $\tan(\theta/2)$ is known as the shear factor and θ as the rotation angle.

It is suggested to select the image centroid as the rotation center instead of the default upper-left corner. Thus, one quantum image can be divided into two halves, i.e., top-bottom halves by a horizontal reference line or left-right halves by a vertical reference line. Consequently, equations for shear mapping are stated as follows:

1. Shear top half along the negative direction of X-axis (STH_x^-):

$$x_s = x - (Y_{\text{mid}} - y)\tan(\theta/2), \tag{3.41}$$

2. Shear bottom half along the positive direction of X-axis (SBH_x^+):

$$x_s = x + (y - Y_{\text{mid}})\tan(\theta/2), \tag{3.42}$$

3. Shear left half along the positive direction of Y-axis (SLH_y^+):

$$y_s = y + (X_{\text{mid}} - x)\sin\theta, \tag{3.43}$$

4. Shear right half along the negative direction of Y-axis (SRH_y^-):

$$y_s = y - (x - X_{\text{mid}})\sin\theta, \tag{3.44}$$

where x_s and y_s are the pixel position after shear mapping, and X_{mid} and Y_{mid} indicate the reference line, i.e., the median of the X- and Y-axis, respectively. Since pixel points on separated sides around the reference line are displaced in opposite directions, the image rotation with the image centroid as the rotation center works.

Referring to STH_x^- in Eq. (3.41), Fig. 3.15 depicts the solution in terms of a quantum circuit, in which $|x\rangle$ and $|y\rangle$ represent the coordinates of a pixel before the shear. $|Y\rangle$ represents the horizontal median Y_{mid} of the quantum image, and $|a\rangle$ represents the shear factor, i.e., $|\tan(\theta/2)\rangle$.

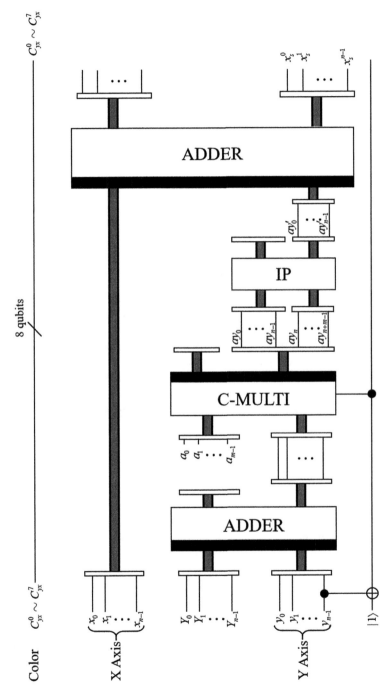

Fig. 3.15 Circuit to realize horizontal shear to the top half of the quantum image [26]

The quantum circuit to compute horizontal shear mapping on the top-half quantum image is illustrated as follows [26]:

Step 1:   Constrained by a CNOT gate, the horizontal shear acts within the top-half image when the control qubit is $|0\rangle$. An adder module labeled with the left-side black bar is deployed to execute the subtraction operation (cf. Sect. 3.3.1). With the subtraction, $|Y_{\text{mid}}\rangle - |y\rangle$ is computed similarly.

Step 2:   With the result of Step 1 as an input, $|a\rangle = |\tan\theta/2\rangle$ is also used as an input to the C-MULTI module to obtain the multiplication result of $(|Y_{\text{mid}}\rangle - |y\rangle)$ and $|\tan(\theta/2)\rangle$.

Step 3:   The result through Step 2 usually manifests itself as a binary decimal that cannot reflect the precise position of the displaced pixel. Thus, the IP module is used to round the fractional part up or down and to produce the corresponding integer, i.e., $\lceil (|Y_{\text{mid}}\rangle - |y\rangle)| \tan(\theta/2)\rangle \rfloor$.

Step 4:   Another adder module is applied to execute the subtraction operation (where the result obtained in Step 3 is the minuend and the original coordinate value $|x\rangle$ is the subtractor) to achieve the new location of the displaced pixel.

A shear mapping on the pixels at the bottom half of the quantum image is now applied. As shown in Eq. (3.42), the difference to realize SBH_x^+ is to calculate $|y\rangle - |Y_{\text{mid}}\rangle$, first using the subtraction operation in the circuit when the control qubit is $|1\rangle$. In the final operation, the quantum adder module is used to compute the addition of $|x\rangle$ and $(|y\rangle - |Y_{\text{mid}}\rangle)|\tan(\theta/2)\rangle$. The circuit implementing the procedure is shown in Fig. 3.16. After these two phases, the horizontal shear to a quantum image is achieved by taking the image centroid as the shear center. Similar to horizontal shears, to make a vertical shear centered at the image centroid, as in Eqs. (3.43) and (3.44), requires to divide the quantum image into left and right halves [26].

3.3.4   Example of Quantum Image Rotation

To illustrate the procedure of horizontal and vertical shear, a 4×4 NEQR image with different colors for each row [26] is presented in Fig. 3.17. In Fig. 3.17a, the image is divided into halves by the horizontal axis, in which the top two rows are sheared to the negative direction while the bottom two rows are sheared to the positive direction (in this case, the shear factor is $\tan 45° = 1$). As presented in Eqs. (3.41) and (3.42), the displacements of each row are 2, 1, 0, and 1, in that order. The arrowhead and tail indicate the direction and distance of the displacement. The dashed boxes indicate the vacated locations after the pixels have moved out.

Turning the discussion to Fig. 3.17b, the image is divided into halves by the vertical axis, where the left two columns are sheared in the negative direction and the right two columns in the positive direction. The depiction and illustration of Fig. 3.17b are similar to those of Fig. 3.17a.

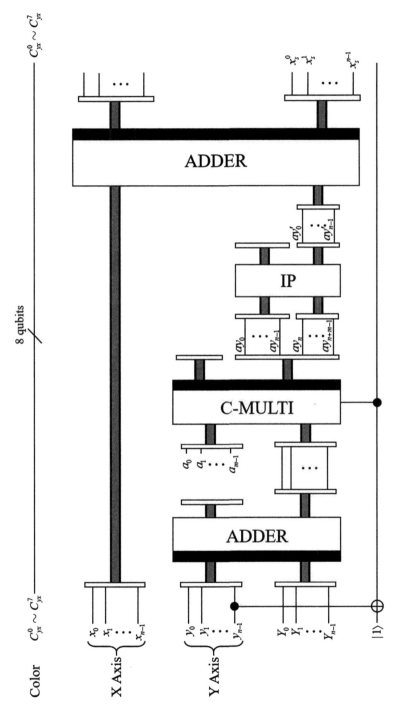

Fig. 3.16 Circuit to realize horizontal shear to the bottom half of the quantum image [26]

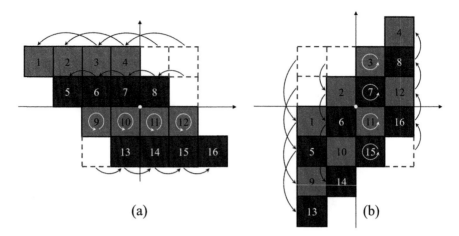

Fig. 3.17 A 4×4 NEQR image to illustrate the (**a**) horizontal and (**b**) vertical shear [26]

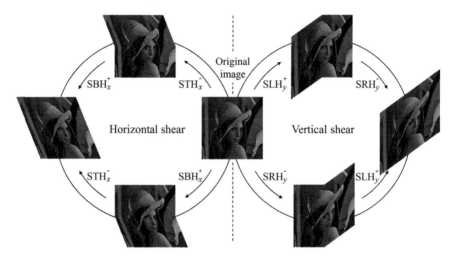

Fig. 3.18 Procedure of shear mappings from the original quantum image [26]

Along three-phase shear mappings for the operation of quantum image rotation, both half images are sheared in opposite directions so as to make the quantum image rotate around the image centroid. With the original quantum Lena image, there are two potential ways of shear mapping: horizontal shear and vertical shear. To operate the horizontal shear, one could use the shear top half (STH) first, and then perform the shear bottom half (SBH), or vice versa [26]. In a similar way, to operate the vertical shear, one could execute the shear left half (SLH) first, and then invoke the shear right half (SRH), or vice versa, as shown in Fig. 3.18.

Utilizing the horizontal shear and the vertical shear separately to rotate the quantum image ensures that each interpolation only concerns two adjacent pixel points along either the X- or Y-axis, which has lower computational complexity than simultaneous interpolations in the two-dimensional plane. In addition, the shear factor in each row or column is invariant so that the relative locations of the pixels in each row or column are preserved. Therefore, the problems of blocking and/or blurring can be avoided during the rotation [26].

To summarize, a novel method of quantum image rotation based on shear transformations on NEQR images was given. To compute the horizontal and vertical shear mappings required for rotation, the quantum self-adder, quantum controlled-multiplier, and quantum interpolation circuits were provided as the basic computing units in the implementation of quantum image rotation.

In this chapter, some advanced quantum image operations are designed in order to realize some meaningful and useful QIMP applications. By employing the quantum properties, notably computational parallelism, the quantum image comparison, scaling, and rotation operations are introduced and their quantum circuit implementations are illustrated. While their classical counterparts have been fully studied, it has been demonstrated how these quantum algorithms perform similar tasks by reducing the required computing resources and accelerating the computing process. Some operations are encapsulated in several QIMP-customized toolkits that are expected to be involved as basic computing modules in more sophisticated calculations.

References

1. Broadbent, A., Kashefi, E.: Parallelizing quantum circuits. Theor. Comput. Sci. **410**(26), 2489–2510 (2009)
2. Draper, T.: Addition on a quantum computer. arXiv:quant-ph/0008033 (2000)
3. Gonzalez, R., Woods, R.: Digital Image Processing, 3rd edn. Pearson Education, London (2008)
4. Iliyasu, A., Le, P., Dong, F., Hirota, K.: A framework for representing and producing movies on quantum computers. Int. J. Quantum Inf. **9**(6), 1459–1497 (2011)
5. Jiang, N., Wang, L.: Quantum image scaling using nearest neighbor interpolation. Quantum Inf. Process. **14**(5), 1559–1571 (2015)
6. Jiang, N., Wang, J., Mu, Y.: Quantum image scaling up based on nearest-neighbor interpolation with integer scaling ratio. Quantum Inf. Process. **14**(11), 4001–4026 (2015)
7. Jiang, N., Lu, X., Hu, H., Dang, Y., Cai, Y.: A novel quantum image compression method based on JPEG. Int. J. Theor. Phys. **57**(3), 611–636 (2018)
8. Li, P., Liu, X.: Bilinear interpolation method for quantum images based on quantum Fourier transform. Int. J. Quantum Inf. **16**(4), 1850031 (2018)
9. Liu, K., Zhang, Y., Lu, K., Wang, X.: Restoration for noise removal in quantum images. Int. J. Theor. Phys. **56**(9), 2867–2886 (2017)
10. MathWorld, W.: Shear factor. http://mathworld.wolfram.com/ShearFactor.html (2019)
11. Moore, C., Nilsson, M.: Parallel quantum computation and quantum codes. SIAM J. Comput. **31**(3), 799–815 (2001)
12. Nagy, M., Akl, S.: Quantum computation and quantum information. Int. J. Parallel Emergent Distrib. Syst. **21**(1), 1–59 (2006)
13. Nielsen, M., Chuang, I.: Quantum Computation and Quantum Information. Cambridge University Press, Cambridge (2000)

14. Paeth, A.: A fast algorithm for general raster rotation. In: Proceedings of Graphics Interface and Vision Interface, pp. 77–81 (1986)
15. Rukundo, O., Cao, H.: Nearest neighbor value interpolation. Int. J. Adv. Comput. Sci. Appl. **3**(4), 25–30 (2012)
16. Sang, J., Wang, S., Niu, X.: Quantum realization of the nearest-neighbor interpolation method for FRQI and NEQR. Quantum Inf. Process. **15**, 37–64 (2016)
17. Sharma, R., Shah, S., Shankar, A.: Algebra I: A Basic Course in Abstract Algebra. Pearson, London (2011)
18. Tanimoto, S.: An Interdisciplinary Introduction to Image Processing. MIT Press, Cambridge (2012)
19. Unser, M., Thevenaz, P., Yaroslavsky, L.: Convolution-based interpolation for fast, high-quality rotation of images. IEEE Trans. Image Process. **4**(10), 1371–1381 (1995)
20. Vedral, V., Barenco, A., Ekert, A.: Quantum networks for elementary arithmetic operations. Phys. Rev. A **54**(1), 147–153 (1996)
21. Venegas-Andraca, S., Bose, S.: Storing, processing, and retrieving an image using quantum mechanics. In: Proceedings of SPIE Conference of Quantum Information and Computation, vol. 5105, pp. 137–147 (2003)
22. Wang, J., Jiang, N., Wang, L.: Quantum image translation. Quantum Inf. Process. **14**(5), 1589–1604 (2015)
23. Yan, F., Iliyasu, A., Fatichah, C., Tangel, M., Betancourt, J., Dong, F., Hirota, K.: Quantum image searching based on probability distributions. J. Quantum Inf. Sci. **2**(3), 55–60 (2012)
24. Yan, F., Le, P., Iliyasu, A., Sun, B., Garcia, J., Dong, F., Hirota, K.: Assessing the similarity of quantum images based on probability measurements. In: IEEE Congress on Evolutionary Computation (CEC), pp. 1–6 (2012)
25. Yan, F., Iliyasu, A., Le, P., Sun, B., Dong, F., Hirota, K.: A parallel comparison of multiple pairs of images on quantum computers. Int. J. Innov. Comput. Appl. **5**(4), 199–212 (2013)
26. Yan, F., Chen, K., Venegas-Andraca, S., Zhao, J.: Quantum image rotation by an arbitrary angle. Quantum Inf. Process. **16**, 1–20 (2017)
27. Zhou, R., Hu, W., Fan, P., Lan, H.: Quantum realization of the bilinear interpolation method for NEQR. Sci. Rep. **7**, 2511 (2017). https://www.nature.com/articles/s41598-017-02575-6
28. Zhou, R., Tan, C., Fan, P.: Quantum multidimensional color image scaling using nearest-neighbor interpolation based on the extension of FRQI. Mod. Phys. Lett. B **31**(17), 1750184 (2017)

Chapter 4
Quantum Image Security

The advent of digital technology has created a heightened need for secure communication. QIMP seeks to facilitate a transition from image processing and applications using traditional (digital) computing to the more sophisticated quantum computing paradigm as well as the potential development of hybrid (i.e., classical-quantum) devices and algorithms for image processing. Indeed, quantum computation and QIMP offer possibilities for secure communication in areas such as encryption, steganography, and watermarking [35]. In this chapter, these QIMP-based security technologies are introduced.

4.1 QIMP-Based Security Technologies

As highlighted in the opening section of this book, QIMP is built on the extension of digital image processing to the quantum computing realm, leading to the realization of secure, efficient, and advanced technologies for cryptography and information hiding. Figure 4.1 provides an outline of quantum image security technologies within these two broad areas.

As a direct application in the science of cryptography, encryption is considered as the process of obscuring information to make it unreadable without special knowledge [29]. This is usually done for secrecy, and typically for confidential communications. Cryptography is about protecting the content of messages, whereas information hiding focuses on concealing their very existence [17]. Hiding information using strategies such as steganography and watermarking seems more secure because such techniques are not easily noticed by attackers. However, among its main constraints is its high demand related to the amount of information that can

---

© Portions of this chapter are reprinted from ref. [33], with permission of Springer.

© Springer Nature Singapore Pte Ltd. 2020
F. Yan, S. E. Venegas-Andraca, *Quantum Image Processing*,
https://doi.org/10.1007/978-981-32-9331-1_4

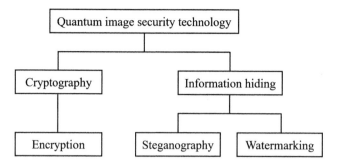

Fig. 4.1 Outline of quantum image security technologies

be hidden inside a cover image without distortions to its visible imperceptibility. While steganography and watermarking are interrelated, they differ in terms of purpose and/or applications, and in terms of the requirements of those purposes [17].

1. In watermarking, the conspicuous (or visible) content is the carrier image, whereas the copyright or ownership is hidden and subject to authentication. The objective of steganography is to securely communicate a secret message by camouflaging it as a meaningless part of a carrier image without triggering any suspicions from third-party adversaries.
2. In watermarking, information is hidden in the form of a stochastic serial number or some image, such as a logo. Therefore, watermarked images usually carry a small amount of information about the copyright ownership. Since the objective of steganography is to camouflage the presence of the hidden message, it often requires large carrying capacity in terms of the carrier image.
3. In watermarking, the watermarked content is susceptible to numerous types of infringements, such as cropping, filtering, or channel noise, which are not of concern in stego images.

   In the remainder of this section, several advances in quantum image security protocols in the areas of watermarking, encryption, and steganography are discussed [35].

4.1.1 Algorithms for Quantum Watermarking

Like digital watermarking, quantum watermarking aims to protect the copyright of an image and authenticate its ownership using visible or invisible signals (mostly logos) embedded in the cover (or carrier) image. Figure 4.2 presents the schematic outlining the approach used in quantum watermarking.

Based on the description of a quantum image and the resulting interpretation of QIMP in Chap. 2, for FRQI representation in particular, the work of Iliyasu et

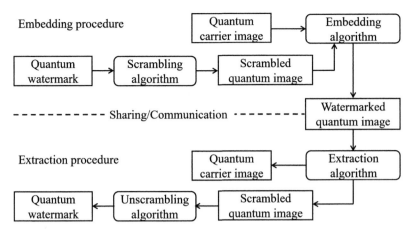

Fig. 4.2 Schematic for quantum watermarking algorithms

al. [8] is credited as the first quantum image security protocol. In that study, a scheme called watermarking and authentication of quantum images (WaQI) was proposed based on restricted geometric transformations on the images. Proposed as an invisible watermarking strategy, WaQI is thought to be a secure, keyless, blind, and computationally efficient scheme that can perfectly authenticate ownership of watermarked images. WaQI is based on the use of a cover and watermark image to produce a watermark embedding circuit that is used to randomly hide the watermark inside the carrier image. This same circuit is reversed to recover the original (unmarked) image during the validation of copyright ownership. Its grayscale version, gray WaQI [9], was proposed as a two-tier watermark strategy that facilitates embedding a conspicuous watermark logo in a predetermined subarea of the cover image; the same watermark signal (logo) is also embedded to cover the rest of the image in an obscure manner.

The original WaQI scheme has proven effective in authenticating ownership of watermarked images, but it has the drawback that the content of the watermark is required to realize the watermark authentication circuit, which is needed to validate the ownership of the marked images. Many of the studies that followed focused on eliminating this shortcoming. In [41], the quantum Fourier transform (QFT) was used to extract the watermarking image without having to know what it looked like. However, this approach has its own drawbacks, since as a result of the computation, the hitherto normalized quantum image state is lost. This is attributed to the fixed embedding strength controlling parameter [40, 41]. In addition, two dynamic watermarking schemes, i.e., quantum Wavelet transform (QWT)-based watermarking [25] and Hadamard transform-based watermarking [26], were proposed. Instead of the fixed embedding strength parameter used in [41], this scheme utilizes dynamic vectors to control the embedding strength. This improves on previous efforts in the form of a better trade-off between visual quality and embedding capacity.

The quantum watermarking strategies reviewed thus far are all based on FRQI representation for the carrier images and watermark logos. Using the multi-channel extension of FRQI representation, i.e., MCQI representation, a multi-channel extension of the WaQI scheme (MC-WaQI) was proposed [33]. In MC-WaQI, two keys are generated from the color and position information of an MCQI image in the preprocessing stage. Following this, two watermark images are embedded in the spatial and frequency domains, respectively, of the cover image. The adoption of MCQI representation for the carrier and watermark images facilitates the protection of colored quantum images and improves the capability of watermarked images to withstand malicious attacks.

In extending quantum watermarking to grayscale images, Miyake et al. proposed the use of simple and small-scale quantum circuits to embed a scrambled image in the carrier image using the XOR (exclusive or) operation [22]. Simulation-based results presented in the study validated the performance of the proposed scheme in terms of visual quality, robustness, and computational complexity. More recently, a new watermarking strategy stored the carrier and the watermark images in the θ and φ phases, respectively, of the same qubit [18]. The study claims that visual imperceptibility is guaranteed regardless of the size of the embedded image, i.e., the embedding capacity of the carrier image.

4.1.2 Algorithms for Quantum Image Encryption

Encryption is pivotal to secure communication and information sharing, especially in warfare, military communication, politics, and even the daily lives of ordinary people, as necessitated by the ubiquity of information, notably images and video, sharing and storage. Quantum image encryption technologies could be broadly classified as spatial or frequency domain-based strategies, whose schematic is shown in Fig. 4.3.

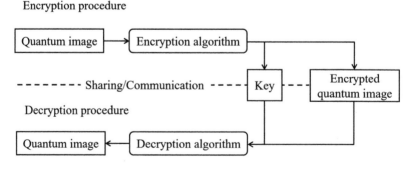

Fig. 4.3 Schematic for quantum image encryption algorithms

Information about the spatial domain of a quantum image is also described by its position information (pixel position) and color information (pixel value). Therefore, algorithms for quantum image encryption are mainly focused on these two parameters [35]. Image encryption methods often used in this regard are the scrambling approach (to transform pixel positions to disorder an image) and replacement approach (to transform pixel values to alter the statistical properties of the encrypted image). Indeed, the combination of these two methods is also an available solution.

Popular scrambling algorithms used on position information include the Hilbert, Arnold, and Fibonacci transforms. These traditional approaches have been extended to encryption applications in the QIMP domain. The Arnold and Fibonacci scrambling circuits [13] take advantage of the plain adder and adder modulo N by modifying operations on the input and output in order to scramble the images, while the Hilbert scrambling circuit [12] uses the Hilbert scanning matrix that is generated by a recursive algorithm. Preceding this, an encryption and decryption algorithm using geometric transformations on FRQI images was investigated to reverse the correlations among adjacent pixels, but the encrypted images were not noise-like, and the sketches could be identified visually [42].

In addition to position space scrambling, algorithms utilizing or combining the replacement approach have also been studied. Zhou et al. (2015) proposed a quantum image gray-code and bit-plane scrambling scheme based on NEQR representations [43]. The scheme's reported cost was rather low, and the scrambling speed was very high compared to other quantum image scrambling methods, such as quantum Hilbert scrambling [12]. Moreover, the encryption scheme in [27] used geometric transformations to shuffle the codes of pixel positions, and further color transformations were performed to recode the color codings in the FRQI images. Targeting the RGB-based MCQI image, [34] introduced a method that applies both color and geometric transformations to an image, where the color information is transformed by quantum rotation operations and the geometric information is scrambled using an improved partition scrambling method, thereby ensuring the security of the quantum images. Finally, a novel quantum image encryption algorithm combining the generalized affine transform with a logistic map was studied [19], by which the gray-level information of the quantum image is encrypted by the XOR operation with a key generator controlled by the logistic map, while the position information of the quantum image is encoded by the generalized affine transform. The proposed algorithm is considered robust, with better performance than its classical counterpart in terms of computational complexity [19].

Turning to frequency domain-based quantum image encryption protocols, the double random-phase encoding technique was generalized to the quantum computing realm, and it was used together with the QFT to realize a robust quantum image encryption method [37]. Similarly, a novel encryption algorithm for FRQI images based on the QWT and double diffusions was discussed in [31]. In another effort, quantum encryption and decryption methods for color images were proposed, whose encryption process can be realized by performing secret random-phase encoding operations in the input and the QFT planes [38]. Meanwhile, in [39], a novel quantum image encryption algorithm was proposed, which can be realized by subtly constructing the evolution rules of one-dimensional quantum cellular automata. The algorithm's complexity was claimed to be lower than that of other quantum image encryption schemes based on QFT.

4.1.3   Algorithms for Quantum Image Steganography

As discussed earlier, image steganography is a technique for information hiding focused on concealing a secret message in a carrier image [5]. Figure 4.4 provides the general schematic for quantum image steganography protocols, while the remainder of this section highlights some advances based on them.

In 2014, Jiang et al. proposed a Moiré pattern-based NEQR image steganography strategy [11]. The strategy was designed primarily as a steganographic algorithm with corresponding quantum circuits to hide a binary image in a grayscale image. The embedding algorithm begins with the choice of an initial Moiré grating, i.e., a stochastic image, as the cover image. The initial Moiré grating is then modified according to the secret image, and the deformed Moiré grating is regarded as the Moiré pattern. Finally, the Moiré pattern is altered to obtain the stego image.

Following that study, an enhanced version using two blind least significant bit (LSB) steganography algorithms in the form of quantum circuits based on NEQR representations [14] was proposed. The first algorithm is anchored on the standard (or plain) LSB, which uses message qubits to directly substitute for the pixels' LSB. While the standard LSB steganography system is simple, its robustness is poor. The other algorithm is block LSB, which embeds a message qubit to a number of pixels that belong to one image block. The block LSB steganography network aims to improve the robustness and undetectability of the standard LSB scheme. This is accomplished by partitioning the cover image into blocks, each hiding one message

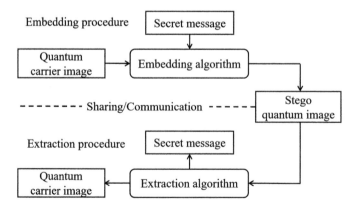

Fig. 4.4 Schematic for quantum image steganography algorithms

qubit instead of a pixel. The experimental results presented in that study demonstrate that the invisibility is good, and the balance between the capacity and robustness can be adjusted according to the needs of applications.

Elsewhere, a least significant qubit (LSQb) information hiding algorithm for NEQR images was proposed by Wang et al. [32]. This algorithm embeds a secret message qubit stream into the last qubit of the color information of a quantum cover image. To further enhance security, they proposed an LSQb frequency domain-based information hiding algorithm. QFT is executed on the cover image, and then the qubit of color encoding information in the secret image is compared with the last qubit of color encoding information in the QFTed cover image using the two-qubit quantum comparator (which will be introduced in Sect. 4.4.2.1). According to the outputs of the quantum comparator circuit, different unitary transformations will facilitate the secret information to be embedded into the QFTed cover image.

To summarize, the study of quantum image security technologies (e.g., watermarking, encryption, and steganography) has become widely popular within the QIMP community. Some more recent studies are recommended to those seeking further understanding of developments in this field [1, 3, 4, 7, 20, 23, 44]. Advances in QIMP have inspired studies to extend watermarking, encryption, and steganography applications to related media, i.e., quantum movies and audio. With recent efforts related to quantum movie/audio representation and accompanying operations, it seems worthwhile to explore the encryption of quantum movies and quantum audio. While these subareas are not as advanced as QIMP, activity is taking on renewed intensity. Some of this work on multimedia is discussed in Chap. 6.

4.2 Duple Watermarking Strategy for Quantum Images

In this section, a double-key, double-domain, multi-channel watermarking strategy for quantum images (MC-WaQI) [33] is introduced, such that verification of the authentic owner of the image is guaranteed without compromising the security of the content of the cover image. In the MC-WaQI strategy, both the watermark image and carrier image are encoded in MCQI representation.

4.2.1 Double Information Key Generation

4.2.1.1 Two Watermark Information

In the MC-WaQI strategy, the secret information is embedded in both the frequency and spatial domains of the carrier image; hence, there is the need to generate two sets of data from the original carrier image with the additional requirement that

Fig. 4.5 (a) Separations of
MCQI watermark image in R,
G, and B channels and (b)
their combination [33]

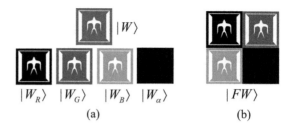

$|W\rangle$

$|W_R\rangle$ $|W_G\rangle$ $|W_B\rangle$ $|W_\alpha\rangle$ $|FW\rangle$

(a)   (b)

these data should be half the size of the carrier image. Assuming the size of the
carrier image is $n \times n$, the size of the watermark image is supposed to be $n/2 \times n/2$; otherwise, the stratagem requires that the watermark image be "polished" by
adding/reducing some redundancies [41].

The MCQI image is a multiple channel quantum image with the original RGB
channels and α channel for processing the color information, as shown in Eqs. (2.33)
and (2.34). The watermark images in different channels are presented in Fig. 4.5a,
where the α channel is the redundant channel with all of the black pixels of the same
size as the watermark. The separations of watermark information in R, G, B, and α
channels are combined to constitute a grayscale image $|FW\rangle$ for the watermarking
in the frequency domain, as shown in Fig. 4.5b. Notice that $|W_R\rangle$, $|W_G\rangle$, and $|W_B\rangle$
are grayscale quantum images in FRQI representation, and $|FW\rangle$ is twice as large
as the original watermark image $|W\rangle$.

4.2.1.2 Color Information Key Generation

As presented in Sect. 1.1.2.1, a measurement applied on a superposition state $\alpha|0\rangle + \beta|1\rangle$ will lead to the collapse of this state to produce the result 0 with probability
$|\alpha|^2$ or 1 with probability $|\beta|^2$, where $|\alpha|^2 + |\beta|^2 = 1$. The color information key
(CIK) is generated by means of such a basic property, which is defined below [33].

Definition 4.1 A CIK in MC-WaQI is a sequence of numbers assigned by an
encoding rule, which is used to transform the color information on the watermark
image.

Since the CIK is generated by performing quantum measurements, it is updated
every time the watermark image is measured. Therefore, the CIK is regarded as an
"unknown" key to public users. A simple example of how a CIK is generated is
presented in Fig. 4.6. First, according to the MC-PPT in Sect. 2.3.2, the watermark
image is prepared and stored as a quantum state, and then a quantum measurement
is applied on each channel of the watermark image to lead the different color
information to collapse to a certain color, as shown in the post-measurement image
in Fig. 4.6a. The circuit structure of this measurement is presented in Fig. 4.6b.

To further clarify the collapse of the color information, consider, for example,
the purple pixel in Fig. 4.7, which is composed of R (128), G (64), and B (128), but

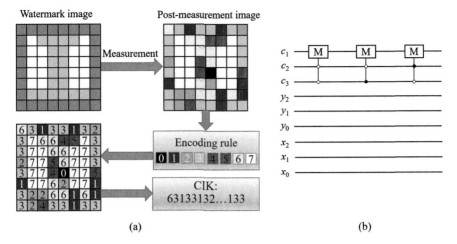

Fig. 4.6 (**a**) Generation procedure of CIK and (**b**) its circuit realization [33]

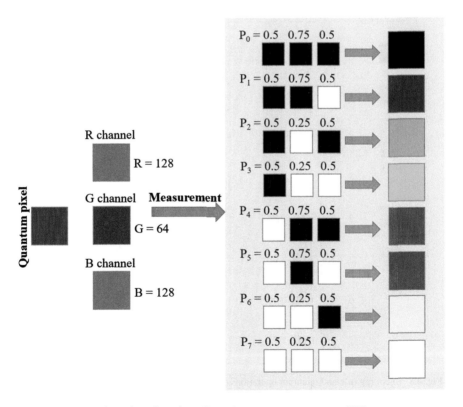

Fig. 4.7 An example to show the color collapse in quantum measurement [33]

collapses to either black or white with probabilities (indicated as P_0–P_7) on each channel after the measurement on these three channels. It is trivial to see from this that there are only eight possible colors in the post-measurement image according to the composition of basic colors in the RGB color model [33].

Eight indices are assigned, from 0 to 7, to the different colors from black through white; based on this, an encoding rule is generated for the CIK, which is presented in Fig. 4.8. The CIK is obtained by the quantum measurement, and it has the same length as the number of pixels in the post-measurement image. For example, the length of CIK in Fig. 4.6 is 64, which is the same size as the watermark image. The first element in that CIK is 6, the second is 3, the third is 1, and so on. Each number in the CIK is assigned a different operation based on a specified COI or CS operation (as presented in Sect. 2.3.3) so that the color information in the watermark image can be transformed. The rule set governing the relationship between the value of the CIK and the color operation, including a brief description of the operations, is presented in Fig. 4.8. Specifically, the COI operation (COI_R, COI_G, or COI_B) changes the grayscale value of one channel (R, G, or B) of an image, and the CS operation

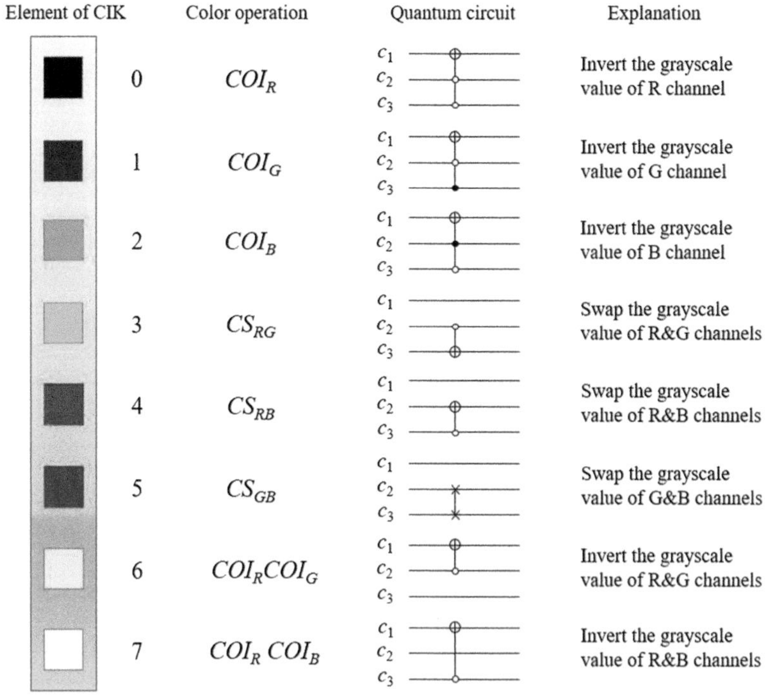

Element of CIK	Color operation	Quantum circuit	Explanation
0	COI_R	c_1, c_2, c_3	Invert the grayscale value of R channel
1	COI_G	c_1, c_2, c_3	Invert the grayscale value of G channel
2	COI_B	c_1, c_2, c_3	Invert the grayscale value of B channel
3	CS_{RG}	c_1, c_2, c_3	Swap the grayscale value of R&G channels
4	CS_{RB}	c_1, c_2, c_3	Swap the grayscale value of R&B channels
5	CS_{GB}	c_1, c_2, c_3	Swap the grayscale value of G&B channels
6	$COI_R COI_G$	c_1, c_2, c_3	Invert the grayscale value of R&G channels
7	$COI_R COI_B$	c_1, c_2, c_3	Invert the grayscale value of R&B channels

Fig. 4.8 Encoding rule and quantum operations corresponding to different elements in CIK [33]

$(CS_{RG}, CS_{RB},$ or $CS_{GB})$ swaps the grayscale value between two channels (RG, RB, or GB).

4.2.1.3 Position Information Key Generation

The position information key (PIK) is used to protect the position information on the watermark image, and is defined as follows [33].

Definition 4.2 A PIK in MC-WaQI is a sequence combining two random permutations M and N, sized m and n, respectively, to scramble the position information on the watermark image.

Specifically, given an $m \times n$-sized image, there are two random permutations M and N (where M and N build up the PIK) of size m and n, respectively. The pixel $(M(i), N(j))$ of the watermark image replaces the pixel at position (i, j) in the original image, where $M(i)$ and $N(j)$ are the i-th and j-th elements of M and N, respectively. After traversing all of the pixels of an image, the position information of the image is scrambled to produce a meaningless image [41]. Considering a 4×4-sized quantum image in Fig. 4.9, the original alphabet sequence is from A through P. If one lets $M = 3, 0, 1, 2; N = 1, 2, 0, 3$, then the alphabet is rearranged to "H E F G P M N O D A B C L I J K." In the quantum circuit in Fig. 4.9c, the last two qubits of the X- and Y-axis are ancilla states prepared in the standard states $|0\rangle$ and they are transformed into the scrambled image at the output.

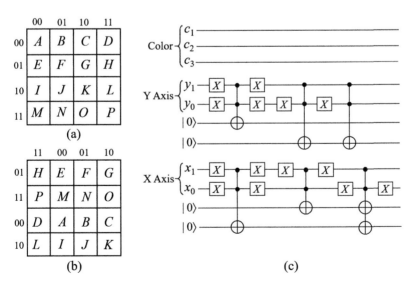

Fig. 4.9 Image scrambling method on (**a**) a 4×4 quantum image; (**b**) the scrambled image; and (**c**) the circuit implementation (reprinted from ref. [41], with permission of Springer)

4.2.2   Watermark Image Embedding and Extraction

A color image consists of many pixels, and the color information of each pixel can be separated into its three channels. According to Eq. (2.33), an MCQI image state can be rewritten as

$$|I\rangle = \sum_{i=0}^{N-1} (X_R^i|0\rangle + X_G^i|1\rangle + X_B^i|2\rangle + X_\alpha|3\rangle)|i\rangle, \tag{4.1}$$

where i is the position information, N is the number of pixels in the image, X_R^i, X_G^i, and X_B^i are color channel information, and X_α is made to carry no information. The watermark image will be embedded in both the frequency domain (QFT coefficients) and spatial domain (RGB channels) of the carrier image, so the embedding and extraction procedures from these two domains are discussed separately.

1. Embedding in frequency domain

    Based on the above image scrambling method and the PIK, the watermark image is embedded in the frequency domain of the carrier image. To guarantee that the pixel values of the embedded carrier image $|I'\rangle$ are still real, the revised value of the QFT coefficients should be symmetric. If the size of carrier image is $m \times n$, then the revised values of the QFT coefficients should meet the conditions:

$$CE_X(i, j) = CE_X(m-1-i, n-1-j), \quad X \in \{R, G, B, \alpha\}, \tag{4.2}$$

where $CE_X(i, j)$ is the revised value of the QFT coefficients in the X channel of the carrier image. Accordingly, the watermark image $|W\rangle$ to be embedded in the carrier image should also be symmetric implies that:

$$W_X(i, j) = W_X(m-1-i, n-1-j). \tag{4.3}$$

    In addition, the image $|W\rangle$ used for embedding in the frequency domain should be twice the size of the image $|I\rangle$ because of the symmetric property of QFT [24]. Using the scrambling method discussed in Sect. 4.2.1.3, image $|FW\rangle$ is processed, with the resultant image $|FW'\rangle$, as shown in Fig. 4.10. The whole procedure of embedding in the frequency domain is as follows [33]:

    (a) Preprocessing of watermark image yields the procedure $W \rightarrow |W\rangle \rightarrow |FW\rangle \rightarrow |FW'\rangle$, as introduced earlier.
    (b) Execute QFT on the carrier image to obtain its QFT coefficients.
    (c) Embed each channel of image $|FW'\rangle$ in the corresponding channels of the QFT coefficients of image $|I\rangle$. The embedding procedure is implemented by performing the phase-rotation operation on the carrier image [36].
    (d) Execute the inverse QFT on each channel of the embedded image to get the intermediate watermarked image $|I'\rangle$.

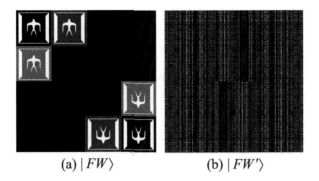

(a) $|FW\rangle$ (b) $|FW'\rangle$

Fig. 4.10 (**a**) Resized watermark image and (**b**) its scrambled version [33]

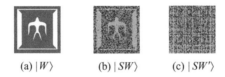

(a) $|W\rangle$ (b) $|SW\rangle$ (c) $|SW'\rangle$

Fig. 4.11 (**a**) Original watermark image; (**b**) color-transformed image; and (**c**) position-scrambled image [33]

2. Embedding in spatial domain.

As stated previously, the procedure of embedding in the spatial domain includes the following steps [33]:

(a) Preprocessing on watermark image $|W\rangle$, as introduced earlier. First, CIK operations are applied on image $|W\rangle$ to transform it to $|SW\rangle$, then an optional PIK operation is used to further scramble the position information of $|SW\rangle$ to obtain $|SW'\rangle$. Resulting images in this process are presented in Fig. 4.11.

(b) Embed each channel of image $|SW'\rangle$ in the corresponding channel of image $|I'\rangle$ to obtain the final watermarked image $|I''\rangle$. In particular, the COI operator in Sect. 4.2.1.2 is adopted to shift the grayscale value of the R, G, or B channel in $|I'\rangle$. According to Eqs. (2.37) and (2.38), the final watermarked image $|I''\rangle$ will have all of its colors coming from $|I'\rangle$ and $|SW'\rangle$.

Using the generated CIK and related operations, it is apparent that the color information of image $|W\rangle$ has been protected. Such an embedding method in spatial domain ensures that the key will be updated every time watermark information is produced, which means that illegal users will find it hard to steal keys. It is different from the available literature [41] in that the key is assigned by the copyright owner. However, the position information in $|SW\rangle$ is still exposed after the color transformation using CIK operations. The PIK introduced in Sect. 4.2.1.3 can be used to further scramble the position information of $|SW\rangle$ in order to improve the security of the carrier image, as presented in Fig. 4.11c.

In the procedure of watermark extraction, the watermark images are extracted from both the frequency and spatial domains by means of two kinds of extraction circuits [33, 36]. The procedure is basically the inverse of watermark embedding in the frequency and spatial domains. This procedure is feasible because all of the quantum gates involved in the implementation of watermark embedding are invertible operations.

4.2.3   Metric for Estimating Congruity Between Quantum Images

In QIMP applications, most researchers are content to adopt the classical peak-signal-to-noise-ratio (PSNR) image quality measure to benchmark and validate their approaches (i.e., to assess likeness between two or more quantum images). This is mainly attributed to the absence of a quantum-based metric equivalent to the PSNR. However, the often confounding contrariety between classical and quantum information processing makes the widely accepted PSNR ill-suited to the quantum computing framework, hence, these classical metrics are insufficient to effectively quantify the fidelity between two or more quantum images [10].

An enhanced quantum-based image fidelity metric, the QIFM, is introduced in [10] as a tool to assess the "congruity" between two or more quantum images. Unlike the aforementioned image quality measures, the QIFM is calibrated as a pixel difference-based image quality measure that is sensitive to the intricacies of QIMP. The design of QIFM moderates its execution cost in order to estimate the congruity between two or more quantum images. A statistical analysis also shows that the QIFM has a better correlation with the digital expectation of likeness between images than other available quantum image quality measures. Therefore, the QIFM is an effective substitute for the PSNR as an image quality measure in the quantum computing framework, thereby providing a tool to effectively assess the fidelity between images in quantum watermarking, quantum movie aggregation, and other applications in QIMP.

To summarize, a new multi-channel watermarking strategy that integrates a double-key and double-domain idea, aimed at enhancing the security of quantum images, was presented in this section. The hidden watermark logo in the spatial and frequency domains can be retrieved by using CIK and PIK that are unaccessible to unauthorized users, hence safeguarding the published versions of an image from illicit tampering. Finally, a quantum-based image fidelity metric was mentioned to assess the fidelity between images in QIMP applications.

4.3   Quantum Image Encryption Using One-Dimensional Quantum Cellular Automata

In any encryption scheme, the sender encrypts and transmits data in a public environment, and only the designated receiver should be able to decrypt the data using the decryption key. In contrast to watermarking, the attacker can detect the existence of the secret information but cannot receive it. In this section, a quantum cellular automata (QCA)-based quantum image encryption method [39] is introduced as a quantum counterpart of classical encryption schemes.

4.3.1   Quantum Cellular Automata

In the QCA algorithm [15], each cell comprises two qubits, i.e., the x-qubit and y-qubit. The state of the i-th QCA cell at computation step t is defined as

$$|y_i^t x_i^t\rangle = c_{0,i}^t |00\rangle + c_{1,i}^t |01\rangle + c_{2,i}^t |10\rangle + c_{3,i}^t |11\rangle, \tag{4.4}$$

where $|c_{k,i}^t\rangle$, $k = 0, 1, 2, 3$, are the coefficients of four basis states for each cell, for which $\sum_{k=0}^{3} |c_{k,i}^t|^2 = 1$. Therefore, during QCA evolution, the state of a cell may be a superposition of these four basis states.

The global state of the QCA at computation step t is the tensor product of the states of its n cells, which is expressed as

$$|S^t\rangle = |y_{n-1}^t x_{n-1}^t y_{n-2}^t x_{n-2}^t \cdots y_0^t x_0^t\rangle. \tag{4.5}$$

The cell states of the QCA evolve based on a global unitary rule R. The global state's evolution from computation step t to $t + 1$ is given by

$$|S^{t+1}\rangle = R|S^t\rangle. \tag{4.6}$$

The evolution operator R has two phases [39]. In the interaction phase, the state of the x-qubit in each cell is controlled by the states of the y-qubits in the neighboring cells by the application of controlled quantum gates. In the evaluation phase, a two input quantum gate or a combination of quantum gates is applied to the x- and y-qubit in each cell, thereby facilitating information flow in the QCA lattice and the simultaneous change of all x-qubit states. Therefore, Eq. (4.6) can be rewritten as

$$|S^{t+1}\rangle = R|S^t\rangle = R_E R_I |S^t\rangle, \tag{4.7}$$

where R_I and R_E are two unitary operators associated with the evolution rule R which are in the interaction and evaluation phases, respectively [16].

4.3.2   Scheme of Quantum Image Encryption Operation

The one-step evolution rule R is operated on the original quantum image, as presented in Fig. 4.12. In the interaction phase, a Toffoli gate is applied to every three neighboring cells. The control qubits are the y-qubits of the $(j + 1)$-th and $(j - 1)$-th cells, while the target qubit is the x-qubit of the j-th cell. In the evaluation phase, a quantum gate U (which is a rotation operation as defined in Eq. (3.39)) is applied to the x- and y-qubit in each cell. In this phase, the operator R_I is composed by a series of tensor products of Toffoli gates,

$$R_I = T \otimes T \otimes \cdots \otimes T, \tag{4.8}$$

and R_E is defined as

$$R_E = U \otimes U \otimes \cdots \otimes U. \tag{4.9}$$

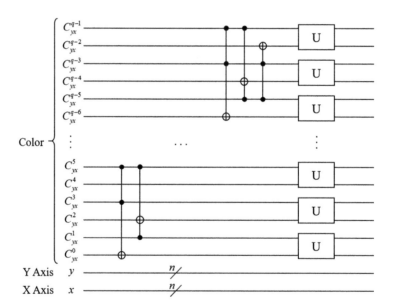

Fig. 4.12 Quantum circuit for one-step evolution rule R (reprinted from ref. [39], with permission of Elsevier)

Therefore, the QCA-based quantum image encryption scheme is described as follows [39]:

Step 1:   Encode plaintext image $|I\rangle$ (as defined in Eq. (2.55)) to obtain $|M^1\rangle$ using the R_I operation, i.e.,

$$|M^1\rangle = (R_I \otimes I)|I\rangle$$

$$= (R_I \otimes I)\frac{1}{2^n}\sum_{y=0}^{2^n-1}\sum_{x=0}^{2^n-1}\bigotimes_{i=0}^{q-1}|C_{yx}^i\rangle|yx\rangle$$

(4.10)

$$= \frac{1}{2^n}\sum_{y=0}^{2^n-1}\sum_{x=0}^{2^n-1}R_I|C_{yx}^0 C_{yx}^1 \cdots C_{yx}^{q-1}\rangle|yx\rangle.$$

Step 2:   Encode confused image $|M^1\rangle$ to obtain $|I^1\rangle$, using the R_E operation, i.e.,

$$|I^1\rangle = (R_E \otimes I)|M^1\rangle$$

$$= (R_E \otimes I)\frac{1}{2^n}\sum_{y=0}^{2^n-1}\sum_{x=0}^{2^n-1}R_I|C_{yx}^0 C_{yx}^1 \cdots C_{yx}^{q-1}\rangle|yx\rangle$$

(4.11)

$$= \frac{1}{2^n}\sum_{y=0}^{2^n-1}\sum_{x=0}^{2^n-1}R_E R_I|C_{yx}^0 C_{yx}^1 \cdots C_{yx}^{q-1}\rangle|yx\rangle.$$

Step 3:   Repeat above two steps for t times. The encrypted quantum image then changes to

$$|I^t\rangle = \bigotimes_{i=1}^{t}(R \otimes I)|I\rangle = \bigotimes_{i=1}^{t}(R_E R_I \otimes I)|I\rangle,$$

(4.12)

where the value of t should depend on the trade-off between computational complexity and encryption effect.

Since all the quantum operations are invertible, the decryption process is the inverse of the encryption process; that is, if the encrypted quantum image is $|I^t\rangle$, then the decryption process is

$$|I\rangle = \bigotimes_{i=1}^{t}(R^\dagger \otimes I)|I\rangle = \bigotimes_{i=1}^{t}(R_I^\dagger R_E^\dagger \otimes I)|I^t\rangle,$$

(4.13)

where $R^\dagger$ is the conjugate-transpose matrix of R, as defined in Sect. 1.1.3.2.

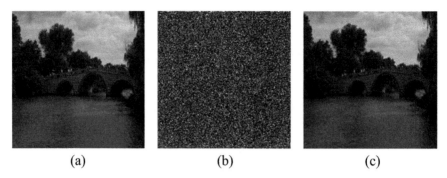

(a)   (b)   (c)

Fig. 4.13 Example of quantum image encryption: (**a**) original image; (**b**) encrypted image; and (**c**) decrypted image (reprinted from ref. [39], with permission of Elsevier)

4.3.3   Example of Quantum Image Encryption

In the simulation, an image with 256×256 pixels is taken as the original image [39], as shown in Fig. 4.13a, and the encrypted image is shown in Fig. 4.13b. The image encryption process can be achieved through subtle construction of the evolution rules of one-dimensional QCA. The encryption algorithm provided has a complexity $O(n)$, which is superior to the complexity $O(n^2)$ of existing QFT-based quantum image encryption schemes [39].

To summarize, a quantum cellular automata (QCA)-based quantum image encryption method has been introduced in this section. The algorithm, supported by the results of detailed numerical simulation and theoretical analysis, is shown to have advantages in security, computational complexity, and robustness over classical counterparts and some existing representative quantum image encryption schemes.

4.4   LSB-Based Quantum Image Steganography Algorithm

In digital steganography, sensitive messages may be concealed by manipulating and storing information in the LSB of an image or sound file [6]. In this section, two blind LSB steganography algorithms in the form of quantum circuits are provided based on the NEQR images [14]. One of these algorithms is plain LSB, which uses the message qubits to substitute for the pixels' LSB directly, and the other is block LSB, which embeds a message qubit in a number of pixels belonging to a single image block.

4.4.1 Plain LSB Steganography Operation

Assume the cover image is a $2^n \times 2^n$ quantum image $|I\rangle$ with gray range 2^q (as defined in Eq. (2.55)), and the message is a $2^n \times 2^n$ binary quantum image $|M\rangle$, as presented below:

$$|M\rangle = \frac{1}{2^n} \sum_{i=0}^{2^{2n}-1} |m_i\rangle \otimes |i\rangle, \tag{4.14}$$

where

$$m_i \in \{0, 1\}, i = 0, 1, \cdots, 2^{2n} - 1. \tag{4.15}$$

The embedding circuit of plain LSB algorithm is presented in Fig. 4.14a, in which $2n$ CNOT gates are used to test whether or not the position information of $|I\rangle$ and $|M\rangle$ is the same. If the position information is identical, that of $|M\rangle$ is changed to $|00\cdots0\rangle$. Therefore, under their control, the LSB of $|I\rangle$ (i.e., $|C_i^0\rangle$) is swapped with the message qubit $|m_i\rangle$ to obtain the stego image $|I'\rangle$.

The extraction circuit is shown in Fig. 4.14b, where $2n$ Hadamard gates are utilized to transform the initial state (i.e., a sequence of $|0\rangle$) to a blank image. Similar

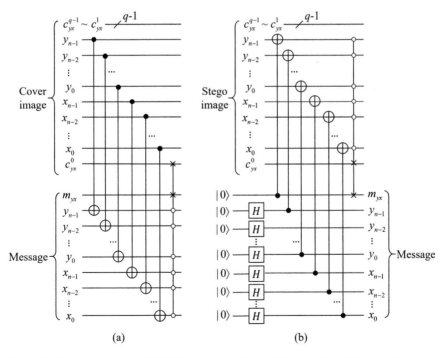

Fig. 4.14 Quantum circuit of plain LSB algorithm: (a) embedding circuit and (b) extraction circuit (reprinted from ref. [14], with permission of Springer)

with the embedding circuit, when the position information of $|I\rangle$ and $|M\rangle$ is equal, the LSB of $|I\rangle$ (i.e., $|C_i^0\rangle$) is swapped with the message qubit $|m_i\rangle$ to obtain the message $|M\rangle$.

4.4.2   Block LSB Steganography Operation

Although the plain LSB steganography algorithm is simple, it exhibits poor robustness [14]. To improve the robustness and undetectability of the LSB scheme, the block LSB steganography algorithm divides the cover image into blocks, each block (instead of each pixel) hides one message qubit. Actually, plain LSB steganography can be viewed as a special case of block LSB in which every block only accommodates one pixel.

4.4.2.1   Quantum Counter and Comparator

(1) Quantum counter

   A quantum counter circuit [21] is shown in Fig. 4.15, where $|b\rangle$ is the input qubit and $b \in \{0, 1\}$. $|a_{n-1} \cdots a_1 a_0\rangle$ is a counter with initial value $|0 \cdots 00\rangle$. If the input qubit $|b\rangle$ is $|1\rangle$, then $|a_{n-1} \cdots a_1 a_0\rangle$ increases by 1; otherwise, $|a_{n-1} \cdots a_1 a_0\rangle$ remains unchanged.

(2) Quantum comparator

   A quantum comparator circuit [30] is shown in Fig. 4.16. The comparator compares a and b, where $|a\rangle = |a_{n-1} \cdots a_1 a_0\rangle$ and $|b\rangle = |b_{n-1} \cdots b_1 b_0\rangle$, $a_i, b_i \in \{0, 1\}$, $i = 0, 1, \cdots, n-1$. Qubits $|e_1\rangle$ and $|e_0\rangle$ are outputs. If $e_1 e_0 = 10$, then $a > b$; if $e_1 e_0 = 01$, then $a < b$; and if $e_1 e_0 = 00$, then $a = b$. The usage and its optical implementation are presented in [2] and [28].

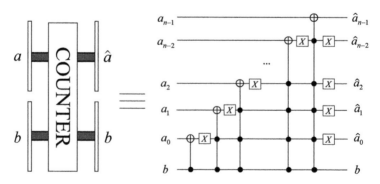

Fig. 4.15 Quantum counter circuit

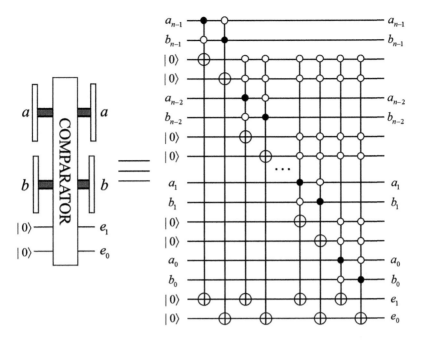

Fig. 4.16 Quantum comparator circuit

4.4.2.2   Block Embedding Procedure

In block LSB scheme, the $2^n \times 2^n$ cover image $|I\rangle$ (shown in Eq. (2.55)) must be divided into $2^{n-p_1} \times 2^{n-p_2}$ blocks, each block of size $2^{p_1} \times 2^{p_2}$, where $p_1, p_2 \in \{0, 1, \cdots, n\}$. The image block $|B\rangle$ can be defined as

$$|B_{k,l}\rangle = \frac{1}{2^n} \sum_{k=0}^{2^n-1} \sum_{l=0}^{2^n-1} |b_{k,l}\rangle \otimes |kl\rangle, \tag{4.16}$$

where

$$|k\rangle = |y_{n-1}y_{n-2}\cdots y_{p_1}\rangle, \ |l\rangle = |x_{n-1}x_{n-2}\cdots x_{p_2}\rangle. \tag{4.17}$$

Assume the message is a binary quantum image, as presented in Eq. (4.14). Its size is $2^{n-p_1} \times 2^{n-p_2}$, and the color information $m_{k,l} \in \{0, 1\}$, where $k = y_{n-1}y_{n-2}\cdots y_{p_1}$ and $l = x_{n-1}x_{n-2}\cdots x_{p_2}$. The embedding procedure is as follows [14]:

Step 1:   The cover image $|I\rangle$ is scrambled to enhance its undetectability in the scheme. The quantum Hilbert image scrambling algorithm [12] is used in this process.

Step 2:   If the position information $|y_{n-1}y_{n-2}\cdots y_{p_1}x_{n-1}x_{n-2}\cdots x_{p_2}\rangle$ of $|I\rangle$ is equal to that of $|M\rangle$, then the embedding operation swaps the LSB of $|I\rangle$ (i.e., $|C_{yx}^0\rangle$) and the message qubit $|m_{k,l}\rangle$.

Step 3:   The inverse Hilbert scrambling is used to recover from the scrambled image.

4.4.2.3   Block Extraction Procedure

Following the embedding of every message qubit 2^p times (where $p = p_1 + p_2$), the stego image can be attacked maliciously, which might change some of the LSB values. This will result in the sum of all of the pixels' LSBs belonging to one block to be equal not to 0 or 2^p, but rather to a value between them.

Determining whether the extracted message qubit is 0 or 1 according to the sum value is facilitated by setting a threshold. If the sum is greater than or equal to the threshold, then the message qubit is 1; otherwise, the message qubit is 0. The extraction procedure is as follows [14]:

Step 1:   This is the same as Step 1 of the embedding procedure.

Step 2:   A control circuit (i.e., partition module, shown in Fig. 4.19) is used to separate the stego image into $2^{n-p_1} \times 2^{n-p_2} = 2^{2n-p_1-p_2}$ blocks. In addition, the circuit includes $2^{2n-p_1-p_2}$ control layers, each corresponding to one image block.

Step 3:   Quantum counters (see Sect. 4.4.2.1) are used to sum all of the pixels' LSBs that belong to one block. It contains $2^{2n-p_1-p_2}$ counters, and the counting numbers are represented as $a_{y_{n-1}\cdots y_{p_1}x_{n-1}\cdots x_{p_2}}$.

Step 4:   Since each block comprises 2^p pixels, the counting number from Step 3 should be compared with 2^{p-1}, which is the threshold T that is set by using the quantum comparator (in Sect. 4.4.2.1). If $a_{y_{n-1}\cdots y_{p_1}x_{n-1}\cdots x_{p_2}} \geq 2^{p-1}$, then the extracted message is 1; otherwise, the extracted message is 0.

4.4.3   Example of Quantum Image Steganography

In this subsection, an example is provided to describe the steganography algorithm [14]. Considering a simple 4×4 cover image and an 8-bit message, 00110110, which is the ASCII code of the character "6," the cover image is partitioned into eight blocks sized 1×2 (in this case, in Eqs. (4.16) and (4.17), $n = 2$, $p_1 = 0$, $p_2 = 1$) and the message is rearranged into a 4×2 binary image [14], as shown in Fig. 4.17.

Figure 4.18 shows the block LSB embedding circuit, which consists of three parts corresponding to the three steps detailed in Sect. 4.4.2.2. The first and third parts accomplish Hilbert image scrambling and its inverse operation [12].

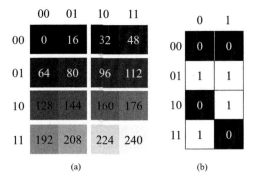

Fig. 4.17 (a) Cover image and (b) message image of the example (the numbers in the pixels are their gray values)

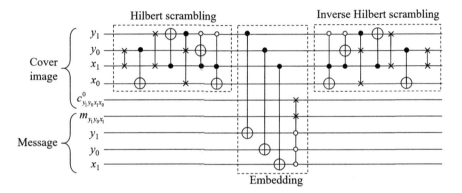

Fig. 4.18 Block LSB embedding circuit of the example (reprinted from ref. [14], with permission of Springer)

The block LSB extraction circuit (in Fig. 4.19) includes four parts, which correspond to the four steps in Sect. 4.4.2.3. The Hilbert scrambling part is the same as in the embedding operation. The partition module is a control circuit that determines which counter $C_{y_1y_0x_1x_0}^0$ enters. For instance, if the control value is 000, then $C_{000x_0}^0$ swaps with the first auxiliary qubit $|0\rangle$, i.e., it enters the first counter. The counting module consists of $2^{n-p_1} \times 2^{n-p_2} = 8$ counters, which correspond to the eight blocks. Each counter $a_{y_1y_0x_1}$ sums the LSB of the pixels of block $B_{y_1y_0x_1}$. Since each block has two pixels, the maximum value of $a_{y_1y_0x_1}$ is 2, so two qubits are enough, i.e., $|a_{y_1y_0x_1}\rangle = |a_{y_1y_0x_1}^1 a_{y_1y_0x_1}^0\rangle$. In addition, the comparing part contains $2^{n-p_1} \times 2^{n-p_2} = 8$ comparators, which compare $a_{y_1y_0x_1}$ with the threshold $2^{p-1} = (01)_2$. As presented in Sect. 4.4.2.1, if $a_{y_1y_0x_1} > 01$, then the bottom two qubits of each comparator are 10, and so on. Hence, one only needs to invert the bottom qubit to obtain the message qubit $|m_{y_1y_0x_1}\rangle$.

To summarize, two LSB-based steganography algorithms for quantum images were introduced. They differ by whether the message qubit is embedded in a pixel or

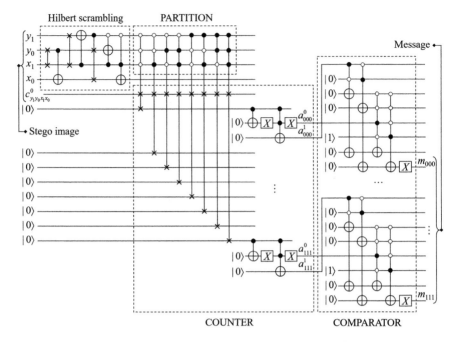

Fig. 4.19 Block LSB extraction circuit of the example (reprinted from ref. [14], with permission of Springer)

a block of the cover image. Both algorithms are blind, i.e., the extraction procedure does not need the original cover or the original message. Analysis and simulation-based experimental results demonstrate that the invisibility of the algorithms is good, and there is an inherent trade-off between their capacity and robustness.

In this chapter, the discussion is started by dividing quantum image security techniques into the two categories of cryptography and information hiding. Specifically, the background and advances of quantum image scrambling, encryption, watermarking, and steganography are discussed. In addition to the fast computing speed brought by parallel computation, the main emphases in these techniques are on ensured security (by means of quantum measurement) compared to their classical counterparts. The schematics of the embedding/extraction and encryption/decryption procedures are depicted to show the implementation and distinctiveness of these algorithms.

References

1. Abd-El-Atty, B., El-Latif, A., Venegas-Andraca, S.: An encryption protocol for NEQR images based on one-particle quantum walks on a circle. Quantum Inf. Process. **18**(9), 272 (2019)
2. Cheng, S., Wang, C.: Quantum switching and quantum merge sorting. IEEE Trans. Circuits Syst. Regul. Pap. **53**(2), 316–325 (2006)

3. Du, S., Qiu, D., Mateus, P., Gruska, J.: Enhanced double random phase encryption of quantum images. Results Phys **13**(102161) (2019)
4. El-Latif, A., Abd-El-Atty, B., Hossain, M.: Efficient quantum information hiding for remote medical image sharing. IEEE Access **6**, 21075–21083 (2018)
5. El-Latif, A., Abd-El-Atty, B., Venegas-Andraca, S.: A novel image steganography technique based on quantum substitution boxes. Opt. Laser Technol. **116**, 92–102 (2019)
6. Gupta, S., Goyal, A., Bhushan, B.: Information hiding using least significant bit steganography and cryptography. Int. J. Mod. Educ. Comput. Sci. **6**, 27–34 (2012)
7. Heidari, S., Vafaei, M., Houshmand, M., Tabatabaey-Mashadi, N.: A dual quantum image scrambling method. Quantum Inf. Process. **18**(9) (2019)
8. Iliyasu, A., Le, P., Dong, F., Hirota, K.: Watermarking and authentication of quantum images based on restricted geometric transformations. Inf. Sci. **186**(1), 126–149 (2012)
9. Iliyasu, A., Le, P., Yan, F., Sun, B., Garcia, J., Dong, F., Hirota, K.: A two-tier scheme for greyscale quantum image watermarking and recovery. Int. J. Innov. Comput. Appl. **5**(2), 85–101 (2013)
10. Iliyasu, A., Yan, F., Hirota, K.: Metric for estimating congruity between quantum images. Entropy **18**(10), 360 (2016)
11. Jiang, N., Wang, L.: A novel strategy for quantum image steganography based on Moiré pattern. Int. J. Theor. Phys. **54**(3), 1021–1032 (2015)
12. Jiang, N., Wang, L., Wu, W.: Quantum Hilbert image scrambling. Int. J. Theor. Phys. **53**(7), 2463–2484 (2014)
13. Jiang, N., Wu, W., Wang, L.: The quantum realization of Arnold and Fibonacci image scrambling. Quantum Inf. Process. **13**(5), 1223–1236 (2014)
14. Jiang, N., Zhao, N., Wang, L.: LSB based quantum image steganography algorithm. Int. J. Theoret. Phys. **55**(1), 107–123 (2016)
15. Karafyllidis, I.: Definition and evolution of quantum cellular automata with two qubits per cell. Phys. Rev. A **70**(4), 044301 (2004)
16. Karafyllidis, I.: Quantum computer simulator based on the circuit model of quantum computation. IEEE Trans. Circuits Syst. Regul. Pap. **52**(8), 1590–1596 (2005)
17. Katzenbeisser, S., Petitcolas, F.: Information Hiding Techniques for Steganography and Digital Watermarking. Artech House Print on Demand, Norwood (1999)
18. Li, P., Xiao, H., Li, B.: Quantum representation and watermark strategy for color images based on the controlled rotation of qubits. Quantum Inf. Process. **15**, 4415–4440 (2016)
19. Liang, H., Tao, X., Zhou, N.: Quantum image encryption based on generalized affine transform and logistic map. Quantum Inf. Process. **15**, 2701–2724 (2016)
20. Liu, X., Xiao, D., Xiang, Y.: Quantum image encryption using intra and inter bit permutation based on logistic map. IEEE Access **7**, 6937–6946 (2018)
21. Ma, L., Lu, J.: Construction of controlled quantum counter. Chin. J. Quantum Electr. **20**(1), 47–50 (2003)
22. Miyake, S., Nakamae, K.: A quantum watermarking scheme using simple and small-scale quantum circuits. Quantum Inf. Process. **15**(5), 1849–1864 (2016)
23. Naseri, M., Abdolmaleky, M., Laref, A., Parandin, F., Celik, T., Farouk, A., Mohamadi, M., Jalalian, H.: A new cryptography algorithm for quantum images. Optik **171**, 947–959 (2018). https://www.sciencedirect.com/science/article/pii/S0030402618309227
24. Nielsen, M., Chuang, I.: Quantum Computation and Quantum Information. Cambridge University Press, Cambridge (2000)
25. Song, X., Wang, S., Liu, S., Abd El-Latif, A., Niu, X.: A dynamic watermarking scheme for quantum images using quantum wavelet transform. Quantum Inf. Process. **12**(2), 3689–3706 (2013)
26. Song, X., Wang, S., Abd El-Latif, A., Niu, X.: Dynamic watermarking scheme for quantum images based on Hadamard transform. Multimedia Systems **20**(4), 379–388 (2014)
27. Song, X., Wang, S., Abd El-Latif, A., Niu, X.: Quantum image encryption based on restricted geometric and color transformations. Quantum Inf. Process. **13**(8), 1765–1787 (2014)

28. Sousa, C., Silva, J., Ramos, R.: Optical quantum bit string comparator. Opt. Quant. Electron. **51**, 28 (2019). https://link.springer.com/article/10.1007/s11082-018-1732-5
29. Walker, M.: Cryptography and Encryption Overview. CEH Certified Ethical Hacker All-in-One Exam Guide (2011)
30. Wang, D., Liu, Z., Zhu, W., Li, S.: Design of quantum comparator based on extended general Toffoli gates with multiple targets. Comput. Sci. **39**(9), 302–306 (2012)
31. Wang, S., Song, X., Niu, X.: A novel encryption algorithm for quantum images based on quantum wavelet transform and diffusion. In: Intelligent Data Analysis and its Applications, Volume II, Advances in Intelligent Systems and Computing, vol. 298, pp. 243–250 (2014)
32. Wang, S., Sang, J., Song, X., Niu, X.: Least significant qubit (LSQb) information hiding algorithm for quantum images. Measurement **73**, 352–359 (2015)
33. Yan, F., Iliyasu, A., Sun, B., Venegas-Andraca, S., Dong, F., Hirota, K.: A duple watermarking strategy for multi-channel quantum images. Quantum Inf. Process. **14**(5), 1675–1692 (2015)
34. Yan, F., Guo, Y., Iliyasu, A., Jiang, Z., Yang, H.: Multi-channel quantum image scrambling. J. Adv. Comput. Intell. Intell. Inf. **20**(1), 163–170 (2016)
35. Yan, F., Iliyasu, A., Le, P.: Quantum image processing: A review of advances in its security technologies. Int. J. Quantum Inf. **15**(3), 1730001 (2017)
36. Yang, Y., Jia, X., Xu, P., Tian, J.: Analysis and improvement of the watermark strategy for quantum images based on quantum Fourier transform. Quantum Inf. Process. **12**(8), 2765–2769 (2013)
37. Yang, Y., Xia, J., Jia, X., Zhang, H.: Novel image encryption/decryption based on quantum Fourier transform and double phase encoding. Quantum Inf. Process. **12**(11), 3477–3493 (2013)
38. Yang, Y., Jia, X., Sun, S., Pan, Q.: Quantum cryptographic algorithm for color images using quantum Fourier transform and double random-phase encoding. Inf. Sci. **277**, 445–457 (2014)
39. Yang, Y., Tian, J., Lei, H., Zhou, Y., Shi, W.: Novel quantum image encryption using one-dimensional quantum cellular automata. Inf. Sci. **345**, 257–270 (2016)
40. Zhang, W., Gao, F., Liu, B., Jia, H.: A quantum watermark protocol. Int. J. Theor. Phys. **52**(2), 504–513 (2013)
41. Zhang, W., Gao, F., Liu, B., Wen, Q., Chen, H.: A watermark strategy for quantum images based on quantum Fourier transform. Quantum Inf. Process. **12**(2), 793–803 (2013)
42. Zhou, R., Wu, Q., Zhang, M., Shen, C.: Quantum image encryption and decryption algorithms based on quantum image geometric transformations. Int. J. Theor. Phys. **52**(6), 1802–1817 (2013)
43. Zhou, R., Sun, Y., Fan, P.: Quantum image gray-code and bit-plane scrambling. Quantum Inf. Process. **14**(5), 1717–1734 (2014)
44. Zhou, N., Hu, Y., Gong, L., Li, G.: Quantum image encryption scheme with iterative generalized Arnold transforms and quantum image cycle shift operations. Quantum Inf. Process. **16**, 164 (2017)

Chapter 5
Quantum Image Understanding

Image understanding transforms data extracted from images to certain commonly understood descriptions, and it makes subsequent decisions and actions according to the interpretation of the images [6]. Image understanding is a broad area of research. In the QIMP field, it includes quantum image classification [12], morphology [15, 22], pseudocolor [7], registration [18], and synthesis [5]. Some typical contributions related to this field are discussed, namely quantum feature extraction [20], filtering [8], and segmentation [4].

5.1 Local Feature Point Extraction for Quantum Images

Feature extraction is aimed at detecting and isolating various desired portions or shapes (features) of digital images [6]. A novel quantum image edge extraction algorithm (QSobel) was proposed in 2014 [21] that is based on FRQI representation and the classical edge extraction algorithm Sobel. QSobel was proved capable of extracting edges of computational complexity $O(n^2)$ for a FRQI image of size $2^n \times 2^n$. The same research group later proposed a quantum feature extraction framework based on a NEQR representation [20]. Their framework, utilizing the quantum addition/subtraction operations and several quantum image transformations, showed that the feature points (i.e., corner points) could be extracted by comparing and thresholding the pixel gradients. This feature extraction framework is introduced below.

© Springer Nature Singapore Pte Ltd. 2020
F. Yan, S. E. Venegas-Andraca, *Quantum Image Processing*,
https://doi.org/10.1007/978-981-32-9331-1_5

5.1.1 Quantum Image Color Transformations

Three types of color operations used in the design of a feature extraction algorithm are discussed. The first is the complement operation U_C, which is important in designing a quantum image subtraction operation. This operation changes all the grayscales of the pixels in an NEQR image to their complementary values on 2^q. For details of the operation and its circuit implementation, see Sect. 2.4.2.1.

The second operation is the halving operation U_H, which reduces the grayscale of all of the pixels in an NEQR image by half [20]. Equation (5.1) expresses the transformation of the quantum operation U_H as

$$
\begin{aligned}
U_H(|I\rangle) &= U_H \left(\frac{1}{2^n} \sum_{y=0}^{2^n-1} \sum_{x=0}^{2^n-1} |f(y,x)\rangle |y\rangle |x\rangle \right) \\
&= U_H \left(\frac{1}{2^n} \sum_{y=0}^{2^n-1} \sum_{x=0}^{2^n-1} \bigotimes_{i=0}^{q-1} |C_{yx}^i\rangle |y\rangle |x\rangle \right) \\
&= \frac{1}{2^n} \sum_{y=0}^{2^n-1} \sum_{x=0}^{2^n-1} \left(|C_{yx}^0\rangle \bigotimes_{i=0}^{q-2} |C_{yx}^{i+1}\rangle |y\rangle |x\rangle \right) \\
&= \frac{1}{2^n} \sum_{y=0}^{2^n-1} \sum_{x=0}^{2^n-1} |C_{yx}^0\rangle |f(y,x)/2\rangle |y\rangle |x\rangle.
\end{aligned}
\tag{5.1}
$$

The third operation is the classification operation U_T of all of the pixels in an image [20]. A threshold T is set, and all the pixels with grayscale values less than the threshold belong to one group, while the remaining pixels belong to the other group. An auxiliary qubit (initialized as $|0\rangle$) is needed to store the classification result, which should be integrated with the image state. This operation U_T is executed as

$$
\begin{aligned}
U_T(|I\rangle|0\rangle) &= U_T \left(\frac{1}{2^n} \sum_{y=0}^{2^n-1} \sum_{x=0}^{2^n-1} |f(y,x)\rangle |yx\rangle |0\rangle \right) \\
&= \frac{1}{2^n} \left(\sum_{f(y,x)\geq T} |f(y,x)\rangle |yx\rangle |1\rangle + \sum_{f(y,x)<T} |f(y,x)\rangle |yx\rangle |0\rangle \right).
\end{aligned}
\tag{5.2}
$$

Generally, when a threshold T is chosen, the auxiliary qubit corresponding to all of the pixels with grayscale values no less than T should be inverted (from $|0\rangle$ to $|1\rangle$). For simplicity, taking an image with a gray range $[0, 2^q - 1]$, a threshold equaling a power of 2 is often selected, and it is thus easy to design the quantum circuit [20].

5.1.2   Quantum Image Addition and Subtraction Operations

To compute the gradients for all the pixels in the quantum image [10] and further extract its feature points, focus must be directed to the addition and subtraction operations of two quantum images in the NEQR model [20]. Regarding the image addition operation on the two images, the pixels of the resultant image incur the arithmetic additions of the grayscales of the corresponding pixels in the two images.

Consider that the two quantum images $|I_A\rangle$ and $|I_B\rangle$ are both of size $2^n \times 2^n$, with a gray range $[0, 2^q - 1]$, i.e.,

$$|I_A\rangle = \frac{1}{2^n} \sum_{yx=0}^{2^{2n}-1} |A_{yx}\rangle |yx\rangle, \tag{5.3}$$

and

$$|I_B\rangle = \frac{1}{2^n} \sum_{yx=0}^{2^{2n}-1} |B_{yx}\rangle |yx\rangle, \tag{5.4}$$

where $|A_{yx}\rangle = \otimes_{i=0}^{q-1} |a_i\rangle$ and $|B_{yx}\rangle = \otimes_{i=0}^{q-1} |b_i\rangle$. Further consider that the resulting quantum image is $|I_C\rangle$ as

$$|I_C\rangle = \frac{1}{2^n} \sum_{yx=0}^{2^{2n}-1} |C_{yx}\rangle |yx\rangle = \frac{1}{2^n} \sum_{yx=0}^{2^{2n}-1} |A_{yx} + B_{yx}\rangle |yx\rangle. \tag{5.5}$$

For every pixel (y, x) in $|I_C\rangle$, the grayscale C_{yx} is equal to the sum of A_{yx} and B_{yx}. Since $A_{yx}, B_{yx} \in [0, 2^q - 1]$, it is known that $C_{yx} \in [0, 2^{q+1} - 2]$, and, therefore, that $q + 1$ qubits are required to store the result, i.e., $|C_{yx}\rangle = \otimes_{i=0}^{q} |c_i\rangle$.

A quantum adder (see Sect. 3.3.2.1) is then used to compute the arithmetic result $|C_{yx}\rangle = |A_{yx} + B_{yx}\rangle$ of the two quantum states $|A_{yx}\rangle$ and $|B_{yx}\rangle$. Therefore, the quantum image addition operation of $|I_A\rangle$ and $|I_B\rangle$ can be carried out using a quantum adder on the two color qubit sequences of the two images to obtain the resulting image $|I_C\rangle$, which is defined as

$$|I_C\rangle = \text{add}(|I_A\rangle, |I_B\rangle). \tag{5.6}$$

To compute the result of the subtraction of two quantum images $|I_A\rangle$ and $|I_B\rangle$, an image complementing operation can be applied to $|I_B\rangle$ to obtain $|I_{\bar{B}}\rangle$ (where

$|I_{\bar{B}}\rangle = U_C|I_B\rangle)$. Therefore, the quantum image subtraction operation can be defined as

$$|I_C\rangle = \mathrm{sub}(|I_A\rangle, |I_B\rangle)$$

$$= \mathrm{add}(|I_A\rangle, |I_{\bar{B}}\rangle)$$

$$= \frac{1}{2^n} \sum_{yx=0}^{2^{2n}-1} |A_{yx} - B_{yx}\rangle|yx\rangle. \tag{5.7}$$

Similarly, $q + 1$ qubits are required to store the grayscale values of the pixels of the resulting image $|I_C\rangle$. The highest qubit being $|0\rangle$ implies that $A_{yx} \geq B_{yx}$; otherwise, $A_{yx} < B_{yx}$. If the highest qubit is neglected, then the operation will be to compute the absolute value of the subtraction of A_{yx} and B_{yx} [20].

5.1.3   Scheme of Quantum Image Feature Extraction

In this subsection, the feature points to be extracted from the images are the corner pixels that have grayscales that differ from the neighborhood pixels in all directions. Generally, the gradient of every direction of a single pixel is used to represent the degree of difference from its neighbors.

One simple method of computing the pixel gradients is the 1-order differential coefficient [9], which uses the 3×3 neighborhood of the pixel, as shown in Fig. 5.1. The framework of the quantum image feature extraction based on the NEQR model is then given [20].

Fig. 5.1 3×3 neighborhood pixels of pixel (y, x); $G1$–$G4$ are the subgradients of the four common orientations in this mask

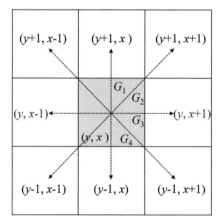

Step 1: Generate the eight shifted quantum images using cycle-shift operations (cf. Sect. 5.2.1) on $|I_{yx}\rangle$. The quantum image set is now expressed as

$$\begin{aligned}
\Big\{ &|I_{yx}\rangle, |I_{y-1x}\rangle, |I_{y+1x}\rangle, |I_{y-1x-1}\rangle, |I_{yx-1}\rangle, \\
&|I_{y+1x-1}\rangle, |I_{y-1x+1}\rangle, |I_{yx+1}\rangle, |I_{y+1x+1}\rangle \Big\}.
\end{aligned} \tag{5.8}$$

The eight shifted images are computed and stored in the quantum states; in contrast, in traditional methods, only one temporal image is used and the neighboring pixels are not stored separately.

Step 2: Obtain the 1-order differential coefficient of the image by using a sequence of quantum image addition and subtraction operations on the relative images in the quantum image set (in Step 1), and compute the gradient of every pixel using the halving operation U_H on the image.

When implementing the zero-cross method [9], the subgradients of four directions of every pixel must be computed, as shown in Fig. 5.1. For pixel (y, x), the gradients are computed based on its 3×3 neighborhood information. The procedure used to compute all four subgradients for all the pixels in the quantum image is presented as

$$\begin{aligned}
|G_1\rangle &= U_H\Big\{ \text{sub}\big[\text{add}\big(|I_{yx}\rangle, |I_{yx}\rangle\big), \text{add}\big(|I_{y+1x}\rangle, |I_{y-1x}\rangle\big)\big]\Big\}, \\
|G_2\rangle &= U_H\Big\{ \text{sub}\big[\text{add}\big(|I_{yx}\rangle, |I_{yx}\rangle\big), \text{add}\big(|I_{y+1x+1}\rangle, |I_{y-1x-1}\rangle\big)\big]\Big\}, \\
|G_3\rangle &= U_H\Big\{ \text{sub}\big[\text{add}\big(|I_{yx}\rangle, |I_{yx}\rangle\big), \text{add}\big(|I_{yx+1}\rangle, |I_{yx-1}\rangle\big)\big]\Big\}, \\
|G_4\rangle &= U_H\Big\{ \text{sub}\big[\text{add}\big(|I_{yx}\rangle, |I_{yx}\rangle\big), \text{add}\big(|I_{y+1x-1}\rangle, |I_{y-1x+1}\rangle\big)\big]\Big\}.
\end{aligned} \tag{5.9}$$

Step 3: Construct the quantum circuit of the classification operation U_T in this scheme, which, since it depends on the threshold value, requires setting a fixed threshold before extracting the image features. Four auxiliary qubits ($|z_i\rangle$, $1 \leq i \leq 4$) are used to record whether the four subgradients of every pixel (in Step 2) are larger than the threshold and store the classification results of these subgradients.

Step 4: Produce the entanglement state of the position qubit sequence and the four classification result qubits $|z\rangle$, which is expressed as

$$|\varphi\rangle = \frac{1}{2^n} \sum_{yx=0}^{2^{2n}-1} |yx\rangle \otimes |z\rangle. \tag{5.10}$$

It is known that the feature points are the pixels having grayscales significantly different than the neighborhood pixels in all directions. This indicates that a pixel can be considered to be a feature point only when every classification result $|z_i\rangle$ (in Step 3) is equal to $|1\rangle$.

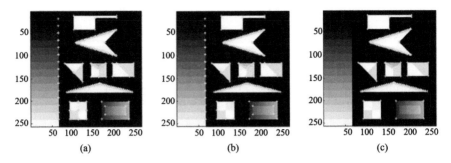

Fig. 5.2 Feature extraction result from the test image using the zero-cross method, where T denotes the threshold and N is the number of extracted feature points: (**a**) $T = 8, N = 304$; (**b**) $T = 16, N = 298$; and (**c**) $T = 32, N = 236$ (reprinted from ref. [20], with permission of Springer)

Based on the above discussion, the method used to compute the gradient and the selected threshold are the two important factors influencing the performance of the feature extraction algorithm. The feature extraction results using the zero-cross method and different thresholds ($T = 8$, 16, and 32) for the test image [13] are shown in Fig. 5.2. It has been claimed that since only the 3×3 neighborhood information is used in the simple zero-cross method, some incorrect features are inevitable in the resulting images [20].

To summarize, a quantum feature extraction framework has been introduced based on the NEQR model. Since the pixels' color information is stored in the basis state of a qubit sequence in the NEQR model, the quantum image addition and subtraction operations can be carried out flexibly using a quantum adder. The gradients of all the pixels can then be computed simultaneously through a sequence of quantum arithmetic operations. Finally, the feature points can be effectively extracted from the quantum image by setting a certain gradient threshold.

5.2   Quantum Image Median Filtering in Spatial Domain

The aim of image filtering is to suppress noise without loss of image details and features, and it is an indispensable operation in image preprocessing [6]. In 2013, Caraiman et al. elucidated a method of achieving quantum image filtering by exploiting QFT and the quantum oracle principle [2]. Yuan et al. recently proposed a spatial filtering method for quantum images [16]. In this method, however, the specific values of the filter coefficients must be known before each filtering operation. Moreover, this method is only suitable for integer filter coefficients [17]. It is noteworthy that these two methods only apply to mean filtering and not to median filtering. In this section, spatial filtering of a quantum image, with emphasis on the design of the quantum median filter and its application to image denoising [8], is introduced.

5.2.1 Quantum Modules for Median Filter

To complete the quantum image median filtering operation, several basic modules, namely the cycle-shift, sort, and median calculation modules, are used [8].

(1) Cycle-shift modules

The four cycle-shift modules used here are represented as S_{y-}, S_{y+}, S_{x-}, and S_{y+}. They are used to translate all the pixels in the image by one unit. For example, for an $2^n \times 2^n$-sized NEQR image, and assuming the position qubit to be $|y\rangle|x\rangle$, the roles of these four modules can be described as follows [8]:

$$S_{y-}(|y\rangle) = |(y-1) \bmod 2^n\rangle,$$
$$S_{y+}(|y\rangle) = |(y+1) \bmod 2^n\rangle,$$
$$S_{x-}(|x\rangle) = |(x-1) \bmod 2^n\rangle,$$
$$S_{x+}(|x\rangle) = |(x+1) \bmod 2^n\rangle.$$
(5.11)

Figure 5.3 shows the quantum circuits and examples of these four modules. In accordance with Eq. (5.11), this operation is a cycle addition of the edge pixels of the image; that is, during the operation S_{x+}, the pixels located at the right edges will move to the left edge in the transformed image [14, 20].

(2) Sort module

The sort module sorts two integers in ascending order and consists of a comparator and swap sub-module (see Fig. 5.4a). In this module [8], the quantum comparator (see Sect. 4.4.2.1) is used to compare two input integers a and b. A decision is then made whether to swap a and b according to the value of $e_1 e_0$; if and only if $e_1 e_0 = 10$ (i.e., $a > b$), a is swapped with b using the swap module (see Fig. 5.4b). At this point, in the module output, $\hat{a}$ and $\hat{b}$ are the sorting results of a and b.

(3) Median calculation module

The median calculation module calculates the median of the nine integers and is composed of 30 sort sub-modules [8]. Figure 5.5 shows its quantum circuit structure, in which $c_1, c_2, \ldots, c_9$ are nine integers that are inputted to this module. In brief, in operation it first obtains the median of the nine integers, based on the bubble-sort principle, and uses the 30 sort sub-modules to order the nine integers $c_1, c_2, \ldots, c_9$. After sorting, the fifth integer $\hat{c}_5 = M$ is clearly the median of the nine integers.

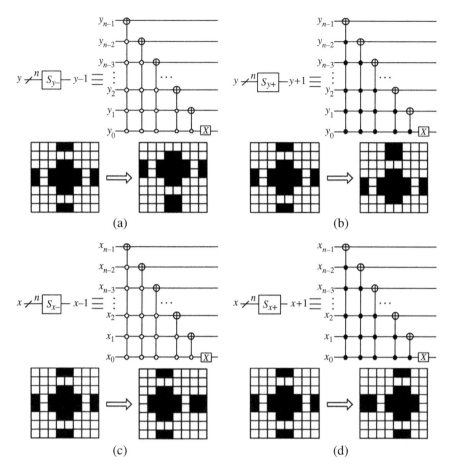

Fig. 5.3 Cycle-shift modules: quantum circuit that translates all of the pixels in the image to the (**a**) top; (**b**) bottom; (**c**) left; and (**d**) right by one unit

5.2.2   Circuit Implementation of Median Filtering Operation

5.2.2.1   Background on Median Filtering Technique

Median filters replace a pixel's value with the median of the intensity values in the neighborhood of that pixel, which are capable of excellent noise reduction for certain types of random noise [6]. To perform median filtering at a point in an image, the values of the pixels are first sorted in the neighborhood, their median determined, and that value assigned to the corresponding pixel in the filtered image. Therefore, the main function of median filters is to force points with distinct intensity levels to be more like their neighbors.

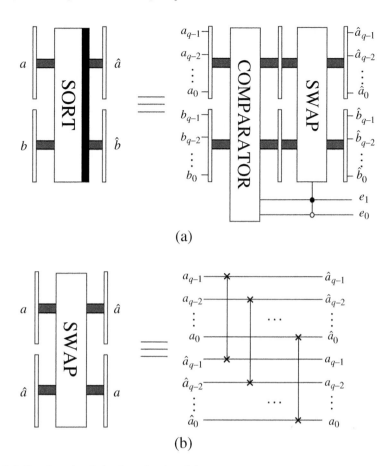

Fig. 5.4 Quantum circuit structure of sort module

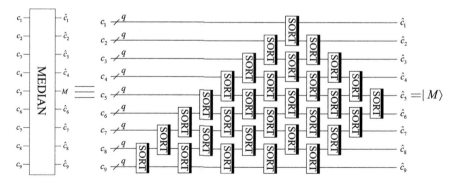

Fig. 5.5 Median calculation module, where $|M\rangle$ in the output indicates the median of nine integers (reprinted from ref. [8], with permission of Springer)

As similarly discussed in Sect. 5.1.3, the original image is first translated by one unit in eight directions (up, down, left, right, up-left, up-right, down-left, and down-right). Then, for the nine images (the original image $|I\rangle$ and the transposed eight images $|I_1\rangle \sim |I_8\rangle$)), nine pixels with the same position (e.g., $|c_{yx}\rangle$, $|c_{y_1x_1=yx}\rangle$, $|c_{y_2x_2=yx}\rangle$, $|c_{y_3x_3=yx}\rangle$, $|c_{y_4x_4=yx}\rangle$, $|c_{y_5x_5=yx}\rangle$, $|c_{y_6x_6=yx}\rangle$, $|c_{y_7x_7=yx}\rangle$, and $|c_{y_8x_8=yx}\rangle$)) are exactly the same as nine pixels encompassed by a 3×3 filtering mask in the original image (i.e., $|c_{yx}\rangle$, $|c_{(y-1)x}\rangle$, $|c_{(y+1)x}\rangle$, $|c_{y(x-1)}\rangle$, $|c_{y(x+1)}\rangle$, $|c_{(y-1)(x-1)}\rangle$, $|c_{(y-1)(x+1)}\rangle$, $|c_{(y+1)(x-1)}\rangle$, and $|c_{(y+1)(x+1)}\rangle$)). Therefore, the median of nine pixels from the same position of the nine images is the grayscale value of the corresponding position of the filtered image [8].

5.2.2.2 Quantum Median Filtering Circuits

The complete quantum circuits of the quantum image median filtering method are shown in Fig. 5.6. This comprises three types of modules: 12 cycle-shift, 16

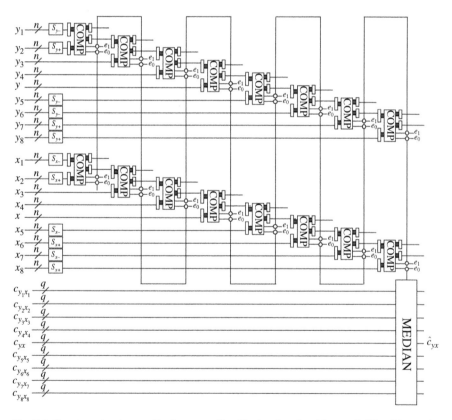

Fig. 5.6 Quantum circuit to realize image median filtering (reprinted from ref. [8], with permission of Springer)

comparator (shortened to "COMP" in the figure), and one median calculation module [8].

The procedure of quantum median filtering circuits is detailed as follows. The input is nine identical quantum images, including the original image as

$$|I\rangle = \frac{1}{2^n} \sum_{y=0}^{2^n-1} \sum_{x=0}^{2^n-1} |c_{yx}\rangle |y\rangle |x\rangle, \qquad (5.12)$$

and eight to be transposed images as

$$|I_i\rangle = \frac{1}{2^n} \sum_{y_i=0}^{2^n-1} \sum_{x_i=0}^{2^n-1} |c_{y_i x_i}\rangle |y_i\rangle |x_i\rangle, \qquad (5.13)$$

where if $y_i x_i = yx$ then $c_{y_i x_i} = c_{yx}$, $i = 1, 2, \ldots, 8$. That is to say, these nine quantum images are exactly the same.

First, with $|I\rangle$ kept constant, a total of 12 cycle-shift modules are applied to execute cycle-shift operations on the other eight images ($|I_1\rangle \sim |I_8\rangle$) to obtain nine images (one original image and eight shifted images), some of which are shown as

$$
\begin{cases}
S_{y-}|I_1\rangle = \dfrac{1}{2^n} \sum\limits_{y_1=0}^{2^n-1} \sum\limits_{x_1=0}^{2^n-1} |c_{y_1 x_1}\rangle S_{y-}|y_1\rangle |x_1\rangle \\[2mm]
\qquad\quad = \dfrac{1}{2^n} \sum\limits_{y_1=0}^{2^n-1} \sum\limits_{x_1=0}^{2^n-1} |c_{y_1 x_1}\rangle |(y_1 - 1) \bmod 2^n\rangle |x_1\rangle \\[2mm]
\qquad\quad = \dfrac{1}{2^n} \sum\limits_{\hat{y}_1=0}^{2^n-1} \sum\limits_{\hat{x}_1=0}^{2^n-1} |c_{\hat{y}_1 \hat{x}_1}\rangle |\hat{y}_1\rangle |\hat{x}_1\rangle \\[2mm]
\qquad\qquad\qquad \vdots \\[2mm]
S_{y+}S_{x+}|I_8\rangle = \dfrac{1}{2^n} \sum\limits_{y_8=0}^{2^n-1} \sum\limits_{x_8=0}^{2^n-1} |c_{y_8 x_8}\rangle S_{y+}|y_8\rangle S_{x+}|x_8\rangle \\[2mm]
\qquad\quad = \dfrac{1}{2^n} \sum\limits_{y_8=0}^{2^n-1} \sum\limits_{x_8=0}^{2^n-1} |c_{y_8 x_8}\rangle |(y_8 + 1) \bmod 2^n\rangle |(x_8 + 1) \bmod 2^n\rangle \\[2mm]
\qquad\quad = \dfrac{1}{2^n} \sum\limits_{\hat{y}_8=0}^{2^n-1} \sum\limits_{\hat{x}_8=0}^{2^n-1} |c_{\hat{y}_8 \hat{x}_8}\rangle |\hat{y}_8\rangle |\hat{x}_8\rangle.
\end{cases}
$$

$$(5.14)$$

Following completion of the image cyclic shift, another 16 comparator modules are invoked to compare the positions with the aim of finding the pixels with the same position in the nine images. Taking Eq. (5.14) as an example, if $y = \hat{y}_1 = \cdots = \hat{y}_8$ and $x = \hat{x}_1 = \cdots = \hat{x}_8$, then $c_{yx}, c_{\hat{y}_1\hat{x}_1}, \ldots, c_{\hat{y}_8\hat{x}_8}$ are the grayscale values of the nine pixels with the same position. Then, using the output of the 16 comparators as a control condition (as shown in Fig. 5.6), a median calculation module is executed to produce the median grayscale value of the nine pixels ($\hat{c}_{yx}$) with the same position. Therefore, by referring to Eq. (5.12), the median filtered quantum image ($|\hat{I}\rangle = \frac{1}{2^n} \sum_{y=0}^{2^n-1} \sum_{x=0}^{2^n-1} |\hat{c}_{yx}\rangle|y\rangle|x\rangle$) is obtained.

5.2.3   Example of Quantum Image Filtering

By use of the NEQR model in Sect. 2.4.1, a 4×4 quantum image (shown in Fig. 5.7a) is used to illustrate a specific median filtering process [8], which is presented as

$$
\begin{aligned}
|I\rangle = \frac{1}{4}(&|111\rangle|0,0\rangle + |130\rangle|0,1\rangle + |172\rangle|0,2\rangle + |159\rangle|0,3\rangle \\
&+ |107\rangle|1,0\rangle + |243\rangle|1,1\rangle + |68\rangle|1,2\rangle + |92\rangle|1,3\rangle \\
&+ |73\rangle|2,0\rangle + |35\rangle|2,1\rangle + |145\rangle|2,2\rangle + |138\rangle|2,3\rangle \\
&+ |233\rangle|3,0\rangle + |69\rangle|3,1\rangle + |121\rangle|3,2\rangle + |176\rangle|3,3\rangle).
\end{aligned}
\tag{5.15}
$$

Corresponding to the quantum circuit in Fig. 5.6 and Eq. (5.14), the whole median filtering process of the NEQR image $|I\rangle$ is presented in Fig. 5.7b–i, and Fig. 5.7j shows the final median filtered quantum image $|\hat{I}\rangle$.

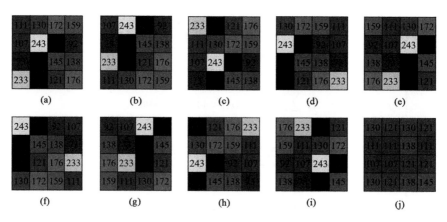

Fig. 5.7 Median filtering process for a 4 × 4 NEQR image; (**a**) $|I\rangle$; (**b**) $S_{y-}|I\rangle$; (**c**) $S_{y+}|I\rangle$; (**d**) $S_{x-}|I\rangle$; (**e**) $S_{x+}|I\rangle$; (**f**) $S_{x-}S_{y-}|I\rangle$; (**g**) $S_{x+}S_{y-}|I\rangle$; (**h**) $S_{x-}S_{y+}|I\rangle$; (**i**) $S_{x+}S_{y+}|I\rangle$; and (**j**) $|\hat{I}\rangle$ (reprinted from ref. [8], with permission of Springer)

To summarize, a quantum median filtering method was introduced in this section. Classical median filtering is achieved by sliding the filtering mask over the entire image, while in the presented method the original image is first translated by one unit in eight directions, after which, for nine images (the original image and eight transposed images), the median of nine pixels with the same position is calculated. This median is that of the corresponding pixels in the filtered image. Using the parallelism of quantum computing allows all the median calculations to be performed simultaneously, so the operation can be completed more quickly than its classical counterpart.

5.3 Threshold-Based Quantum Image Segmentation

The image segmentation process separates the foreground of one or more objects in a digital image from the background [6]. In the QIMP field, in 2014, Caraiman et al. proposed a quantum algorithm for threshold estimation and a segmentation algorithm based on iterative thresholding [3]. Both algorithms exhibit significant increases in speed compared to the analogous classical procedures because they exploit the quantum mechanism of amplitude amplification and the QFT. In 2015, Caraiman et al. proposed another threshold-based segmentation method, one that applies a quantum oracle in a single computational step [4]. This method enables accurate retrieval of the segmented image using a finite number of quantum measurement operations. This segmentation method is introduced in this section.

5.3.1 CQIR Representation and Initialization

Similar to NEQR representation in that a qubit sequence is used to encode the color information in quantum images [19], Caraiman et al. proposed an approach designated CQIR that facilitates histogram equalization of a quantum image that is particularly useful for improved processing in operations such as computing negatives, binarization, and histograms [1]. The CQIR representation is expressed as

$$|I\rangle = \frac{1}{2^n} \sum_{i=0}^{2^{2n}-1} \sum_{j=0}^{2^m-1} \alpha_{ij} |j\rangle |i\rangle, \tag{5.16}$$

where pixel positions are encoded in a register using $2n$ qubits, while each pixel's color information is represented using $m = \lceil \log_2 L \rceil$ qubits encoding the L gray-level colors. Coefficients α_{ij}, with $\sum_{j=0}^{2^m-1} |\alpha_{ij}|^2 = 1$ for all $0 \le i \le 2^{2n} - 1$, are used to express the color of a pixel with position i via a superposition of all the possible colors. For a given pixel i, coefficient α_{ij} will have a value of 1 if the color

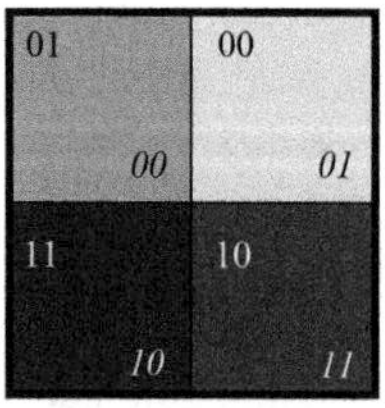

$$|I\rangle = \frac{1}{\sqrt{2^2}} \sum_{i=0}^{2^2-1} \sum_{j=0}^{2^2-1} \alpha_{ij} |j\rangle|i\rangle$$

$$= \frac{1}{2}(|01\rangle|00\rangle + |00\rangle|01\rangle + |11\rangle|10\rangle + |10\rangle|11\rangle)$$

$$\alpha_{00} = 0, \alpha_{01} = 1, \alpha_{02} = 0, \alpha_{03} = 0, \alpha_{10} = 1, \alpha_{11} = 0, \alpha_{12} = 0, \alpha_{13} = 0$$

$$\alpha_{20} = 0, \alpha_{21} = 0, \alpha_{22} = 0, \alpha_{23} = 1, \alpha_{30} = 0, \alpha_{31} = 0, \alpha_{32} = 1, \alpha_{33} = 0$$

Fig. 5.8 A 2×2 CQIR image and its quantum state (reprinted from ref. [4], with permission of Springer)

of the pixel is j, and 0 otherwise [2]. This is shown in Fig. 5.8 by a simple example of a 2×2 image with four colors, in which two qubits are used to represent the color information and two qubits to encode the position of each pixel.

The initialization of CQIR and some possible transformations were discussed in [1]. Also see Sect. 2.1 for a discussion of the similarities and differences between CQIR and other available image representations.

5.3.2 Circuit Implementation of Segmentation Operation

Image segmentation operation partitions the image into a set of nonoverlapping regions covering it and these regions correspond to one or more objects of interest and the background. Thresholding relies on color similarity of pixels belonging to different regions in an image, which makes it more simple and convenient among various segmentation methods [6].

The quantum procedure for threshold-based image segmentation uses the principles of quantum parallelism by applying a thresholding function f: $\{0, 1, \ldots, 2^{m+2n} - 1\} \rightarrow \{0, 1\}$ in the form of an oracle operator U_f on the state $|I\rangle \otimes |0\rangle$, where $|I\rangle$ is the quantum image represented in Eq. (5.16). The operator U_f is built using the function:

$$f(z) = \begin{cases} 0, & \text{if } z \gg 2n < T \\ 1, & \text{if } z \gg 2n \geq T \end{cases}, \tag{5.17}$$

where z in binary representation is $z = c_{m-1}c_{m-2} \cdots c_0 p_{2n-1}p_{2n-2} \cdots p_0$, where qubits $c_{m-1}c_{m-2} \cdots c_0$ code the color, qubits $p_{2n-1}p_{2n-2} \cdots p_0$ code pixel positions, "$\gg$" is the bitwise right-shift operator, and T is the segmentation threshold [4].

The quantum circuit (in Fig. 5.9) carries out a threshold-based segmentation of a CQIR image $|I_{in}\rangle$. The thresholding function is implemented using the oracle operator U_f in Eq. (5.17). The output image is represented by the quantum state $|I_{out}\rangle$, where pixels with intensities below the threshold T are black and others are

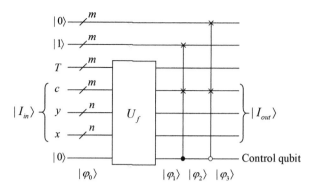

Fig. 5.9 Quantum circuit that performs threshold-based segmentation of a quantum image (reprinted from ref. [4], with permission of Springer)

white. This procedure is now analyzed and the state at each step of the quantum image segmentation circuit described [4].

In Fig. 5.9, the input state $|\varphi_0\rangle$ mainly consists of the segmentation threshold $|T\rangle$ with m qubits, input image $|I_{in}\rangle$ with $m+2n$ qubits, and control qubit $|0\rangle$ as follows:

$$|\varphi_0\rangle = |1\rangle^{\otimes m}|0\rangle^{\otimes m}|T\rangle_m|I_{in}\rangle_{m+2n}|0\rangle. \tag{5.18}$$

Further, the input image $|I_{in}\rangle$ can be interpreted as a superposition of two states: a state, $|I_{in}^{bg}\rangle$, corresponding to background pixels having a gray level less than the threshold, and one, $|I_{in}^{obj}\rangle$, corresponding to object pixels with a gray level greater than or equal to the threshold:

$$|I_{in}\rangle = \frac{\sqrt{2^{2n}-t}}{2^n}|I_{in}^{bg}\rangle + \frac{\sqrt{t}}{2^n}|I_{in}^{obj}\rangle, \tag{5.19}$$

where

$$|I_{in}^{bg}\rangle = \frac{1}{\sqrt{2^{2n}-t}}\sum_{y=0}^{2^n-1}\sum_{x=0}^{2^n-1}\sum_{j=0}^{T-1}\alpha_{yxj}|j\rangle|y\rangle|x\rangle, \tag{5.20}$$

$$|I_{in}^{obj}\rangle = \frac{1}{\sqrt{t}}\sum_{y=0}^{2^n-1}\sum_{x=0}^{2^n-1}\sum_{j=T}^{2^m-1}\alpha_{yxj}|j\rangle|y\rangle|x\rangle, \tag{5.21}$$

and t is the number of object pixels. Using the oracle operator U_f on this superposition state produces:

$$\begin{aligned}|\varphi_1\rangle &= |1\rangle^{\otimes m}|0\rangle^{\otimes m}U_f(|T\rangle|I_{in}\rangle|0\rangle))\\ &= |1\rangle^{\otimes m}|0\rangle^{\otimes m}|T\rangle\left(|I_{in}^{bg}\rangle|0\rangle + |I_{in}^{obj}\rangle|1\rangle\right).\end{aligned} \tag{5.22}$$

Thus far, the control qubit has distinguished between the two quantum states $|I_{in}^{bg}\rangle$ and $|I_{in}^{obj}\rangle$. This is used next to assign different gray levels to the image pixels relying on whether they belong to the background or to the objects of interest [4]. The final image will contain black pixels (the background) and white pixels (the segmented objects), which can be achieved using controlled-swap (also known as Fredkin) gates.

Two Fredkin gates are employed in the quantum circuit in Fig. 5.9 to set the state of the color register $|c_{obj}\rangle$ to $|1\rangle^{\otimes m}$ (white pixels) and $|c_{bg}\rangle$ to $|0\rangle^{m}$ (black pixels) when the control qubit is $|1\rangle$ and $|0\rangle$, respectively. Consequently,

$$|\varphi_2\rangle = \frac{\sqrt{2^{2n}-t}}{2^n}|1\rangle^{\otimes m}|0\rangle^{\otimes m}|T\rangle|I_{in}^{bg}\rangle|0\rangle + \frac{\sqrt{t}}{2^n}|c_{obj}\rangle|0\rangle^{\otimes m}|T\rangle|I_{out}^{obj}\rangle|1\rangle, \quad (5.23)$$

$$|\varphi_3\rangle = \frac{\sqrt{2^{2n}-t}}{2^n}|1\rangle^{\otimes m}|c_{bg}\rangle|T\rangle|I_{out}^{bg}\rangle|0\rangle + \frac{\sqrt{t}}{2^n}|c_{obj}\rangle|0\rangle^{\otimes m}|T\rangle|I_{out}^{obj}\rangle|1\rangle, \quad (5.24)$$

where

$$\left|I_{out}^{bg}\right\rangle = \frac{1}{\sqrt{2^{2n}-t}} \sum_{y=0}^{2^n-1} \sum_{x=0}^{2^n-1} |0\rangle^{\otimes m}|y\rangle|x\rangle, \quad (5.25)$$

$$\left|I_{out}^{obj}\right\rangle = \frac{1}{\sqrt{t}} \sum_{y=0}^{2^n-1} \sum_{x=0}^{2^n-1} |1\rangle^{\otimes m}|y\rangle|x\rangle, \quad (5.26)$$

are the background pixels and object pixels in the output image $|I_{out}\rangle$.

5.3.3 Example of Quantum Image Segmentation

To illustrate the above quantum segmentation algorithm, a simple example of a 2×2 CQIR image with four possible colors ($n = 1$, $m = 2$ in Eq. (5.16)) is explored, and the state of the quantum system at each step mathematically described [4]. The image presented in Fig. 5.8 is considered, and the value $T = 2$ used for the segmentation threshold. Hence, the input state is

$$|\varphi_0\rangle = |11\rangle|00\rangle|10\rangle\frac{1}{2}(|0100\rangle + |0001\rangle + |1110\rangle + |1011\rangle)|0\rangle. \quad (5.27)$$

The quantum circuit that implements the comparison operator U_{cmp} can be realized using the approach of Oliveira et al. [11] (an earlier version of the quantum

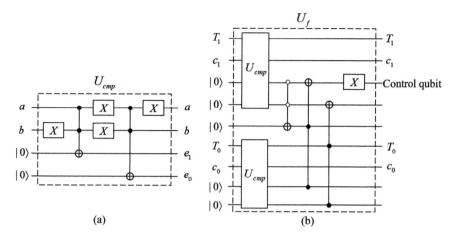

Fig. 5.10 Quantum circuit that implements (**a**) the comparison operator U_{cmp} and (**b**) the oracle operator U_f built atop U_{cmp} (reprinted from ref. [4], with permission of Springer)

comparator introduced in Sect. 4.4.2.1). The comparison of two quantum states $|a\rangle$ and $|b\rangle$ can be implemented by

$$U_{cmp}|a\rangle|b\rangle|0\rangle^{\otimes p}|0\rangle|0\rangle = |a\rangle|b\rangle|\psi\rangle|e_1\rangle|e_0\rangle, \qquad (5.28)$$

where $p + 2$ ancilla qubits are involved in the input states, and $|e_1\rangle$ and $|e_0\rangle$ encode the comparison result at the output. To satisfy the function in Eq. (5.17), it is concluded if $e_0 = 0$, then $a \geq b$; otherwise, $a < b$. The quantum circuits that implement this comparison operator U_{cmp} and the oracle operator U_f that flips the control qubit if $c \geq T$, where $|c\rangle = |c_1\rangle|c_0\rangle$ encodes the gray level and $|T\rangle = |T_1\rangle|T_0\rangle$ indicates the threshold, are shown in Fig. 5.10.

Application of U_f on the input image state to transform $|\varphi_0\rangle$ to

$$|\varphi_1\rangle = |11\rangle|00\rangle|10\rangle\frac{1}{2}(|0100\rangle|0\rangle + |0001\rangle|0\rangle + |1110\rangle|1\rangle + |1011\rangle|1\rangle)$$

$$= \frac{1}{2}|11\rangle|00\rangle|10\rangle|0100\rangle|0\rangle + \frac{1}{2}|11\rangle|00\rangle|10\rangle|0001\rangle|0\rangle \qquad (5.29)$$

$$+ \frac{1}{2}|11\rangle|00\rangle|10\rangle|1110\rangle|1\rangle + \frac{1}{2}|11\rangle|00\rangle|10\rangle|1011\rangle|1\rangle.$$

The two Fredkin gates swap the color sub-states first with $|11\rangle$ when the control qubit is $|1\rangle$, and then with $|00\rangle$ when the control qubit is $|0\rangle$, which are shown as

$$|\varphi_2\rangle = \frac{1}{2}|11\rangle|00\rangle|10\rangle|0100\rangle|0\rangle + \frac{1}{2}|11\rangle|00\rangle|0001\rangle|0\rangle$$

$$+ \frac{1}{2}|11\rangle|00\rangle|10\rangle|1110\rangle|1\rangle + \frac{1}{2}|10\rangle|00\rangle|10\rangle|1111\rangle|1\rangle. \qquad (5.30)$$

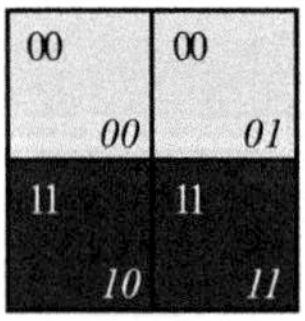

$$| I_{out} \rangle = \frac{1}{2}(|00\rangle|00\rangle + |00\rangle|01\rangle + |11\rangle|10\rangle + |11\rangle|11\rangle)$$

Fig. 5.11 Quantum segmentation result of the CQIR image in Fig. 5.8

$$|\varphi_3\rangle = \frac{1}{2}|11\rangle|01\rangle|10\rangle|0000\rangle|0\rangle + \frac{1}{2}|11\rangle|00\rangle|0001\rangle|0\rangle$$
$$+ \frac{1}{2}|11\rangle|00\rangle|10\rangle|1110\rangle|1\rangle + \frac{1}{2}|10\rangle|00\rangle|10\rangle|1111\rangle|1\rangle. \tag{5.31}$$

Figure 5.11 depicts the state of the output quantum image. The pixels with a gray level less than the threshold ($|T\rangle = |10\rangle$) in the original image are colored with the minimum gray level of zero, while the others are colored with the maximum gray level of 3.

To summarize, a quantum circuit to carry out threshold-based image segmentation can be built using a quantum oracle that implements the thresholding function. The circuit implementation of the oracle operator was discussed and examples of segmenting synthetic images provided. The superiority of the quantum image segmentation over its classical counterpart is its increased speed owing to the inherent computational parallelism in quantum information processing.

In this chapter, by referring to the classical image understanding techniques, quantum image filtering, feature extraction, and segmentation algorithms are introduced. In such algorithms, to interpret and describe the images, thresholding and sampling must always be taken into account, and quantum computing modules for image translation, addition, and comparison always employed. Although image understanding is a broad area, QIMP research in this field is still restricted to several limited topics. To enhance understanding of these algorithms, an example and a corresponding circuit implementation for each technique have been provided.

References

1. Caraiman, S., Manta, V.: Image processing using quantum computing. In: 16th International Conference on System Theory, Control and Computing (ICSTCC), pp. 1–6 (2012)
2. Caraiman, S., Manta, V.: Quantum image filtering in the frequency domain. Adv. Electr. Comput. Eng. **13**(3), 77–84 (2013)
3. Caraiman, S., Manta, V.: Histogram-based segmentation of quantum images. Theor. Comput. Sci. **529**, 46–60 (2014)
4. Caraiman, S., Manta, V.: Image segmentation on a quantum computer. Quantum Inf. Process. **14**(5), 1693–1715 (2015)
5. Du, S., Qiu, D., Gruska, J., Mateus, P.: Synthesis of quantum images using phase rotation. ArXiv:1811.05170 [quant-ph] (2018)

6. Gonzalez, R., Woods, R.: Digital Image Processing, 3rd edn. Pearson Education, London (2008)
7. Jiang, N., Wu, W., Wang, L., Zhao, N.: Quantum image pseudocolor coding based on the density-stratified method. Quantum Inf. Process. **14**(5), 1735–1755 (2015)
8. Li, P., Liu, X., Xiao, H.: Quantum image median filtering in the spatial domain. Quantum Inf. Process. **17** (2018)
9. Marr, D., Hildreth, E.: Theory of edge detection. In: Proceedings of the Royal Society of London, pp. 187–217 (1980)
10. Mehrotra, R., Nichani, S., Ranganathan, N.: Corner detection. Pattern Recogn. **23**(11), 1223–1233 (1990)
11. Oliveira, D., Ramos, R.: Quantum bit string comparator: circuits and applications. Quantum Comput. Comput. **7**(1), 17–26 (2007)
12. Ruan, Y., Chen, H., Tan, J., Li, X.: Quantum computation for large-scale image classification. Quantum Inf. Process. **15**(10), 4049–4069 (2016)
13. Smith, S., Brady, J.: Susan-a new approach to low level image processing. Int. J. Comput. Vis. **23**(1), 45–48 (1997)
14. Wang, J., Jiang, N., Wang, L.: Quantum image translation. Quantum Inf. Process. **14**(5), 1589–1604 (2015)
15. Yuan, S., Mao, X., Li, T., Xue, Y., Chen, L., Xiong, Q.: Quantum morphology operations based on quantum representation model. Quantum Inf. Process. **14**(5), 1625–1645 (2015)
16. Yuan, S., Mao, X., Zhou, J., Wang, X.: Quantum image filtering in the spatial domain. Int. J. Theor. Phys. **56**(8), 2495–2511 (2017)
17. Yuan, S., Lu, Y., Mao, X., Luo, Y., Yuan, J.: Improved quantum image filtering in the spatial domain. Int. J. Theor. Phys. **57**(3), 804–813 (2018)
18. Zhang, Y., Lu, K., Gao, Y., Xu, K.: A novel quantum representation for log-polar images. Quantum Inf. Process. **12**(9), 3103–3126 (2013)
19. Zhang, Y., Lu, K., Gao, Y., Wang, M.: NEQR: a novel enhanced quantum representation of digital images. Quantum Inf. Process. **12**(8), 2833–2860 (2013)
20. Zhang, Y., Lu, K., Xu, K., Gao, Y., Wilson, R.: Local feature point extraction for quantum images. Quantum Inf. Process. **14**(5), 1573–1588 (2015)
21. Zhang, Y., Lu, K., Gao, Y.: QSobel: a novel quantum image edge extracting algorithm. Sci. China Inf. Sci. **58**(1), 1–13 (2015)
22. Zhou, R., Chang, Z., Fan, P., Li, W., Huang, T.: Quantum image morphology processing based on quantum set operation. Int. J. Theor. Phys. **54**(6), 1974–1986 (2015)

Chapter 6
Quantum Multimedia Techniques

Although QIMP is still in its infancy, researchers could not wait to tackle other multimedia techniques, such as movies and audio. Although research of these two techniques is proceeding slowly, some advances have been made. In this chapter, the chromatic framework of quantum movies [21] and the flexible representation of quantum audio signals [20] are introduced. In addition, some typical operations and applications of these quantum multimedia techniques are discussed.

6.1 Chromatic Framework for Quantum Movies and Applications

Motivated by the dominance of TV and movies and advances in the QIMP subdiscipline, in 2011, Iliyasu et al. explored a conceptual scheme to represent and produce movies on quantum computers [7]. Relying somewhat on classical technical jargon, Iliyasu's quantum movie scheme (QMS) is introduced as a prelude to a discussion on the development of quantum movies.

6.1.1 Grayscale Quantum Movie Scheme

Classically, a movie comprises a sequence of multiple images, and every movie was at some stage a script, i.e., a collection of predetermined dialogues and instructions required to convey a storyline to the audience [6]. Four levels of detail are required

---

© Springer Nature Singapore Pte Ltd. 2020
F. Yan, S. E. Venegas-Andraca, *Quantum Image Processing*,
https://doi.org/10.1007/978-981-32-9331-1_6

to convey this larger narrative of a movie [4]. At the lowest level, a movie consists of a set of almost identical images called *frames*, which at the next level are grouped into *shots*. Each shot is delineated by two or more key frames that bear little resemblance to each other. Consecutive shots are aggregated into *scenes* based on their pertinence. A scene could have a single shot, and usually all of the shots in a single scene have a common background. A sequence of all of the scenes together composes a *movie* [7].

This classical terminology and these roles are extended to the representation and production of movies on quantum computers. In QMS, a key frame is defined as an FRQI image, shown in Eq. (2.1), that captures the broad content from which the additional information required to convey a single shot (or a part of it) in a movie is obtained [7]. When one or more key frames are set, the motion dictated by the movie script generates the in-between content called viewing frames, resulting in a smooth change of the content over time. When a scene cannot be adequately conveyed by transforming a preceding key frame, a third type of frame, the makeup frame, is included in the movie sequence. The main difference between a key frame and a makeup frame is that viewing frames cannot be realized from makeup frames [7]. The key, makeup, and viewing frames, which are all FRQI quantum states as defined in Eq. (2.1), are encoded in a collection of 2^m-ending frames as required to capture the information necessary to represent the shots and scenes of a quantum movie.

Several conceptual devices, i.e., quantum CD, quantum player, and movie reader, were proposed by Iliyasu et al. to achieve the preparation, manipulation, and measurement of the QMS [7]. Quantum CD prepares, initializes, and stores as many key frames and their ancillary information conveying the movie script; quantum player manipulates the contents of the key frames in order to interpolate the missing viewing frames to depict the shots and scenes of the movie; and movie reader measures the contents of the sequence of key, viewing, and makeup frames to retrieve their classical versions. At appropriate frame transition rates, this sequence creates the impression of continuity as in a movie. The trio of the quantum CD, player, and movie reader combine to produce the QMS on quantum computers. Furthermore, a simple motion operation is applied to the key frames to effectively convey two-dimensional movement of every point in the frame and the movie enhancement stage of the movie reader demonstrates the need to enhance the content of each frame before being viewed by the audience [7].

In QMS, multiple FRQI images are stacked and encoded as frames of a movie strip. While conceived with sensitivity to the intricacies of quantum computing, QMS resembles early movie production, with two limitations on its use [21]. First, disregarding decoherence and measurement issues in recovering movie content, the entire movie is encoded in grayscale, hence the result will be monochrome. Second, QMS makes no provision for storing audio information, which limits it to silent movies. These concepts are discussed below.

6.1.2   Chromatic Framework for Quantum Movies

To enhance the visual cum esthetic perception of Iliyasu's QMS [7], a chromatic framework for quantum movies (CFQM) that integrates chromatic descriptions of individual frames and merges them with the time information that tags each frame and binds them into a quantum register (i.e., a movie strip) is discussed [21].

6.1.2.1   CFQM Framework Based on MCQI Images

As noted earlier, Yan et al. replaced the FRQI format used to encode movie frames in QMS with MCQI images. The resulting movie strip comprising 2^m frames is then bound to the time tag associated with each frame in the quantum register, and subsequently evolves into a CFQM framework, which is formulated as

$$|M(m,n)\rangle = \frac{1}{2^{\frac{m}{2}}} \sum_{t=0}^{2^m-1} |F_t(n)\rangle \otimes |t\rangle, \tag{6.1}$$

where $|t\rangle$, $t = 0, 1, \ldots, 2^m - 1$, are 2^m-dimensional quantum basis states to represent the time information in the entire movie and $|F_t(n)\rangle$ is the movie frame at time $|t\rangle$ which is presented as an MCQI image (defined in Sect. 2.3) in the form:

$$|F_t(n)\rangle = \frac{1}{2^{n+1}} \sum_{i=0}^{2^{2n}-1} |c_{t,i}\rangle \otimes |i\rangle, \tag{6.2}$$

where $|c_{t,i}\rangle$ encodes the color information of the image in R, G, B, and α channels, and is defined as

$$|c_{t,i}\rangle = \cos\theta_{t,i}^R|000\rangle + \cos\theta_{t,i}^G|001\rangle + \cos\theta_{t,i}^B|010\rangle + \cos\theta_{t,i}^\alpha|011\rangle$$
$$+ \sin\theta_{t,i}^R|100\rangle + \sin\theta_{t,i}^G|101\rangle + \sin\theta_{t,i}^B|110\rangle + \sin\theta_{t,i}^\alpha|111\rangle, \tag{6.3}$$

where $\{\theta_{t,i}^R, \theta_{t,i}^G, \theta_{t,i}^B, \theta_{t,i}^\alpha\} \in \{0, \pi/2\}$ are four angles encoding the colors of the R, G, B, and α channels, respectively, of the i-th pixel. A simple four-frame movie framework (each frame is a 2×2 MCQI image) as well as its quantum state is shown in Fig. 6.1.

Fig. 6.1 A four-frame
CFQM framework and its
quantum state

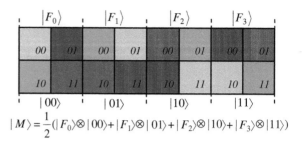

$$|M\rangle = \frac{1}{2}(|F_0\rangle \otimes |00\rangle + |F_1\rangle \otimes |01\rangle + |F_2\rangle \otimes |10\rangle + |F_3\rangle \otimes |11\rangle)$$

6.1.2.2   Initialization of the CFQM Framework

The preparation procedure to transform a quantum computer from its initialized
state (usually a sequence of basis states $|0\rangle$) to a desired quantum state is the first
step in quantum movie representation and production [7, 10].

To initialize a CFQM framework, $m + 2n + 3$ basis states $|0\rangle$ (denoted by
$|0\rangle^{\otimes m+2n+3}$) are employed, where m is the number of qubits that will be used to
encode the temporal (time) information depicting the time lapse in the entire movie,
$2n$ qubits will be used to encode the spatial (position) information of each frame,
which is essentially a $2^n \times 2^n$ MCQI image, and the remaining three qubits are used
to store the chromatic (color) information in the movie framework. The preparation
procedure for the CFQM framework consists of the following three steps [21]:

Step 1:   Apply the transformation $G = I \otimes H^{\otimes m+2n+2}$ on the initialized state
$|0\rangle^{\otimes m+2n+3}$ to generate an intermediate state $|K\rangle$, as follows:

$$G(|0\rangle^{m+2n+3}) = |0\rangle \otimes (H^{\otimes 2}|0\rangle^{\otimes 2}) \otimes (H^{\otimes 2n}|0\rangle^{2n}) \otimes (H^{\otimes m}|0\rangle^{\otimes m})$$

$$= |0\rangle \otimes \frac{1}{2}\sum_{c=0}^{3}|c\rangle \otimes \frac{1}{2^n}\sum_{i=0}^{2^{2n}-1}|i\rangle \otimes \frac{1}{2^{\frac{m}{2}}}\sum_{t=0}^{2^m-1}|t\rangle \qquad (6.4)$$

$$= |K\rangle,$$

where two kinds of unitary matrices, i.e., a two-dimensional identity matrix I
and Hadamard matrix H, are used. In addition, $H^{\otimes m+2n+2}$ indicates the tensor
product of $m + 2n + 2$ Hadamard matrices, as used in Sect. 2.2.1.

Step 2:   Initialize the movie frame, i.e., the MCQI image, at time $|t\rangle$. Rotation
matrices are utilized in the operation, which is formalized as

$$R_y(2\theta) = \begin{pmatrix} \cos\theta & -\sin\theta \\ \sin\theta & \cos\theta \end{pmatrix}, \theta \in \{\theta_{t,i}^R, \theta_{t,i}^G, \theta_{t,i}^B\}. \qquad (6.5)$$

Based on the transform in Eq. (6.5), three 8×8 controlled-rotation operations, $R_{t,i}^R$, $R_{t,i}^G$, and $R_{t,i}^B$, are required to initialize the color information in the R, G, and B channels at the position of $|i\rangle$, as follows:

$$R_{t,i}^R = I \otimes \sum_{c=1}^{3} |c\rangle\langle c| + R(2\theta_{t,i}^R) \otimes |0\rangle\langle 0|,$$

$$R_{t,i}^G = I \otimes \sum_{c=0,c\neq 1}^{3} |c\rangle\langle c| + R(2\theta_{t,i}^G) \otimes |1\rangle\langle 1|, \qquad (6.6)$$

$$R_{t,i}^B = I \otimes \sum_{c=0,c\neq 2}^{3} |c\rangle\langle c| + R(2\theta_{t,i}^B) \otimes |2\rangle\langle 2|.$$

Figure 6.2 shows that each of the $R_{t,i}^R$, $R_{t,i}^G$, and $R_{t,i}^B$ operations in Eq. (6.6) is a three-qubit gate. In addition, the $C^2(R_y(2\theta))$ operation can be constructed from elementary gates, as shown in Fig. 6.2d. When these three rotations are considered as a whole, the RGB information of a pixel $|i\rangle$ in a frame can be initialized by

$$R_{t,i} = I^{\otimes 3} \otimes \sum_{j=0,j\neq i}^{2^{2n}-1} |j\rangle\langle j| + (R_{t,i}^R R_{t,i}^G R_{t,i}^B) \otimes |i\rangle\langle i|. \qquad (6.7)$$

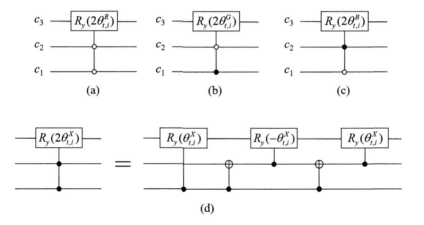

Fig. 6.2 Controlled-rotation operations: (a) $R_{t,i}^R$; (b) $R_{t,i}^G$; (c) $R_{t,i}^B$; and (d) their implementations [21]

An MCQI image contains $2^n \times 2^n$ pixels; therefore, to execute the operation $R_{t,i}$ in Eq. (6.7) requires the traversal of all 2^{2n} pixels in the image. The entire operation can be generalized in the form:

$$\mathfrak{R}_t = \prod_{i=0}^{2^{2n}-1} R_{t,i}.$$

(6.8)

Based on the operation $\mathfrak{R}_t$ in Eq. (6.8), in the CFQM framework, a frame tagged at time $|t\rangle$ in the strip can be initialized as

$$H_t = I^{\otimes 2n+3} \otimes \sum_{s=0,s\neq t}^{2^m-1} |s\rangle\langle s| + \mathfrak{R}_t \otimes |t\rangle\langle t|,$$

(6.9)

where H_t is a unitary matrix, implying that $H_t H_t^\dagger = I^{\otimes m+2n+3}$. Specifically, when the p-th frame is initialized in the CFQM framework, an operation H_p is applied on the intermediate state $|K\rangle$ in Eq. (6.4) to obtain:

$$H_p(|K\rangle) = H_p \left(|0\rangle \otimes \frac{1}{2} \sum_{c=0}^{3} |c\rangle \otimes \frac{1}{2^n} \sum_{i=0}^{2^{2n}-1} |i\rangle \otimes \frac{1}{2^{\frac{m}{2}}} \sum_{t=0}^{2^m-1} |t\rangle \right)$$

$$= \frac{1}{2^{\frac{m}{2}+n+1}} \left[|0\rangle \otimes \sum_{c=0}^{3} |c\rangle \otimes \sum_{i=0}^{2^{2n}-1} |i\rangle \otimes \sum_{t=0,t\neq p}^{2^m-1} |t\rangle \right.$$

$$\left. + \mathfrak{R}_p \left(|0\rangle \otimes \sum_{c=0}^{3} |c\rangle \otimes \sum_{i=0}^{2^{2n}-1} |i\rangle \right) \otimes |p\rangle \right]$$

$$= \frac{1}{2^{\frac{m}{2}+n+1}} \left[|0\rangle \otimes \sum_{c=0}^{3} |c\rangle \otimes \sum_{i=0}^{2^{2n}-1} |i\rangle \otimes \sum_{t=0,t\neq p}^{2^m-1} |t\rangle \right.$$

$$\left. + \prod_{i=0}^{2^{2n}-1} R_{p,i} \left(|0\rangle \otimes \sum_{c=0}^{3} |c\rangle \otimes \sum_{i=0}^{2^{2n}-1} |i\rangle \right) \otimes |p\rangle \right].$$

(6.10)

So far, in the strip of the entire CFQM framework, the p-th frame has been initialized while the other frames remain vacant, i.e., up to this stage, the other frames contain position and time information, with no color content.

Step 3: A CFQM framework is composed of 2^m MCQI images, hence the preparation of a CFQM framework can be divided into 2^m sub-operations, and each MCQI image is prepared in each sub-operation. Analogous to the operation in Eq. (6.10), when one continues to initialize the second, i.e., the q-th, frame in the CFQM framework, an operation H_q is applied on the quantum states in Eq. (6.10), resulting in

$$H_q H_p |K\rangle = H_q (H_p |K\rangle)$$

$$= \frac{1}{2^{\frac{m}{2}+n+1}} \left[|0\rangle \otimes \sum_{c=0}^{3} |c\rangle \otimes \sum_{i=0}^{2^{2n}-1} |i\rangle \otimes \sum_{\substack{t=0, \\ t\neq q, t\neq p}}^{2^m-1} |t\rangle \right.$$

$$+ \mathfrak{R}_q \left(|0\rangle \otimes \sum_{c=0}^{3} |c\rangle \otimes \sum_{i=0}^{2^{2n}-1} |i\rangle \right) \otimes |q\rangle$$

$$\left. + \mathfrak{R}_p \left(|0\rangle \otimes \sum_{c=0}^{3} |c\rangle \otimes \sum_{i=0}^{2^{2n}-1} |i\rangle \right) \otimes |p\rangle \right]. \tag{6.11}$$

Consequently, the procedure to transform the quantum computer from the initialized state $|0\rangle^{\otimes m+2n+3}$ to the desired state $|M(m, n)\rangle$ is generalized as

$$\prod_{t=0}^{2^m-1} H_t G \left(|0\rangle^{\otimes m+2n+3} \right) = \frac{1}{2^{\frac{m}{2}}} \sum_{t=0}^{2^m-1} |F_t(n)\rangle \otimes |t\rangle \tag{6.12}$$

$$= |M(m, n)\rangle.$$

Following initialization, the retrieval steps must be undertaken in quantum movie production [7]. In the CFQM framework, the color information of each frame is encoded in a three-qubit entangled state $|c_3 c_2 c_1\rangle$, as shown in Eq. (6.3). Therefore, similar to the retrieval of the MCQI state in Sect. 2.3.2, any attempt to retrieve it (i.e., the eight coefficients of $|c_3 c_2 c_1\rangle$) requires multiple measurements on these three qubits to reveal the probability for each state [21]. Specifically, as shown in Fig. 6.2, the angle $\theta_{t,i}^X$ encodes the grayscale value in the X channel and is controlled by c_2 and c_1 when they are in the state $|00\rangle$, $|01\rangle$, and $|10\rangle$ (where X can be R, G, or B). Multiple measurements on the state of c_3 retrieve an outcome of either 0 with probability $\cos^2 \theta_{t,i}^X$ or 1 with probability $\sin^2 \theta_{t,i}^X$. Based on the probability, one can retrieve the grayscale value of the color information in the X channel, and by performing this operation iteratively, all of the quantum information in the CFQM framework can be retrieved.

6.1.3 Quantum Operations to Achieve Montages

The word "montage" originates from the French word "monter," which translates to "to mount" or "to cut." In this application, it is a movie editing technique where short clips (shots) are edited into a sequence. By cutting and assembling the shots in the movie, montages condense space, time, and information [8, 11]. This subsection will introduce the implementation of quantum movie montages using innovative transformations such as frame-to-frame (FTF), color of concern (COC), and sub-block swapping (SBS) operations [21].

6.1.3.1 FTF Operation to Achieve Psychological Montages

As presented in Sect. 6.1.2, a unique time tag is integrated into each frame of the CFQM framework to determine the playing order (time lapse) of a movie clip. By altering the time tag of a frame (or group of frames), the playing order of a movie's content can be manipulated to realize essential operations such as deletion, playback, and extraction [21]. Based on the formulation of the CFQM framework in Eq. (6.1), the FTF_c operator that is used to transit the t-th frame $|F_t(n)\rangle$ to $(t \pm c)$-th frame $|F_{t\pm c}(n)\rangle$ is defined as

$$
FTF_c|M(m,n)\rangle = \frac{1}{2^{\frac{m}{2}}} \sum_{t=0}^{2^m-1} |F_t(n)\rangle \otimes FTF_c|t\rangle
$$

$$
= \frac{1}{2^{\frac{m}{2}}} \sum_{t=0}^{2^m-1} |F_{t\pm c}(n)\rangle \otimes |t \pm c \bmod 2^m\rangle,
$$

(6.13)

where $|t\rangle$ represents the time information tagging each frame to the CFQM framework, and $c \in \{0, 1, \ldots, 2^m - 1\}$ indicates the number of shift steps that move from the t-th frame to the $(t \pm c)$-th frame in the CFQM framework.

It should be clarified that in an actual movie the script comes to life as time elapses. Thus, the storyline is developed and with it, the causality and depiction of the plots and relations between the main characters in the movie become more complicated. A lengthy shot is insufficient to convey the ideas of the director, so it is necessary to play several shots alternately (e.g., with interludes after each shot) to capture the transition between shots. The FTF operation facilitates abridgment in the content, connects shots, and replays certain frames. To use such an operation in a flexible and purposeful manner can realize some useful content that otherwise may not be conveyed.

A possible application of the FTF operation is the psychological montage. The FTF operation can be used to repeat one or more frames at different instances to convey the inner world, reminiscences, and cogitations of a character. The FTF operation can eliminate the need to duplicate a frame when it is required elsewhere

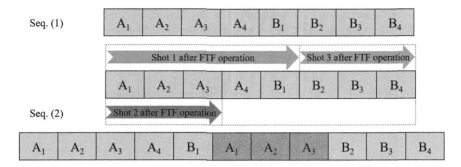

Fig. 6.3 FTF operation to realize psychological montages [21]

in a movie. A simple example of such a use of the FTF operation is presented in Fig. 6.3.

As shown in Seq. (1) in Fig. 6.3, the FTF operation makes it easy to return to or playback an earlier action, say from frame B_1 to A_1. The movie will replay from frame A_1 until A_3, then play from frame A_3 to B_2, and continue to play the other frames in the order shown in Seq. (1). This is akin to inserting frames A_1, A_2, and A_3 between frames B_1 and B_2 in Seq. (1). The arrows and their annotations indicate the playing order after the FTF operation, while the final movie sequence is presented in Seq. (2).

6.1.3.2 COC Operation to Achieve Comparative Montages

The COC operation, which focuses mainly on manipulating the color of some specific channel (R, G, or B), has been successfully implemented in many MCQI-based QIMP applications. Since the 2^m-ending movie strip is composed of MCQI images, it is expedient to consider utilizing the COC operation in some advanced MCQI-based quantum movie (i.e., CFQM) applications that are based on manipulations to the chromatic content, such as the color conversion of an image (or parts of it) by manipulating its RGB channel [21]. The COC_X operator shifts the grayscale value of a preselected R, G, or B channel as defined below:

$$COC_X = I^{\otimes 2n+3} \otimes \sum_{t=0,t\neq k}^{2^m-1} |t\rangle\langle t| + COI_X \otimes |k\rangle\langle k|, \tag{6.14}$$

where COI_X is realized by using the $U_X = C^2 R_y(2\theta)$ gate, as discussed in Sect. 2.3.3.1. Applying the COC_X operator to the CFQM framework in Eq. (6.1) would yield

$$COC_X|M(m,n)\rangle = \frac{1}{2^{\frac{m}{2}}} \sum_{t=0, t\neq k}^{2^m-1} |F_t(n)\rangle \otimes |t\rangle + \frac{1}{2^{\frac{m}{2}}} COI_X |F_k(n)\rangle \otimes |k\rangle$$

$$= \frac{1}{2^{\frac{m}{2}}} \sum_{t=0, t\neq k}^{2^m-1} |F_t(n)\rangle \otimes |t\rangle$$

$$+ \frac{1}{2^{\frac{m}{2}}} \left(U_X \otimes I^{\otimes 2n} \right) \left(\frac{1}{2^{n+1}} \sum_{i=0}^{2^{2n}-1} |c_{t,i}\rangle \otimes |i\rangle \right) \otimes |k\rangle$$

$$= \frac{1}{2^{\frac{m}{2}}} \sum_{t=0, t\neq k}^{2^m-1} |F_t(n)\rangle \otimes |t\rangle + \frac{1}{2^{\frac{m}{2}}} \left(\frac{1}{2^{n+1}} \sum_{i=0}^{2^{2n}-1} |c_{t,i}^X\rangle \otimes |i\rangle \right) \otimes |k\rangle$$

$$= \frac{1}{2^{\frac{m}{2}}} \sum_{t=0, t\neq k}^{2^m-1} |F_t(n)\rangle \otimes |t\rangle + \frac{1}{2^{\frac{m}{2}}} |F_k'(n)\rangle \otimes |k\rangle,$$

$$(6.15)$$

where the $|c_{t,i}\rangle$ state encodes the RGB information as defined in Eq. (6.3), and $|c_{t,i}^X\rangle$ is the color state after applying the COC_X operator, which is defined as

$$|c_{t,i}^R\rangle = \cos(\theta_{t,i}^R - \theta)|000\rangle + \cos\theta_{t,i}^G|001\rangle + \cos\theta_{t,i}^B|010\rangle + \cos\theta_{t,i}^\alpha|011\rangle$$
$$+ \sin(\theta_{t,i}^R - \theta)|100\rangle + \sin\theta_{t,i}^G|101\rangle + \sin\theta_{t,i}^B|110\rangle + \sin\theta_{t,i}^\alpha|111\rangle,$$

$$|c_{t,i}^G\rangle = \cos\theta_{t,i}^R|000\rangle + \cos\left(\theta_{t,i}^G - \theta\right)|001\rangle + \cos\theta_{t,i}^B|010\rangle + \cos\theta_{t,i}^\alpha|011\rangle$$
$$+ \sin\theta_{t,i}^R|100\rangle + \sin\left(\theta_{t,i}^G - \theta\right)|101\rangle + \sin\theta_{t,i}^B|110\rangle + \sin\theta_{t,i}^\alpha|111\rangle,$$

$$|c_{t,i}^B\rangle = \cos\theta_{t,i}^R|000\rangle + \cos\theta_{t,i}^G|001\rangle + \cos(\theta_{t,i}^B - \theta)|010\rangle + \cos\theta_{t,i}^\alpha|011\rangle$$
$$+ \sin\theta_{t,i}^R|100\rangle + \sin\theta_{t,i}^G|101\rangle + \sin(\theta_{t,i}^B - \theta)|110\rangle + \sin\theta_{t,i}^\alpha|111\rangle.$$

$$(6.16)$$

It should be noted that the frame $|F_k'(n)\rangle$ in Eq. (6.15) is the frame at time $|k\rangle$, whose colors all come from the original frame $|F_k(n)\rangle$ by shifting the angle θ on the R, G, or B channel.

Color is an important element that is extensively manipulated for various reasons, such as to reflect the theme and allure of a movie. Due to the established physiological adaptation of the human visual system to color, varying colors at different stages in a movie can convey artistic effects to the audience. Various hues are typically used to produce strong contrast during some frolicsome scenes in a

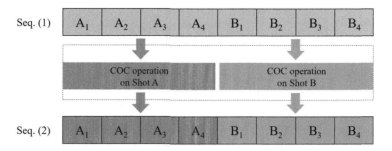

Fig. 6.4 COC operation to realize comparative montages [21]

movie, and warm colors are always used in this case. Certain hues will dampen the color contrast in quiet and elegant scenes, and cool colors are often used in these instances. Comparative montages are often used to set off each other in contrast to exhibit contrastive effects.

In the CFQM framework, the COC operation is used to manipulate all or part of the color information of a movie so as to realize a good distribution of light and shade. Seq. (1) in Fig. 6.4 depicts the original sequence of a two-shot movie consisting of Shot A and Shot B. To generate different results, two kinds of COC operations are applied separately on Shots A and B. As shown in Seq. (2), Shot A is transformed to a much warmer color, and Shot B to a much cooler color. Different color tones will generate a comparative effect so that prominence is to some extent given to the theme of the movie scene.

6.1.3.3   SBS Operation to Achieve Parallel or Cross Montages

The SBS operation is a geometric transformation that targets the position information of sub-blocks in the frames of a CFQM framework [21]. This operation interchanges sub-blocks in two frames from different instances of time within the CFQM framework to manipulate a scene. Mathematically, the SBS_{t_i,t_j} operator is defined as

$$SBS_{t_i,t_j} = I^{\otimes 3} \otimes |B\rangle\langle B| \otimes I^{\otimes m} + I^{\otimes 3} \otimes |B'\rangle\langle B'| \otimes SW_{t_i,t_j}, \tag{6.17}$$

where SW_{t_i,t_j} is a sub-operation that is used to exchange the time information t_i and t_j of the two sub-blocks being swapped, and is defined as

$$SW_{t_i,t_j} = |t_i\rangle\langle t_j| + |t_j\rangle\langle t_i| + \sum_{\substack{k=0, \\ k\neq t_i, k\neq t_j}}^{2^m-1} |k\rangle\langle k|. \tag{6.18}$$

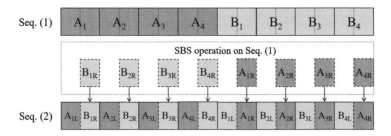

Fig. 6.5 SBS operation to realize parallel or cross montages [21]

Applying the operation SBS_{t_i,t_j} on the CFQM framework in Eq. (6.1) would yield

$$SBS_{t_i,t_j}|M(m,n)\rangle = \frac{1}{2^{\frac{m}{2}}} \sum_{t=0}^{2^m-1} |F_t^B(n)\rangle \otimes |t\rangle + \frac{1}{2^{\frac{m}{2}}} \sum_{t=0}^{2^m-1} |F_t^{B'}(n)\rangle \otimes SW_{t_i,t_j}|t\rangle$$

$$= \frac{1}{2^{\frac{m}{2}}} \sum_{t=0}^{2^m-1} |F_t^B(n)\rangle \otimes |t\rangle$$

$$+ \frac{1}{2^{\frac{m}{2}}} \sum_{t=0}^{2^m-1} |F_t^{B'}(n)\rangle \otimes \left(|t_i\rangle\langle t_j| + |t_j\rangle\langle t_i| + \sum_{\substack{k=0, \\ k\neq t_i, k\neq t_j}}^{2^m-1} |k\rangle\langle k| \right)|t\rangle$$

$$= \frac{1}{2^{\frac{m}{2}}} \sum_{t=0}^{2^m-1} |F_t^B(n)\rangle \otimes |t\rangle + \frac{1}{2^{\frac{m}{2}}} \sum_{t=0}^{2^m-1} |F_t^{B'}(n)\rangle \otimes |t\rangle$$

$$= \frac{1}{2^{\frac{m}{2}}} \sum_{t=0}^{2^m-1} \left(|F_t^B(n)\rangle + |F_t^{B'}(n)\rangle \right) \otimes |t\rangle.$$

$$(6.19)$$

In conveying a storyline, a good movie should be capable of captivating its audience. Where the acting or script falls short, graphics and montages can be effective in conveying certain minutiae and emotions. However, this often requires advanced redesign of the montage operations.

In parallel or cross montages, the presentation of two or more storylines is required in parallel or crosswise, after which they are integrated into the plot to present a unified theme. Therefore, to clip two shots and combine different parts into one unit can allow two storylines to evolve together. In this manner, the movie will present a clear plot that cannot be realized in a single shot. Based on the SBS operation, the content of some frames can be manipulated to realize these advanced montage operations.

As mentioned earlier, one can use the SBS operation to integrate specific content or storylines by clipping and merging different shots in parallel. In Fig. 6.5, Seq.

(1) consists of Shots A and B, each having four frames. This illustrates how parallel or crosswise montages can be realized using the SBS operation. Using the SBS operation, the contents of Shots A and B can be manipulated, in this case clipping each frame into its left and right parts and connecting the left half of each frame in Shot A (A_{1L}, A_{2L}, A_{3L}, A_{4L}) with the corresponding right half in Shot B (B_{1R}, B_{2R}, B_{3R}, B_{4R}). The remaining left halves of Shot B are similarly stitched to the remaining right halves of Shot A. Seq. (2) shows the sequence resulting from the SBS operation.

Finally, in Fig. 6.6, an outline showing the CFQM framework and the requirements for its initialization and transformation to implement a given montage application based on the CFQM framework is presented [21]. In the quantum circuit model of quantum computation, algorithms are implemented by using a sequence of basic gates, such as the NOT, Hadamard, and Toffoli gates, acting on one or more qubits to simultaneously affect each element and perform massive parallel data processing [12]. Then, as shown in Fig. 6.6 (and explained earlier in this section), the CFQM framework is prepared via a series of quantum basis states on which the quantum operations are applied to facilitate the transformations for various montage applications. The equation numbers at the bottom of Fig. 6.6 provide references to the equations that formalize each operation.

To summarize, CFQM improves on an FRQI-based grayscale movie scheme by integrating color into the representation, transformation, and recovery of the

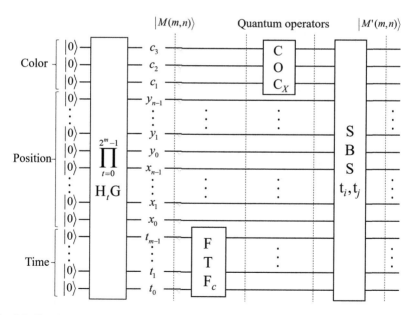

Fig. 6.6 Circuit network for the CFQM framework: showing requirements for its initialization as well as transformations to manipulate its temporal, spatial, and chromatic contents using quantum operations [21]

elements of a movie. Additionally, an assemblage of transformations was used to tailor the implementation of the new framework toward rapid editing of movie content, and special effects to present compressed narrations of a movie, i.e., montages. Specifically, a set of carefully formulated transformations was presented, including the FTF, COC, and SBS operations, to facilitate implementation of psychological, comparative, and parallel (or cross) montage applications that are essential to convey various dialogues in a movie. Other applications, such as for video encryption [13, 17], moving target detection [18], and image stabilization [19], have also been developed.

6.2 Flexible Representation and Manipulation of Quantum Audio Signals

Classical audio processing may arise in either the digital or analog domain. However, most modern audio systems use digital representations because of the power and efficiency of digital signal processing techniques [23]. Focusing on amplitude transformations required to process audio signals on quantum computers, in this section, a flexible representation of quantum audio (FRQA) signals [20] is described.

6.2.1 Quantum Representation for Digital Audio

In electrical engineering and computer science, an analog audio signal is a representation of a sound or longitudinal wave whose core components are frequency, amplitude, wavelength, and phase [9]. Such waves are often simplified to descriptions in terms of sinusoidal plane waves, expressed as

$$y(t) = A \sin(2\pi f t + \varphi), \tag{6.20}$$

where A is the amplitude (the peak deviation of the function from zero); f is the frequency (the number of oscillations, or cycles, that occur per second of time); $\omega = 2\pi f$ is the angular frequency (the rate of change of the function argument in radians per second); and φ is the phase, which specifies (in radians) the position of the oscillation in its cycle at $t = 0$. Furthermore,

$$f = \frac{\omega}{2\pi}, \quad \lambda = \frac{v}{f}, \tag{6.21}$$

where λ is the wavelength and v is the speed of the wave. When φ in Eq. (6.20) is nonzero, the entire waveform appears to be shifted in time by an amount of φ/ω seconds. A negative value represents a delay, while a positive shift represents an advance. Conversely, when φ is zero, the equation reduces to $y(t) = A \sin \omega t$, which simply shows that the waveform depends on frequency, amplitude, and time components.

Moreover, by considering an audio signal as a voltage that varies over time, an analog-to-digital converter (ADC) can be used to discretely take samples from the analog signals at a given frequency (i.e., sampling rate) [9]. According to a given binary sequence length (i.e., resolution), each sampled value is converted to a number based on its voltage level. In this manner, digital audio is produced and represented as a sequence of numbers that express instantaneous amplitudes of a sampled audio signal. A digital audio signal A can generally be expressed in the form:

$$A = [a_0, a_1, \ldots, a_{L-1}], \tag{6.22}$$

where L is the size of the audio signal, $L \in \mathbb{N}$; $a_t \in \{-2^{q-1}, \ldots, -1, 0, 1, \ldots, 2^{q-1} - 1\}$, $q \in \mathbb{N}$, $t = 0, 1, \ldots, L - 1$. Figure 6.7 shows an example of ADC (including the sampling and quantization procedures), where the sampling rate is 7 Hz, with 4-bit quantization [16]. An array $A = [0, 3, 5, 7, 7, 5, 3, 0, -3, -5, -7, -7, -5, -3, 0]$ is used to represent the digital audio.

Building on the digital interpretations in Eq. (6.22) and considering the amplitude component of an L-sized audio signal as a string of nonnegative integers $a_t \in \{0, 1, \ldots, 2^q - 1\}$, where q is the length of the binary sequence used to store each element, a quantum representation for digital audio (QRDA) signals was postulated in [16].

The precept in QRDA representation, and more generally the outcomes from [16], show a first attempt to facilitate audio signal representation and manipulation in the quantum computing domain. Notwithstanding its innovation, the tightly bounded unipolar encoding strategy used in QRDA may hinder accurate compu-

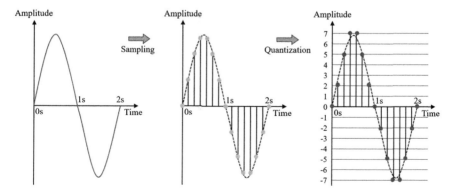

Fig. 6.7 An example of the ADC procedure (reprinted from ref. [16], with permission of Springer)

tation and processing operations in quantum audio processing, for the following
reasons [20]:

(1) In QRDA representation, the amplitude values a_t can only represent nonnega-
    tive numbers. Hence, some arithmetic operations pertaining to amplitude values
    are prone to errors. For instance, when there are two amplitude values a_m and
    a_n (such that $a_m < a_n$), it is virtually impossible to obtain a result from the
    operation $a_m - a_n$.
(2) As a unipolar representation, QRDA is not formulated to display or determine
    the midrange of a waveform in processing operations. Therefore, it is difficult to
    execute some operations because all of the amplitude values are positive (e.g.,
    addition of opposite amplitude values in two waveforms will accumulate to a
    higher amplitude rather than offsetting each other).

Among other reasons, filling in these lapses in the QRDA representation and
further facilitating more basic operations in quantum audio processing are two major
objectives of the FRQA representation.

6.2.2 Flexible Representation of Quantum Audio Signals

Different from the QRDA representation stated above, FRQA representation
encodes the amplitude values in quantum audio in a bipolar (both nonnegative
and negative) manner, i.e., $s_t \in \{-2^{q-1}, \ldots, -1, 0, 1, \ldots, 2^{q-1} - 1\}$. In this
fashion, the formalism of binary logic arithmetic provides the tools needed for
effective quantum audio processing. Equation (6.23) describes the stipulation in the
form:

$$S_t = S_t^0 S_t^1 \ldots S_t^{q-1}, \ S_t^i \in \{0, 1\}, i = 0, 1, \ldots, q - 1, \tag{6.23}$$

where $t = 0, 1, \ldots, 2^l - 1$ denotes the time information of a 2^l-sized quantum
audio signal, and $S_t = S_t^0 S_t^1 \ldots S_t^{q-1}$ is the binary sequence encoding the two's
complement notation of the amplitude value. Two cases of the binary sequence S_t
are as follows:

(1) If the amplitude value is nonnegative, then $S_t^0 = 0$ and S_t are simply represented
    as a binary sequence of the value itself.
(2) If the amplitude value is negative, then $S_t^0 = 1$ and S_t are represented by the
    two's complement mode of its absolute value.

Although one-dimensional, an FRQA signal is described in terms of its amplitude
and time components, and is written as

$$|A\rangle = \frac{1}{2^{l/2}} \sum_{t=0}^{2^l-1} |S_t\rangle \otimes |t\rangle, \tag{6.24}$$

where $|S_t\rangle = |S_t^0 S_t^1 \ldots S_t^{q-1}\rangle$ is the two's complement representation of each amplitude value, and $|t\rangle = |t_0 t_1 \ldots t_{l-1}\rangle$, $t_i \in \{0, 1\}$, is the corresponding time information, and the state $|A\rangle$ is normalized, i.e., $\||A\rangle\| = 1$. It is trivial that, as formalized in Eq. (6.24), FRQA representation requires $q + l$ qubits to represent a quantum audio with 2^l samples [20].

For an L-sized FRQA audio (L cannot be represented by 2^l), to employ l qubits to represent the time information will produce $2^l - L$ audio redundancies [16]. Figure 6.8 shows a segment of an audio signal and its representative expression using FRQA representation. The size of the audio is 13, and $l = \lceil \log_2 13 \rceil = 4$. Hence, three redundancies are generated and the amplitude values of them are set as $|000\rangle$.

Compared with the only known effort to perform audio signal processing on quantum computers (i.e., QRDA), FRQA audio facilitates the effective realization of basic processing operations: (1) FRQA audio allows two sample values to be accurately added (or mixed, in audio parlance), and facilitates the use of quantum circuit elements to handle overflow and warp-around situations that are encountered when the size of a result is greater than the capacity of the register allocated for its storage; and (2) FRQA audio permits signal subtraction using simple logical addition operations on an augend and addend, one of them inverted (negated). In this manner, the FRQA state offers considerable saving in hardware complexity,

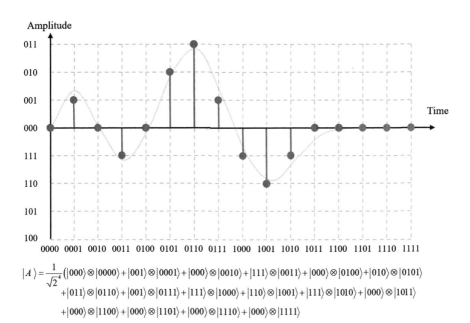

$$|A\rangle = \frac{1}{\sqrt{2}^4}\big(|000\rangle \otimes |0000\rangle + |001\rangle \otimes |0001\rangle + |000\rangle \otimes |0010\rangle + |111\rangle \otimes |0011\rangle + |000\rangle \otimes |0100\rangle + |010\rangle \otimes |0101\rangle$$
$$+ |011\rangle \otimes |0110\rangle + |001\rangle \otimes |0111\rangle + |111\rangle \otimes |1000\rangle + |110\rangle \otimes |1001\rangle + |111\rangle \otimes |1010\rangle + |000\rangle \otimes |1011\rangle$$
$$+ |000\rangle \otimes |1100\rangle + |000\rangle \otimes |1101\rangle + |000\rangle \otimes |1110\rangle + |000\rangle \otimes |1111\rangle$$

Fig. 6.8 A segment of an FRQA audio signal and its representation (blue points are the redundancies) [20]

since the more tedious "borrow" mechanism associated with subtraction is replaced by a "carry" procedure in the addition operation.

6.2.2.1   Initialization of the FRQA Signals

As stated earlier, in digital audio, the value of each sampled point is stored in an assigned q-length binary sequence, $B_t^0 B_t^1 \ldots B_t^{q-1}$, $B_t^i \in \{0, 1\}$, which indicates that the sequence is capable of holding the amplitude values from 0 to $2^q - 1$. To quantize the amplitude value B_t and convert it to the two's complement system $|S_t\rangle$, one must perform the value-setting operation Ω_t, which consists of two sub-operations [20]:

(1) *Quantization*: Using the classical binary representation of B_t as the reference, the initialized states on quantum computer can be transformed to their desired quantum states. The means to accomplish this has been widely discussed in the literature [10, 15].

(2) *Conversion*: To convert the quantum state in (1) to its two's complement equivalent, the CNOT gate operation is applied on the most significant qubit (MSQb) of the qubit sequence (the leftmost qubit in the sequence encoding the audio sample) to produce the desired quantum amplitude state $|S_t\rangle$.

Similar to the ADC, these steps are assumed to be the basic requirements for a possible future quantum computing device, a digital-to-quantum converter (DQC) [20]. To illustrate this procedure, consider the conversion of a three-qubit resolution to the amplitude information in quantum audio, as presented in Table 6.1. The resolution values, ranging from 0 to 7, are held in a three-qubit sequence. These values are then binarized and subsequently quantized in two's complement notation for further computation by other quantum audio processing units.

Table 6.1 Conversion of three-qubit resolution to the amplitude information in quantum audio [20]

Resolution	Binary sequence	Two's complement	Amplitude
7	111	$|011\rangle$	3
6	110	$|010\rangle$	2
5	101	$|001\rangle$	1
4	100	$|000\rangle$	0
3	011	$|111\rangle$	-1
2	010	$|110\rangle$	-2
1	001	$|101\rangle$	-3
0	000	$|100\rangle$	-4

As outlined in this example, the value-setting operation Ω_t can be defined as

$$\Omega_t = \overset{q-1}{\underset{i=0}{\otimes}} \Omega_t^i, \tag{6.25}$$

$$\Omega_t^i \left(|0\rangle \right) = \begin{cases} \overline{|0 \oplus B_t^i\rangle}, & i = 0 \\ |0 \oplus B_t^i\rangle, & i \neq 0 \end{cases}, \tag{6.26}$$

where $\oplus$ is the XOR operation. It is trivial that the operation Ω_t^i works by means of an additional CNOT gate to negate the MSQb only when $B_t^i = 1$; otherwise, it remains unchanged. The amplitude value for each sample is then set as

$$\Omega_t |0\rangle^{\otimes q} = \overline{|0 \oplus B_t^0\rangle} \otimes \left(\overset{q-1}{\underset{i=1}{\otimes}} |0 \oplus B_t^i\rangle \right) \tag{6.27}$$

$$= \overset{q-1}{\underset{i=0}{\otimes}} |S_t^i\rangle = |S_t\rangle.$$

In this manner, a unitary transform that encodes the amplitude information by means of two's complement arithmetic is available during FRQA preparation. The procedure for FRQA preparation is accomplished in the following two steps [20], parts of which are akin to those in FRQI initialization in Sect. 2.2.1:

Step 1: Denoting the tensor products of q two-dimensional identity matrices and l Hadamard matrices by $I^{\otimes q}$ and $H^{\otimes l}$, respectively, the transform $\mathscr{H} = I^{\otimes q} \otimes H^{\otimes l}$ on the initial state $|0\rangle^{\otimes q+l}$ is applied to obtain the intermediate state $|H\rangle$ in the form:

$$|H\rangle = \mathscr{H} \left(|0\rangle^{\otimes q+l} \right) = \frac{1}{\sqrt{2^l}} \sum_{t=0}^{2^l-1} |0\rangle^{\otimes q} |t\rangle. \tag{6.28}$$

Thus far, the time component of the FRQA model has been initialized; therefore, the intermediate state $|H\rangle$ can be regarded as the superposition of all of the samples of an empty digital audio, i.e., with all of the amplitude values set to $|0\rangle$.

Step 2: The value-setting operation Ω_t is used to generate the amplitude information for each sample. Since Ω_t can only handle one sample at a time, considering a 2^l-sized quantum audio, 2^l sub-operations are needed to execute this transformation. R_t is considered an l-controlled Ω_t operation to integrate the amplitude values into each instant of time. For a given sample k, R_k is defined as

$$R_k = \left(I \otimes \sum_{t=0, t \neq k}^{2^l-1} |t\rangle\langle t| \right) + \Omega_k \otimes |k\rangle\langle k|. \tag{6.29}$$

Applying R_k on the intermediate state $|H\rangle$ gives

$$
\begin{aligned}
R_k\left(|H\rangle\right) &= R_k\left(\frac{1}{\sqrt{2^l}}\sum_{t=0}^{2^l-1}|0\rangle^{\otimes q}|t\rangle\right) \\
&= \frac{1}{\sqrt{2^l}}R_k\left(\sum_{t=0,t\neq k}^{2^l-1}|0\rangle^{\otimes q}|t\rangle + |0\rangle^{\otimes q}|k\rangle\right) \\
&= \frac{1}{\sqrt{2^l}}\left(\sum_{t=0,t\neq k}^{2^l-1}|0\rangle^{\otimes q}|t\rangle + \Omega_k|0\rangle^{\otimes q}|k\rangle\right) \\
&= \frac{1}{\sqrt{2^l}}\left(\sum_{t=0,t\neq k}^{2^l-1}|0\rangle^{\otimes q}|t\rangle + |S_k\rangle|k\rangle\right).
\end{aligned}
\tag{6.30}
$$

From Eq. (6.30), it is apparent that for all sub-operations R_t, one has

$$
\mathscr{R}|H\rangle = \left(\prod_{t=0}^{2^l}R_t\right)|H\rangle = \frac{1}{2^{l/2}}\sum_{t=0}^{2^l-1}|S_t\rangle\otimes|t\rangle = |A\rangle.
\tag{6.31}
$$

After the two steps above, the initialized state $|0\rangle^{\otimes q+l}$ is transformed to the desired FRQA state by applying the unitary transform $\mathscr{R}\mathscr{H}$. Subsequently, the complexity of the preparation procedure is the object of focus.

Complexity theory on quantum computation has been studied as regards transformations from the basic gates, hence, the complexity of quantum algorithms is usually computed in terms of quantum gates [1]. Indeed, the circuit complexity depends largely on the strategy employed for circuit decomposition and the basic operation unit [14]. The discussion is confined to the CNOT gate, since it is considered a relatively "expensive" elementary gate that is easily utilized to simulate more complicated gates. The decomposition of complicated circuits into simpler circuit networks composed entirely of basic or elementary quantum gates, i.e., NOT, CNOT, and Toffoli gates, is illustrated in [12]. For instance, an l-controlled NOT gate can be decomposed into $2(l-1)$ Toffoli gates as well as one CNOT gate, and one Toffoli gate can be approximately simulated by six CNOT gates [20].

Based on the above, it is clear that the implementation of transform $\mathscr{H}$ in Step 1 requires l Hadamard gates. In addition, transform $\mathscr{R}$ in Step 2 can be divided into 2^l sub-operations (i.e., R_t) to store the amplitude information for each sample. Therefore, with enough ancillary qubits, each sub-operation R_t can be directly implemented using $2(l-1)$ Toffoli gates and no more than q CNOT gates. Hence, the complexity of preparing a 2^l-sized FRQA state is

$$
2^l\times[2(l-1)\times 6+q] = (12l+q-12)\cdot 2^l,
\tag{6.32}
$$

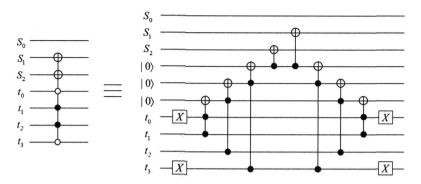

Fig. 6.9 Network to implement the operation R_6 to prepare the sample at $|0110\rangle$ of FRQA audio signal in Fig. 6.8 [20]

which indicates the efficiency of the preparation process [20]. As a further example of the complexity of constructing an FRQA audio, the initialization of the sample is selected at $|0110\rangle$ in Fig. 6.8. The circuit network to implement the operation, i.e., R_6 (when $k = 6$ in Eq. (6.29)), is presented in Fig. 6.9.

6.2.2.2   Retrieval of FRQA Signals

Similar to previous discussions, quantum measurement is a unique tool used to recover classical information from a quantum system. To retrieve the amplitude information of each audio sample, two quantum measurements Γ and M are used:

$$\Gamma = \sum_{t=0}^{2^l-1} I^{\otimes q} \otimes |t\rangle\langle t|, \tag{6.33}$$

$$M = \sum_{m=0}^{2^q-1} m|m\rangle\langle m|. \tag{6.34}$$

First, executing the measurement operation Γ on the time components of the audio content extracts the corresponding information of sample t as $|P_t\rangle$,

$$|P_t\rangle = |S_t\rangle|t\rangle, \tag{6.35}$$

and then the measurement operation M is used to recover the amplitude value from the quantum state:

$$
\begin{aligned}
\langle S_t | M | S_t \rangle &= \langle S_t | \left(\sum_{m=0}^{2^q-1} m |m\rangle \langle m| \right) | S_t \rangle \\
&= \sum_{m=0}^{2^q-1} m \langle S_t | | m \rangle \langle m | | S_t \rangle = S_t.
\end{aligned}
\tag{6.36}
$$

It is apparent that these measurement operations enable the amplitude value of sample k to be recovered. This means that all of the samples in a quantum audio signal can be recovered in the same way, so the original digital audio can be retrieved from the FRQA state.

6.2.3 Quantum Operations to Manipulate Audio Signals

Basic signal operations that propagate more sophisticated applications are the foundations of digital audio processing. The ability to extend similar operations to quantum audio processing is essential to validating the utility of this emerging sub-field of quantum information processing. In this subsection, based on the FRQA representation, a few basic audio signal operations, including signal addition, inversion, delay, and reversal, are presented [20].

6.2.3.1 Signal Addition

Signal addition is among the fundamental operations in audio signal processing. This operation involves the addition of amplitudes of two or more signals at each instant of time. By means of this operation, a series of audio signal processing applications, such as echo, reverb addition, and active noise reduction, can be implemented. Representing the amplitude values in the two's complement system in FRQA audio facilitates the determination of the results of arithmetic operations, and the depiction of the resulting waveforms with respect to the midrange. This arithmetic advantage is exploited to craft the definition of the signal addition operation [20].

Assuming that $|A_x\rangle$ and $|A_y\rangle$ are two 2^l-sized audio segments, which are presented as

$$
|A_x\rangle = \frac{1}{2^{l/2}} \sum_{x=0}^{2^l-1} |S_x\rangle \otimes |t_x\rangle,
\tag{6.37}
$$

where

$$|t_x\rangle = \left|t_x^0 t_x^1 \ldots t_x^{l-1}\right\rangle, t_x^i \in \{0, 1\},$$ (6.38)

$$|S_x\rangle = \left|S_x^0 S_x^1 \ldots S_x^{q-1}\right\rangle, S_x^i \in \{0, 1\},$$ (6.39)

and

$$|A_y\rangle = \frac{1}{2^{l/2}} \sum_{y=0}^{2^l-1} |S_y\rangle \otimes |t_y\rangle,$$ (6.40)

where

$$|t_y\rangle = \left|t_y^0 t_y^1 \ldots t_y^{l-1}\right\rangle, t_y^i \in \{0, 1\},$$ (6.41)

$$|S_y\rangle = \left|S_y^0 S_y^1 \ldots S_y^{q-1}\right\rangle, S_y^i \in \{0, 1\},$$ (6.42)

so the signal addition operation produces the output $|A_z\rangle$:

$$|A_z\rangle = \frac{1}{2^{l/2}} \sum_{z=0}^{2^l-1} |S_z\rangle \otimes |t_z\rangle,$$ (6.43)

where

$$|t_z\rangle = \left|t_z^0 t_z^1 \ldots t_z^{l-1}\right\rangle, t_z^i \in \{0, 1\},$$ (6.44)

$$|S_z\rangle = \left|S_z^0 S_z^1 \ldots S_z^q\right\rangle = |S_x + S_y\rangle, S_z^i \in \{0, 1\},$$ (6.45)

$$t_z = t_x = t_y.$$ (6.46)

To construct a quantum circuit to execute the signal addition operation, two commonly used quantum modules are first introduced. Together with additional control conditions, use of the adder module (in Sect. 3.3.2.1, where the inputs are two q-qubit binary sequences) arises when the addition of amplitude values in two segments of quantum audio at any instant of time is required. The quantum comparator module (in Sect. 4.4.2.1, where the inputs are two l-qubit binary sequences) guarantees that the two operands in the addition are the amplitude values of the two audio segments at the same instant of time.

To formalize, the operation of an FRQA-based signal addition operation $\mathscr{U}_A$ can be written in the form:

$$\mathscr{U}_A : |S_x\rangle|S_y\rangle \rightarrow |S_x\rangle|S_x + S_y\rangle.$$ (6.47)

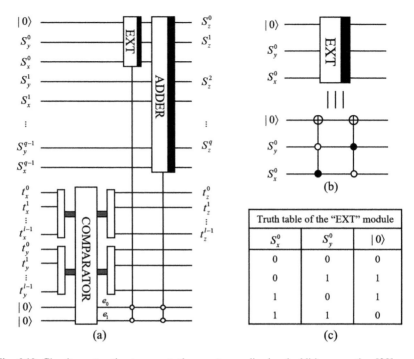

Fig. 6.10 Circuit construction to execute the quantum audio signal addition operation [20]

The quantum circuit to realize the operation $\mathscr{U}_A$ is depicted in Fig. 6.10a, where the adder operation is applied to the amplitude component and the comparator operation is applied to the time component. Additionally, to avoid possible overflow arising from the two's complement addition, a sign-extension module is introduced (EXT in Fig. 6.10b, whose truth table is shown in Fig. 6.10c), which stretches the size of the register (the binary sequence to store the result) while preserving the sign of the operation in the adder module. To conclude the discussion of the signal addition operation, an example of the case when $l = 2$ and $q = 2$ is presented in Fig. 6.11, where the quantum circuit (a) is implemented to add the augend (b) to the addend (c) to produce the output (d).

6.2.3.2 Signal Inversion

Inverting a signal is common and important in signal processing operations. A meaningful use of inversion is to transform signal subtraction to signal addition by means of inverted inputs (audio cancellation is realized as such). In audio signal processing, signal inversion is realized by inverting all of the amplitude values of an audio signal. When amplitude values are represented by bipolar values, the operation essentially reduces to alterations of positive and negative signs of the

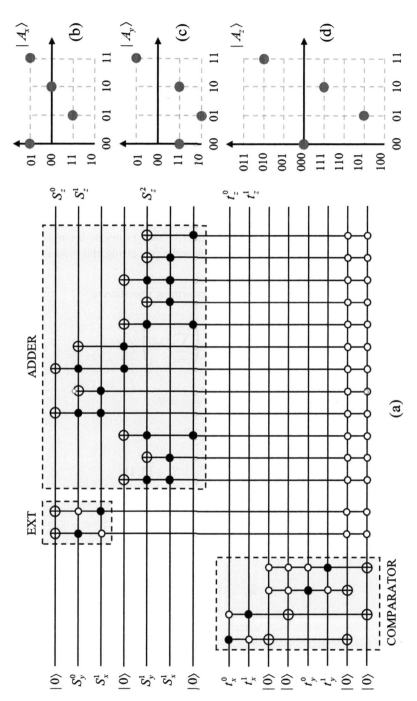

Fig. 6.11 Example of the quantum audio signal addition operation [20]

signals. In this subsection, the FRQA-based signal inversion operation is formalized [20].

Assuming that $|A\rangle$ is an FRQA audio sample in the form presented in Eq. (6.24), the signal inversion operation $\mathcal{U}_I$ applied on $|A\rangle$ will produce the output $|A_I\rangle$ in the form:

$$|A_I\rangle = \frac{1}{2^{l/2}} \sum_{t=0}^{2^l-1} |S_I\rangle \otimes |t\rangle,$$

where

$$|t\rangle = |t_0 t_1 \ldots t_{l-1}\rangle, t_i \in \{0, 1\},$$

$$|S_I\rangle = \left| - S_t^0 S_t^1 \ldots S_t^{q-1} \right\rangle = |- S_t\rangle, S_t^i \in \{0, 1\}. \tag{6.48}$$

Like two's complement arithmetic, an effective way to negate a number is to invert all of the qubits and add "1." In quantum audio processing, this procedure can be explained as follows:

Step 1: Invert all of the qubits in $|S_t\rangle$ by performing operation $\mathcal{U}_I^1$:

$$\mathcal{U}_I^1(|A\rangle) = \frac{1}{2^{l/2}} \mathcal{U}_I^1 \left(\sum_{t=0}^{2^l-1} |S_t\rangle \right) \otimes |t\rangle$$

$$= \frac{1}{2^{l/2}} \sum_{t=0}^{2^l-1} |\overline{S_t}\rangle \otimes |t\rangle,$$

where

$$|S_t\rangle = \left| S_t^0 S_t^1 \ldots S_t^{q-1} \right\rangle, S_t^i \in \{0, 1\},$$

$$|\overline{S_t}\rangle = \left| \overline{S_t^0 S_t^1 \ldots S_t^{q-1}} \right\rangle, \overline{S_t^i} \in \{0, 1\}. \tag{6.49}$$

Step 2: Add "1" to the inverted result $|\overline{S_t}\rangle$ and neglect the overflow by applying operation $\mathcal{U}_I^2$:

$$\mathcal{U}_I^2 : |\overline{S_t}\rangle \rightarrow |S_I\rangle,$$

where

$$|\overline{S_t}\rangle = |\overline{S_t^0 S_t^1 \ldots S_t^{q-1}}\rangle,$$

$$\left| \left(\overline{S_t^0 S_t^1 \ldots S_t^{q-1}} + 1 \right) \bmod 2^q \right\rangle = |S_I\rangle. \tag{6.50}$$

It should be noted that, as is obtained in (classical) digital audio signal processing, a slight skewing of the data range is unavoidable, as the inverted counterpart of $|-2^{q-1}\rangle$ cannot be found in the sampled amplitude values s_t. To overcome this, the discussion is confined to amplitude values within the range from $|-2^{q-1}+1\rangle$ to $|2^{q-1}-1\rangle$. The quantum circuit to invert an FRQA audio signal is shown in Fig. 6.12, where the operation $\mathscr{U}_I^1$ (in Step 1) can be directly implemented using q NOT gates, and in the operation $\mathscr{U}_I^2$ (in Step 2), $q-1$ Toffoli gates and q CNOT gates are required [20].

A simple example to illustrate how a quantum audio signal is inverted will demonstrate the execution of the signal inversion operation. Using the FRQA audio signal $|A_z\rangle$ in Fig. 6.11d as input, the signal inversion circuit in Fig. 6.13a produces the inverted signal $|A_I\rangle$ in Fig. 6.13b.

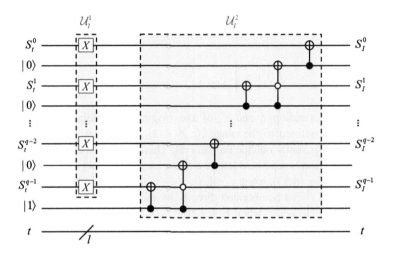

Fig. 6.12 Circuit construction to execute the quantum audio signal inversion operation [20]

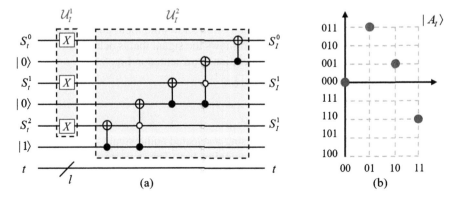

Fig. 6.13 Example of the quantum audio signal inversion operation [20]

6.2.3.3   Signal Delay

Signal delay is an operation that records an input signal and then plays it back after an interval in time. This is a common audio effect that is used to create the sound of a repeating and decaying echo. In this subsection, the FRQA-based signal delay operation is formalized [20].

Assuming $A(t)$ is the original audio signal, then audio signal $B(t)$ is regarded as a delayed version of audio $A(t)$ if

$$A(t) = B(t'), t' = t + \Delta t, \tag{6.51}$$

where t denotes the time information of amplitude values, and Δt is a fixed interval that specifies the desired delay of the system. The signal delay operation $\mathcal{U}_D$ can be described using:

$$\mathcal{U}_D : A(t) \rightarrow B(t'), t' = t + \Delta t, \tag{6.52}$$

$$B(t') = \begin{cases} 0, & 0 \le t' \le \Delta t - 1 \\ A(t), & \Delta t \le t' \le 2^l - 1 \end{cases}. \tag{6.53}$$

The time information t and t' of the original and delayed audio signals, respectively, is confined to the range $[0, 2^l - 1]$, where $\Delta t \le t' = t + \Delta t \le 2^l + \Delta t - 1$ is apparently outside the interval. Therefore, for the current discussion, the time information is separated into two parts, i.e., $[\Delta t, 2^l - 1]$ and $[2^l, 2^l + \Delta t - 1]$.

As shown in Eq. (6.53), when $t' \in [\Delta t, 2^l - 1]$, $B(t') = A(t)$, in which case, the time information t' can be obtained directly by means of the adder module on the time component. However, when $t' \in [2^l, 2^l + \Delta t - 1]$, one needs to employ the carry qubit of the adder module to achieve the interval shift $[2^l, 2^l + \Delta t - 1] - 2^l = [0, \Delta t - 1]$ and set the amplitudes $S_t = 0$ as the delay period.

The general circuit for the quantum audio signal delay operation is presented in Fig. 6.14, which consists of one adder module (applied on the time component) and $2q$ Toffoli gates. In addition, Fig. 6.15 presents a simple example of an FRQA-based signal delay operation, where Fig. 6.15a shows the input audio signal ($l = 3$ and $q = 3$ in Eq. (6.24)) and Fig. 6.15b shows the signal that is delayed by two time units. The quantum circuit for this operation is presented in Fig. 6.16.

6.2.3.4   Signal Reversal

Signal reversal is the process of reversing a selected audio signal such that the end of the signal is heard first and the beginning last. This operation can be used to create interesting sound effects or make small portions of inappropriate language unintelligible. Based on the FRQA state, one can define the signal reversal operation on quantum computers and construct the quantum circuit to accomplish it [20].

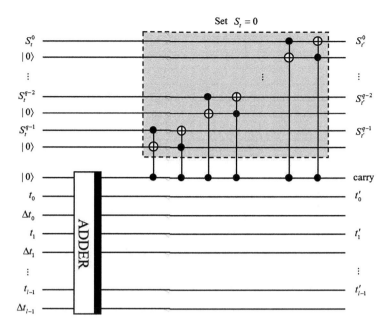

Fig. 6.14 Circuit construction to execute the quantum audio signal delay operation [20]

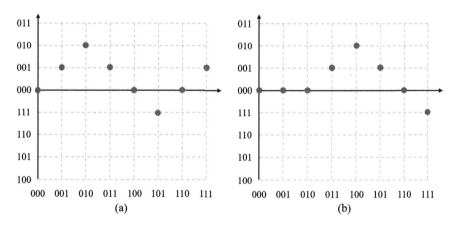

Fig. 6.15 (a) Input quantum audio signal and (b) the signal delayed by two time units [20]

Assuming that $|A\rangle$ is an FRQA audio signal in the form presented in Eq. (6.24), the signal reversal operation $\mathcal{U}_R$ applied on $|A\rangle$ produces an output of the form:

$$|A_R\rangle = \frac{1}{2^{l/2}} \sum_{t=0}^{2^l-1} |S_t\rangle \otimes |\bar{t}\rangle,$$

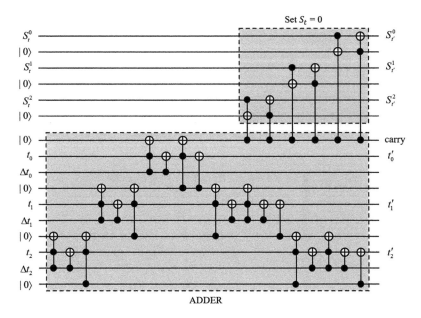

Fig. 6.16 Circuit construction to execute the quantum audio signal delay operation in Fig. 6.15 [20]

where

$$|\bar{t}\rangle = |\overline{t_0 t_1 \dots t_{l-1}}\rangle, \bar{t_i} \in \{0, 1\}. \tag{6.54}$$

Hence the signal reversal operation $\mathscr{U}_R$ can be defined as

$$
\begin{aligned}
\mathscr{U}_R(|A\rangle) &= \frac{1}{2^{l/2}} \sum_{t=0}^{2^l - 1} |S_t\rangle \otimes \mathscr{U}_R(|t\rangle) \\
&= \frac{1}{2^{l/2}} \sum_{t=0}^{2^l - 1} |S_t\rangle \otimes |\bar{t}\rangle.
\end{aligned}
\tag{6.55}
$$

The general circuit to execute the signal reversal operation is presented in Fig. 6.17a. Although this operation can obviously be implemented directly using l NOT gates, to further demonstrate its realization, the quantum audio signal in Fig. 6.15a is used as an input signal, the output of which is presented in Fig. 6.17b. As seen, the result shows that all of the time points are played in a reversed order.

Some control conditions on the time component will allow to confine the execution of the reversal operation $\mathscr{U}_R$ to a desired period. For example, in Fig. 6.18a, the time wire t_0 is employed as the control wire to confine the reversal operation to the last half of the audio signal. As seen from the result in Fig. 6.18b,

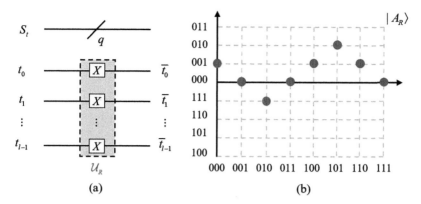

Fig. 6.17 (a) Circuit construction to execute the quantum audio signal reversal operation and (b) a simple example of this operation [20]

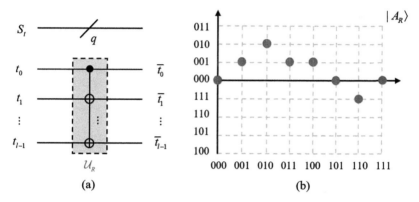

Fig. 6.18 (a) Circuit construction to execute the restricted quantum audio signal reversal operation and (b) a simple example of this operation [20]

only the last four time points (from the original input sample in Fig. 6.15a) are reversed, while the others are retained as in the input signal.

To summarize, as an alternative to QRDA representation, FRQA provides a more intuitive, unrestricted model to accurately represent audio content in the quantum computing domain. The FRQA protocol encodes amplitude values in two's complement notation so that one can exploit its arithmetic advantages to facilitate the construction of quantum circuits for amplitude transformations on audio content. This allows various operations that facilitate advanced audio processing applications. Applications based on the FRQA quantum audio signals, such as quantum audio steganography and watermarking, can be found in [2] and [3].

In this chapter, inspired by QIMP, a timeline of the progress in its two emerging sub-topics, i.e., quantum movie and audio signals, is presented. The formulation, requirements, and applications of both types of media are discussed, leading to the conclusion that they both have potential roles in quantum computation. Learning from experience with digital movies and the quest for talking color quantum movies, the requirements, limitations, and likely impediments to the realization of sound movies in the quantum computing paradigm [5, 22] are assessed.

References

1. Barenco, A., Bennett, C., Cleve, R., Divincenzo, D., Margolus, N., Shor, P., Sleator, T., Smolin, J., Weinfurter, H.: Elementary gates for quantum computation. Phys. Rev. A **52**(5), 3457–3467 (1995)
2. Chen, K., Yan, F., Iliyasu, A., Zhao, J.: Exploring the implementation of steganography protocols on quantum audio signals. Int. J. Theor. Phys. **57**(2), 476–494 (2018)
3. Chen, K., Yan, F., Iliyasu, A., Zhao, J.: Dual quantum audio watermarking schemes based on quantum discrete cosine transform. Int. J. Theor. Phys. **58**(2), 502–521 (2019)
4. Hampapur, A., Weymouth, T., Jain, R.: Digital video segmentation. In: Proceedings of the Second ACM International Conference on Multimedia, pp. 357–364 (1994)
5. Iliyasu, A.: Roadmap to talking quantum movies: a contingent inquiry. IEEE Access **7** (2018)
6. Iliyasu, A., Le, P., Dong, F., Hirota, K.: Restricted geometric transformations and their applications for quantum image watermarking and authentication. In: Proceeding of the 10th Asian Conference on Quantum Information Sciences (AQIS 2010), pp. 96–97 (2010)
7. Iliyasu, A., Le, P., Dong, F., Hirota, K.: A framework for representing and producing movies on quantum computers. Int. J. Quantum Inf. **9**(6), 1459–1497 (2011)
8. Jing, G., Hu, Y., Guo, Y., Yu, Y., Wang, W.: Content-aware video2comics with manga-style layout. IEEE Trans. Multimedia **17**(12), 2122–2133 (2015)
9. Kefauver, A., Patschke, D.: Fundamentals of digital audio. A-R Editions, Middleton (2007)
10. Le, P., Dong, F., Hirota, K.: A flexible representation of quantum images for polynomial preparation, image compression, and processing operations. Quantum Inf. Process. **10**(1), 63–84 (2011)
11. Liao, Z., Yu, Y., Gong, B., Cheng, L.: AudeoSynth: music-driven video montage. ACM Trans. Graphics **34**(4), 1–10 (2015)
12. Nielsen, M., Chuang, I.: Quantum Computation and Quantum Information. Cambridge University Press, Cambridge (2000)
13. Song, X., Wang, H., Venegas-Andraca, S., El-Latif, A.: Quantum video encryption based on qubit-planes controlled-XOR operations and improved logistic map. Phys. A: Stat. Mech. Appl. **537**, 122660 (2020)
14. Vedral, V., Barenco, A., Ekert, A.: Quantum networks for elementary arithmetic operations. Phys. Rev. A **54**(1), 147–153 (1996)
15. Venegas-Andraca, S., Bose, S.: Storing, processing, and retrieving an image using quantum mechanics. In: Proceedings of SPIE Conference of Quantum Information and Computation, vol. 5105, pp. 137–147 (2003)
16. Wang, J.: QRDA: quantum representation of digital audio. Int. J. Theor. Phys. **55**(3), 1622–1641 (2016)
17. Yan, F., Iliyasu, A., Venegas-Andraca, S., Yang, H.: Video encryption and decryption on quantum computers. Int. J. Theor. Phys. **54**(8), 2893–2904 (2015)
18. Yan, F., Iliyasu, A., Khan, A., Yang, H.: Measurements-based moving target detection in quantum video. Int. J. Theor. Phys. **55**(4), 2162–2173 (2016)
19. Yan, F., Iliyasu, A., Hirota, K., Yang, H.: Strategy for quantum image stabilization. Sci. China Inf. Sci. **59**(052102), 1–10 (2016)

20. Yan, F., Iliyasu, A., Guo, Y., Yang, H.: Flexible representation and manipulation of audio signals on quantum computers. Theor. Comput. Sci. **752**, 71–85 (2018)
21. Yan, F., Jiao, S., Iliyasu, A., Jiang, Z.: Chromatic framework for quantum movies and applications in creating montages. Front. Comp. Sci. **12**(4), 736–748 (2018)
22. Yan, F., Iliyasu, A., Chen, K., Yang, H.: Toward realizing talking quantum movies: Synchronization of audio and visual content. Int. J. Inf. Sci. Technol. **3**(4), 24–33 (2019)
23. Zölzer, U.: Digital Audio Signal Processing. Wiley, Hoboken (2008)

Chapter 7
Summary and Discussion

7.1 Concluding Remarks

The notion of quantum computation and quantum information holds expectations of fast and secure computing technologies. Perhaps this is attributable to the parallelism and entanglement properties inherent to information processing on these paradigms. Therefore, extending digital image processing to the quantum computing realm, i.e., QIMP, conjures similar expectations [21].

In earlier chapters, the recent advances in QIMP, including image representations, algorithms required to operate and manipulate the images, and likely applications emanating from them, were highlighted. Notably, the FRQI representation of Le et al. [10] is credited with awakening interest in studies of QIMP, leading to the intensified efforts that have been witnessed recently. Proposed in 2010 and revised a year later [12], this study formulated a universally acceptable formulation to represent an image on a quantum computer. The FRQI representation integrates the spatial and chromatic information required to encode an image in a single formula. In this manner, separate or combined transformations to manipulate the content of such images are easily executable.

Following the successful interpretation of a quantum image, there have been many attempts to utilize (for example, Le et al.'s geometric transformation [9] and color transformation [11]); extend (for example, Sun et al.'s MCQI representation [17] and Zhang et al.'s NEQR representation [22]); and modify (for example, Iliyasu et al.'s quantum movie representation [6] and Wang's quantum audio representation [18]) the FRQI representation for different intents and purposes. Similarly, these

---

©Portions of this chapter are reprinted from Ref. [20], with permission of Springer.

© Springer Nature Singapore Pte Ltd. 2020
F. Yan, S. E. Venegas-Andraca, *Quantum Image Processing*,
https://doi.org/10.1007/978-981-32-9331-1_7

advances have led to many applications in the areas including quantum image security and understanding, and they form the core technologies highlighted in this book.

A search on the Web of Science on the keywords "quantum image processing" shows an obvious increase in papers published since 2010. New research groups and individuals are showing interest in the emerging subdiscipline of QIMP. Research activity is increasing in China, Japan, Mexico, and the USA, while work is emerging from Saudi Arabia, India, Iran, and the UK. These efforts are focused on expanding the applicability of QIMP to realize more classical-like image processing algorithms; propose technologies to physically realize the QIMP hardware; or note challenges that could impede the realization of some QIMP protocols [21].

Inspired by the growing interest in QIMP, efforts to improve on the available literature should be intensified, and similar work in different quantum computing technologies is required. All of these efforts are essential for the realization of smooth, effective, and secure QIMP technologies, to unleash the immense potential of quantum information processing.

7.2   Open Questions and Future Directions

The objectives of the following discussions are twofold. First, targeting researchers already in the area, a few of the open questions emanating from the published literature are identified. The second objective focuses mainly on up and coming researchers who may wish to pursue advanced research in the area. In this regard, several considerations to guide these pursuits have been enumerated. It is hoped that this compendium will invigorate research in the area.

There are several open questions and areas requiring improvement or expansion in QIMP. These include the following [20, 21].

1. In addition to new solutions to pertinent problems, there are untouched areas in which state-of-the-art image-based applications exist in the classical realm. Besides enhancing the algorithmic advantages of existing QIMP protocols, exploration must be intensified to realize applications, such as image registration, mosaic, super-resolution, semantic analysis, reconstruction, enhancement, and fusion, and to solve open problems in science and engineering, such as computer vision, astrophysics, and medicine. Furthermore, advanced toolkits are required to develop quantum algorithms in these fields. These toolkits should include quantum routines for performing basic QIMP tasks.

2. Considering the incipient status of the QIMP subdiscipline, its protocols, and its applications, benchmarks are required to gauge the performance of algorithmic frameworks realizable in the quantum computing realm. For instance, the QIMP algorithms and protocols highlighted in this book rely on the traditional PSNR image quality measure to assess similarity or likeness between images in various applications. As argued in Sect. 4.2.3, given the quantumness inherent to QIMP,

the PSNR image quality is the ill-suited tool to quantify fidelity between quantum images. The QIFM provides the essence for quantum image fidelity assessments. However, similar to advances in digital PSNR, more work is required to improve and concretize its formulation, including experimental validations for its use as an image quality metric on quantum computers.

3. Quantum error correction (QEC) protects quantum information from errors due to decoherence and other quantum noise [16]. QEC is essential in achieving fault-tolerant quantum computation that can deal not only with noise in stored quantum information but also with faults in quantum gates, preparation, and measurements. Most current research on QIMP focuses on image manipulation, with scant attention paid to the physical preparation and retrieval steps of QIMP. These are stages where QEC could make or negate the gains made in the area. It is therefore necessary to consider frameworks for integrating QEC into existing and future QIMP protocols.

4. On digital computers, images and image processing underpinned advanced applications in videos and movies. The quantum movie framework provides a platform to ponder quantum movie representation and production, and it still requires refinement and expansion. Also, text, image, and audio are the main signals humans use in day-to-day interactions. While QIMP has seen tremendous interest and growth, text and audio have received less attention [13]. Recently, however, Wang and Yan separately proposed the quantum representation of digital audio signals. These encouraging efforts, like QIMP, must be scrutinized and enhanced if quantum audio processing is to flourish.

5. QIMP is essentially a strategy for the use of quantum mechanics to store image information. Indeed, one could store any information using a similar strategy. Besides text, audio, and movies, one can study the representation and manipulation of information in quantum machine learning, quantum neural networks, quantum cognition, and quantum cellular automata (as introduced in Sect. 1.2.1). Further, when considered in a more practical manner, research on quantum radar, sensors, robots, and nanoscale materials deserves more attention.

In the hope of stimulating interest in advanced research in QIMP, the following recommendations are made [20, 21]:

1. In this book, several protocols devoted to storing, processing, and retrieving visual information using quantum mechanical systems have been described. Some computational advantages and disadvantages of those protocols arise upon comparison (e.g., the number of qubits used to store images). However, a comprehensive comparative analysis has not yet been produced to clearly exhibit the value and usefulness of those quantum protocols in both theoretical and applied computer science, as well as in engineering applications. For each existing QIMP protocol, one must compute accurate formulae for the computational complexity of algorithms used for storing and retrieving images, as well as the physical resources (both quantum and classical) employed for those tasks. This is crucial for two reasons. First is that the complexity of QIMP algorithms is usually computed in terms of quantum gates, while classical complexity is

usually measured by running time. Second is that quantum hardware designers must clearly identify the amount of classical and quantum resources needed to implement a given QIMP protocol.

2. While advanced classical-like QIMP technologies are desirable, one must be mindful of the contrariety that permeates digital and quantum information processing. The very properties often credited for the power of quantum computation forestall the realization of some classical operations. Consequently, in future research, the temptation to realize the quantum version of every digital image processing application must be resisted. Efforts should focus on areas and applications where the gains of quantum computation can be exploited. Additionally, since QIMP is still in its infancy, it would enhance the literature to identify traditional image processing tasks that cannot be accomplished on the quantum computing paradigm because they violate important postulates.

3. Quantum algorithms can be used to solve problems in the realms of classical or quantum information. Published results in the field have so far focused on processing images in quantum mechanical systems by referring to their classical counterparts. Of course, this work has been of paramount importance to build the foundations of the field and attract the attention of applied computer scientists and engineers who work in related areas. Algorithms developed to process and visualize quantum information can become the building blocks of new methods to present complex data to both experts and the general public [1]. Scrutinizing models and understanding results via data visualization is a fruitful approach for efficient problem solving. First, visualization of experimental results is of great value in many scientific disciplines (e.g., astrophysics, bioinformatics, and nanotechnology). Second, engineering solutions focus on performance and accuracy, either as a result of market demands or as a key technical requirement within a given domain of application (for example, digital processing of medical images [3]). In both contexts, researchers working on QIMP can exploit the physical and mathematical properties of quantum computing (e.g., entanglement and parallelism) and propose novel uses of existing quantum algorithms and protocols (e.g., quantum teleportation [2]) to devise innovative solutions.

4. One of the main goals in quantum computing is to design algorithms that are more efficient (i.e., faster) than their classical counterparts. This usually rests on the implicit assumption that both quantum and classical algorithms are to be executed on general-purpose and universal computers. Unfortunately, the quest for quantum algorithms that run on universal computers has retarded the development of advanced quantum algorithms for specific architectures. No matter how advanced a protocol, it will be less meaningful without physical hardware to utilize it. Although interest in quantum hardware design is growing—both Intel and IBM are working on quantum chip technologies [4, 8]—exploration of quantum computation to support the realization of QIMP-specific hardware remains insufficient to experimentally validate QIMP technologies [7]. The experimental validation of QIMP protocols by improving the synergy between researchers of quantum computation in physics, optics, computer science, and engineering must be encouraged. In our opinion, specific-purpose hardware is

a blue-sky arena for the development of QIMP algorithms as well as to attract funding from industrial partners (for example, QIMP algorithms to run on specific-purpose devices like advanced digital cameras or next-generation TV technology) [15].

5. So far, all of the so-called experimental implementation of QIMP protocols has been restricted to classical computing resources and MATLAB simulations based on linear algebra, with complex vectors as quantum states and unitary matrices as unitary transforms. These offer a rather restrictive implementation of the expected power of quantum computation. Therefore, as efforts to improve and expand QIMP technologies are intensified, it is important to identify the role of quantum computing software in implementing various algorithms so that they can complement the hardware. Although many efforts have been made, e.g., the IBM QISKIT quantum toolkit [5] and other quantum software [19] and simulators [14], much is still required before robust quantum software that can match the advances in digital image processing is realized. In terms of QIMP, insights from computer science and physics must be combined to determine which environment is better suited to certain algorithms.

In conclusion, quantum image processing (QIMP) is an emerging area focused on extending conventional image processing tasks and applications to the quantum computing framework. While increasing numbers of researchers are working in the QIMP field, some fundamental problems remain unsolved. It is hoped that the systematic introduction, open questions, and future directions identified in this book will arouse the interest of more researchers and accelerate efforts toward realizing more sophisticated QIMP-based technologies.

References

1. Borkin, M., Vo, A., Bylinskii, Z., Isola, P.S.S., Oliva, A., Pfister, H.: What makes a visualization memorable? IEEE Trans. Vis. Comput. Graph. **19**(12), 2306–2315 (2013)
2. Bouwmeester, D., Pan, J., Mattle, K., Eibl, M., Weinfurter, H., Zeilinger, A.: Experimental quantum teleportation. Nature **390**, 575–579 (1997)
3. Eklund, A., Dufort, P., Forsberg, D., LaConte, S.: Medical image processing on the GPU—past, present and future. Med. Image Anal. **17**(8), 1073–1094 (2013)
4. Hsu, J.: CES 2018: Intel's 49-Qubit Chip Shoots for Quantum Supremacy. https://spectrum. ieee.org/tech-talk/computing/hardware/intels-49qubit-chip-aims-for-quantum-supremacy (2018)
5. IBM: An Open-source Quantum Computing Framework for Leveraging Today's Quantum Processors in Research, Education, and Business. https://qiskit.org/ (2019)
6. Iliyasu, A., Le, P., Dong, F., Hirota, K.: A framework for representing and producing movies on quantum computers. Int. J. Quantum Inf. **9**(6), 1459–1497 (2011)
7. Iliyasu, A., Le, P., Yan, F., Sun, B., Garcia, J., Dong, F., Hirota, K.: Insights into the viability of using available photonic quantum technologies for efficient image and video processing applications. Int. J. Unconv. Comput. **9**(1-2), 125–151 (2013)
8. Knight, W.: IBM Raises the Bar with a 50-Qubit Quantum Computer. https://www. technologyreview.com/s/609451/ibm-raises-the-bar-with-a-50-qubit-quantum-computer/ (2017)

9. Le, P., Iliyasu, A., Dong, F., Hirota, K.: Fast geometric transformations on quantum images. IAENG Int. J. Appl. Math. **40**(3), 113–123 (2010)
10. Le, P., Dong, F., Hirota, K.: A flexible representation of quantum images for polynomial preparation, image compression, and processing operations. Quantum Inf. Process. **10**(1), 63–84 (2011)
11. Le, P., Iliyasu, A., Dong, F., Hirota, K.: Efficient colour transformations on quantum image. J. Adv. Comput. Intell. Intell. Inform. **15**(6), 698–706 (2011)
12. Le, P., Iliyasu, A., Dong, F., Hirota, K.: A flexible representation and invertible transformations for images on quantum computers. New Adv. Intell. Signal Process. Stud. Comput. Intell. **372**, 179–202 (2011)
13. Li, H., Fan, P., Xia, H., Peng, H., Song, S.: Quantum implementation circuits of quantum signal representation and type conversion. IEEE Trans. Circuits Syst. Regul. Pap. **66**(1), 341–354 (2019)
14. List of QC Simulators. https://quantiki.org/wiki/list-qc-simulators. Accessed 14 Nov 2016
15. Mastriani, M.: Quantum Boolean image denoising. Quantum Inf. Process **14**(5), 1647–1673 (2015)
16. Nielsen, M., Chuang, I.: Quantum Computation and Quantum Information. Cambridge University, Cambridge (2000)
17. Sun, B., Iliyasu, A., Yan, F., Dong, F., Hirota, K.: An RGB multi-channel representation for images on quantum computers. J. Adv. Comput. Intell. Intell. Inform. **17**(3), 404–417 (2013)
18. Wang, J.: QRDA: quantum representation of digital audio. Int. J. Theor. Phys. **55**(3), 1622–1641 (2016)
19. Wecker, D., Svore, K.: LIQUi|⟩: a software design architecture and domain-specific language for quantum computing. arXiv:1402.4467v1 (2014)
20. Yan, F., Iliyasu, A., Venegas-Andraca, S.: A survey of quantum image representations. Quantum Inf. Process. **15**(1), 1–35 (2016)
21. Yan, F., Iliyasu, A., Le, P.: Quantum image processing: a review of advances in its security technologies. Int. J. Quantum Inf. **15**(3), 1730001 (2017)
22. Zhang, Y., Lu, K., Gao, Y., Wang, M.: NEQR: a novel enhanced quantum representation of digital images. Quantum Inf. Process **12**(8), 2833–2860 (2013)

Appendix

The key to understanding the properties of quantum computation is to have a profound knowledge of the mathematical disciplines involved in describing quantum phenomena, namely linear algebra and probability theory. These two fields of mathematics are used to describe the basic behavior of closed quantum systems in the postulates of quantum mechanics.

This appendix is devoted to providing a succinct introduction to the mathematical foundation required in quantum image processing. Quantum computation makes extensive use of complex numbers, the basic operations of which are defined first.

Definition A.1 (The Set of Complex Numbers $\mathbb{C}$) Let $a, b \in \mathbb{R}$ and $i = \sqrt{-1}$. Then, any number of the form $z = a + bi$ is known as a complex number, where a and b are the real and imaginary parts of z, respectively. The set of all complex numbers is denoted by $\mathbb{C}$.

Definition A.2 (Addition and Multiplication in $\mathbb{C}$) Let $z_1, z_2 \in \mathbb{C}$, where $z_1 = a + bi$ and $z_2 = c + di$. The following operations are defined.

1. Addition: $z_1 + z_2 = (a + bi) + (c + di) = (a + c) + (b + d)i$.
2. Multiplication: $z_1 z_2 = (a + bi)(c + di) = (ac - bd) + (bc + ad)i$.

Definition A.3 (Conjugation and Norm in $\mathbb{C}$) Let $z \in \mathbb{C}$, where $z = a + bi$. The following operations are defined.

1. Conjugation: $\bar{z} = a - bi$.
2. Norm: $|z| = \sqrt{a^2 + b^2}$.

The set $\mathbb{C}$ is an example of a fundamental algebraic structure in mathematics noted as a field, which is defined as follows.

Definition A.4 (Field) A field $(\mathbb{F}, +, \cdot)$ is a set $\mathbb{F}$ with two operations known as addition $(+)$ and multiplication $(\cdot)$ that satisfies the following properties.

© Springer Nature Singapore Pte Ltd. 2020
F. Yan, S. E. Venegas-Andraca, *Quantum Image Processing*,
https://doi.org/10.1007/978-981-32-9331-1

1. Closure under addition: $\forall\, x, y \in \mathbb{F} \;\Rightarrow\; x + y \in \mathbb{F}$.
2. Commutativity of addition: $\forall\, x, y \in \mathbb{F} \;\Rightarrow\; x + y = y + x$.
3. Associativity of addition: $\forall\, x, y, z \in \mathbb{F} \;\Rightarrow\; x + (y + z) = (x + y) + z$.
4. Additive identity: $\exists\, 0 \in \mathbb{F}$ such that $\forall\, x \in \mathbb{F} \;\Rightarrow\; x + 0 = 0 + x = x$.
5. Additive inverses: For each $x \in \mathbb{F}$, $\exists -x \in \mathbb{F}$ such that $x + (-x) = -x + x = 0$.
6. Closure under multiplication: $\forall\, x, y \in \mathbb{F} \;\Rightarrow\; xy \in \mathbb{F}$.
7. Commutativity of multiplication: $\forall\, x, y \in \mathbb{F} \;\Rightarrow\; xy = yx$.
8. Associativity of multiplication: $\forall\, x, y, z \in \mathbb{F} \;\Rightarrow\; x(yz) = (xy)z$.
9. Multiplicative identity: $\exists\, 1 \in \mathbb{F}$ such that $\forall\, x \in \mathbb{F} \;\Rightarrow\; x1 = 1x = x$.
10. Multiplicative inverses: For each $x \in \mathbb{F}$, $\exists\, x^{-1} \in \mathbb{F}$ such that $xx^{-1} = x^{-1}x = 1$.
11. Distributivity of multiplication over addition: $\forall\, x, y, z \in \mathbb{F} \;\Rightarrow\; x(y + z) = xy + xz$.

Furthermore, the concept of $\mathbb{R}^2$, the visual representation of which is described as the Cartesian plane, is defined as

$$\mathbb{R}^2(\mathbb{R}) = \left\{ \begin{pmatrix} a \\ b \end{pmatrix} \;\middle|\; a, b \in \mathbb{R} \text{ and scalars } \alpha \in \mathbb{R} \right\}.$$

The set $\mathbb{R}^2$ is an example of a vector space under the typical operations of vector addition and scalar multiplication.

Definition A.5 (Vector Space) A set $\mathbb{V}$, together with a field $\mathbb{F}$ and the operations known as vector addition and scalar multiplication, is defined as a vector space if it satisfies the following axioms.

1. $\forall\, x, y \in \mathbb{V} \Rightarrow x + y \in \mathbb{V}$.
2. $\forall\, x, y \in \mathbb{V} \Rightarrow x + y = y + x$.
3. $\forall\, x, y, z \in \mathbb{V} \Rightarrow x + (y + z) = (x + y) + z$.
4. $\exists! 0 \in \mathbb{V}$ such that $\forall x \in \mathbb{V} \Rightarrow x + 0 = 0 + x = x$.
5. For each $x \in \mathbb{V}$, $\exists! - x \in \mathbb{V}$ such that $x + (-x) = -x + x = 0$.
6. $\forall\, x \in \mathbb{V}, \alpha \in \mathbb{F} \;\Rightarrow\; \alpha x \in \mathbb{V}$.
7. $\forall\, x \in \mathbb{V} \Rightarrow 1x = x$, where 1 is the multiplicative identity of $\mathbb{F}$.
8. $\forall\, x \in \mathbb{V} \Rightarrow 0x = 0$, where 0 is the additive identity of $\mathbb{F}$.
9. $\forall\, x \in \mathbb{V}, \alpha, \beta \in \mathbb{F} \Rightarrow (\alpha + \beta)x = \alpha x + \beta x$.
10. $\forall\, x \in \mathbb{V}, \alpha, \beta \in \mathbb{F} \Rightarrow \alpha(\beta x) = (\alpha\beta)x$.
11. $\forall\, x, y \in \mathbb{V}, \alpha \in \mathbb{F} \Rightarrow \alpha(x + y) = \alpha x + \alpha y$.

In addition to vector addition and scalar multiplication, the dot product in $\mathbb{R}^2$ is always an essential operation.

Definition A.6 (Dot Product in $\mathbb{R}^2$) Let $x, y \in \mathbb{R}^2$, and then

$$x \cdot y = \begin{pmatrix} x_1 \\ x_2 \end{pmatrix} \cdot \begin{pmatrix} y_1 \\ y_2 \end{pmatrix} = x_1 y_1 + x_2 y_2.$$

The set $\mathbb{C}^2$, i.e., the set of ordered pairs with complex entries defined over the set of complex numbers, is defined as

$$\mathbb{C}^2(\mathbb{C}) = \left\{ \begin{pmatrix} a \\ b \end{pmatrix} \ \middle| \ a, b \in \mathbb{C} \text{ and scalars } \alpha \in \mathbb{C} \right\},$$

which is also a vector space under the operations of vector addition and scalar multiplication as defined in the following:

1. Vector addition: $\begin{pmatrix} a_1 \\ b_1 \end{pmatrix} + \begin{pmatrix} a_2 \\ b_2 \end{pmatrix} = \begin{pmatrix} a_1 + a_2 \\ b_1 + b_2 \end{pmatrix}.$

2. Scalar multiplication: $\alpha \begin{pmatrix} a \\ b \end{pmatrix} = \begin{pmatrix} \alpha a \\ \alpha b \end{pmatrix}.$

Definition A.7 (Dot Product in $\mathbb{C}^2$) Let $w, z \in \mathbb{C}^2$, and then

$$w \cdot z = \begin{pmatrix} w_1 \\ w_2 \end{pmatrix} \cdot \begin{pmatrix} z_1 \\ z_2 \end{pmatrix} = (\bar{w}_1, \bar{w}_2) \begin{pmatrix} z_1 \\ z_2 \end{pmatrix} = \bar{w}_1 z_1 + \bar{w}_2 y_2.$$

The dot product of two vectors w and z in $\mathbb{C}^2$ is the usual row-column matrix multiplication, where the entries of the row vector are the complex conjugates of the entries of w (note that $w \cdot z \neq z \cdot w$, in general). It can be straightforwardly generalized to $\mathbb{C}^n$, which is defined as follows.

Definition A.8 (Dot Product in $\mathbb{C}^n$) Let $w, z \in \mathbb{C}^n$, and then

$$w \cdot z = \begin{pmatrix} w_1 \\ w_2 \\ \vdots \\ w_n \end{pmatrix} \cdot \begin{pmatrix} z_1 \\ z_2 \\ \vdots \\ z_n \end{pmatrix} = (\bar{w}_1, \bar{w}_2, \ldots, \bar{w}_n) \begin{pmatrix} z_1 \\ z_2 \\ \vdots \\ z_n \end{pmatrix} = \sum_{i=1}^{n} \bar{w}_i z_i.$$

The dot product is a particular case of a more general concept noted as the inner product, which is presented below.

Definition A.9 (Inner Product) Let $\mathbb{V}(\mathbb{C})$ denote a vector space $\mathbb{V}$ defined over the set of complex numbers $\mathbb{C}$ and $a, b \in \mathbb{V}(\mathbb{C})$. Then, the inner product function $(\ ,\ )$ is defined as

$$(\ ,\ ) : \mathbb{V} \times \mathbb{V} \to \mathbb{C},$$

with the following properties:

1. $\forall a \in \mathbb{V} \Rightarrow (a, a) \geq 0$ and $(a, a) = 0 \Leftrightarrow a = 0.$
2. $\forall a, b \in \mathbb{V} \Rightarrow (a, b) = (b, a)^*.$
3. $\forall a, b_i \in \mathbb{V}, \alpha_i \in \mathbb{C}, i \in \mathbb{N} \Rightarrow (a, \sum_i \alpha_i b_i) = \sum_i \alpha_i (a, b_i).$

Definition A.10 (Hilbert Space) A Hilbert space $\mathcal{H}$ is an inner product vector space defined over the complex number system. An example of a Hilbert space is $\mathbb{C}^2(\mathbb{C})$, i.e., the complex bi-dimensional vector space defined over the field of complex numbers with an inner product.

Using the standard notation in algebra, an element $x \in \mathbb{R}^2$ may be written as

$$x = a\hat{i} + b\hat{j},$$

where

$$\hat{i} = \begin{pmatrix} 1 \\ 0 \end{pmatrix} \text{ and } \hat{j} = \begin{pmatrix} 0 \\ 1 \end{pmatrix},$$

are the canonical bases of $\mathbb{R}^2$.

In quantum mechanics and, as a heritage, in quantum computation, Dirac notation is a most convenient notation with which to write elements of vector spaces and consequently write quantum bits.

The symbol "$| \ \rangle$" is known as a ket (always a column vector) and the symbol "$\langle \ |$" is known as a bra (always a row vector). Therefore, $x = a\hat{i} + b\hat{j}$ would be written in Dirac notation as

$$|x\rangle = a|i\rangle + b|j\rangle = a \begin{pmatrix} 1 \\ 0 \end{pmatrix} + b \begin{pmatrix} 0 \\ 1 \end{pmatrix}.$$

Definition A.11 (Ket and Bra–Dirac Notation) Let $\mathcal{H}$ be a Hilbert space, and then the ket and bra in $\mathcal{H}$ are defined as follows.

1. A vector $\psi \in \mathcal{H}$ is denoted by $|\psi\rangle$ and is referred to as a ket. The elements $|\psi\rangle$ of $\mathcal{H}$ are represented as column vectors by choosing a basis for $\mathcal{H}$. For example, let $\mathcal{H} = \mathbb{C}^2$ and choose the vector basis $\{|0\rangle, |1\rangle\}$, where

$$|0\rangle = \begin{pmatrix} 1 \\ 0 \end{pmatrix} \text{ and } |1\rangle = \begin{pmatrix} 0 \\ 1 \end{pmatrix}.$$

Then, every element $|\psi\rangle \in \mathcal{H}$ can be written as

$$|\psi\rangle = \alpha|0\rangle + \beta|1\rangle = \alpha \begin{pmatrix} 1 \\ 0 \end{pmatrix} + \beta \begin{pmatrix} 0 \\ 1 \end{pmatrix}, \alpha, \beta \in \mathbb{C}.$$

2. Let $|\psi\rangle = \alpha|0\rangle + \beta|1\rangle$. The bra $\langle\psi|$ is defined as

$$\langle\psi| = \alpha^*\langle 0| + \beta^*\langle 1|,$$

where $\alpha^*, \beta^* \in \mathbb{C}$, $\langle 0| = (1, 0)$, and $\langle 1| = (0, 1)$. In other words, $\langle \psi| \leftrightarrow |\psi\rangle$ corresponds to transposition and conjugation. For example, let

$$|\psi\rangle = \frac{i}{\sqrt{2}}|0\rangle + \frac{1}{\sqrt{2}}|1\rangle = \frac{i}{\sqrt{2}}\begin{pmatrix} 1 \\ 0 \end{pmatrix} + \frac{1}{\sqrt{2}}\begin{pmatrix} 0 \\ 1 \end{pmatrix} = \begin{pmatrix} \frac{i}{\sqrt{2}} \\ \frac{1}{\sqrt{2}} \end{pmatrix},$$

and then

$$\langle \psi| = \frac{-i}{\sqrt{2}}\langle 0| + \frac{1}{\sqrt{2}}\langle 1| = \frac{-i}{\sqrt{2}}(1, \ 0) + \frac{1}{\sqrt{2}}(0, \ 1) = \left(\frac{-i}{\sqrt{2}}, \frac{1}{\sqrt{2}} \right).$$

Definition A.12 (Dot Product in $\mathbb{C}^2$ Using Dirac Notation) Let $|w\rangle, |z\rangle \in \mathbb{C}^2$ with $|w\rangle = \begin{pmatrix} w_1 \\ w_2 \end{pmatrix}$ and $|z\rangle = \begin{pmatrix} z_1 \\ z_2 \end{pmatrix}$. The inner product of $|w\rangle$ and $|z\rangle$ is defined as

$$(|w\rangle, |z\rangle) = \langle w||z\rangle = \langle w|z\rangle = \begin{pmatrix} \bar{w}_1, \bar{w}_2 \end{pmatrix}\begin{pmatrix} z_1 \\ z_2 \end{pmatrix} = \bar{w}_1 z_1 + \bar{w}_2 y_2.$$

Definition A.13 (Dot Product in $\mathbb{C}^n$ Using Dirac Notation) Let $|w\rangle, |z\rangle \in \mathbb{C}^n$, and then

$$(|w\rangle, |z\rangle) = \begin{pmatrix} \bar{w}_1, \bar{w}_2, \ldots, \bar{w}_n \end{pmatrix}\begin{pmatrix} z_1 \\ z_2 \\ \vdots \\ z_n \end{pmatrix} = \sum_{i=1}^n \bar{w}_i z_i.$$

Furthermore, the linear operator, a mathematical entity that will be used in quantum computation to design quantum gates and quantum circuits, is defined.

Definition A.14 (Linear Operator) A linear operator between Hilbert spaces $\mathcal{H}_1$ and $\mathcal{H}_2$ is defined as any function $\hat{A} : \mathcal{H}_1 \rightarrow \mathcal{H}_2$ that is linear in its inputs,

$$\hat{A}\left(\sum_i \alpha_i |\psi_i\rangle \right) = \sum_i \alpha_i \hat{A}|\psi_i\rangle.$$

Definition A.15 Let $|\psi\rangle, |a\rangle \in \mathcal{H}_1$ and $|\phi\rangle \in \mathcal{H}_2$, and then the outer product is the linear operator from $\mathcal{H}_1$ to $\mathcal{H}_2$ defined by

$$(|\phi\rangle\langle\psi|)|a\rangle \equiv (\langle\psi|a\rangle)|\phi\rangle.$$

Note that a summation of outer products is also a linear operator.

To exemplify how linear transformations written as summations of outer products interact with kets, the Hadamard operator is defined as

$$\hat{H} = \frac{1}{\sqrt{2}}(|0\rangle\langle 0| + |0\rangle\langle 1| + |1\rangle\langle 0| - |1\rangle\langle 1|).$$

The action of $\hat{H}$ on ket $|0\rangle$ is given by

$$\hat{H}|0\rangle = \left(\tfrac{1}{\sqrt{2}}|0\rangle\langle 0| + \tfrac{1}{\sqrt{2}}|0\rangle\langle 1| + \tfrac{1}{\sqrt{2}}|1\rangle\langle 0| - \tfrac{1}{\sqrt{2}}|1\rangle\langle 1|\right)|0\rangle$$

$$= \tfrac{\langle 0|0\rangle}{\sqrt{2}}|0\rangle + \tfrac{\langle 1|0\rangle}{\sqrt{2}}|0\rangle + \tfrac{\langle 0|0\rangle}{\sqrt{2}}|1\rangle - \tfrac{\langle 1|0\rangle}{\sqrt{2}}|1\rangle$$

$$= \tfrac{1}{\sqrt{2}}|0\rangle + \tfrac{1}{\sqrt{2}}|1\rangle.$$

Finally, the tensor product, a method used to build vector spaces from other vector spaces, is defined, which is crucial to representing multiparticle quantum systems.

Definition A.16 (Tensor Product) Let $\mathbb{V}$ and $\mathbb{W}$ be vector spaces (over a field $\mathbb{F}$) of dimension m and n, respectively, and $\mathbb{X}$ be the tensor product of $\mathbb{V}$ and $\mathbb{W}$, i.e., $\mathbb{X} = \mathbb{V} \otimes \mathbb{W}$. The elements of $\mathbb{X}$ are linear combinations of vectors $|a\rangle \otimes |b\rangle$, where $|a\rangle \in \mathbb{V}$ and $|b\rangle \in \mathbb{W}$. Let $\hat{A}, \hat{B}$ be linear operators on $\mathbb{V}$ and $\mathbb{W}$, respectively, and $\alpha \in \mathbb{F}$. Then,

1. $\alpha(|a_1\rangle \otimes |b_1\rangle) = (\alpha|a_1\rangle) \otimes |b_1\rangle = |a_1\rangle \otimes (\alpha|b_1\rangle)$.
2. $(|a_1\rangle + |a_2\rangle) \otimes |b_1\rangle = |a_1\rangle \otimes |b_1\rangle + |a_2\rangle \otimes |b_1\rangle$.
3. $|a_1\rangle \otimes (|b_1\rangle + |b_2\rangle) = |a_1\rangle \otimes |b_1\rangle + |a_1\rangle \otimes |b_2\rangle$.
4. $\hat{A} \otimes \hat{B}(|a_1\rangle \otimes |b_1\rangle) = \hat{A}|a_1\rangle \otimes \hat{B}|b_1\rangle$.

Shorthand notation for $|a\rangle \otimes |b\rangle$ is simply $|ab\rangle$ or $|a, b\rangle$. In addition, the tensor product of $|a\rangle$ with itself n times $|a\rangle \otimes |a\rangle \otimes \ldots \otimes |a\rangle$ can also be conveniently written as $|a\rangle^{\otimes n}$.

A handy and simple matrix representation of the tensor product is the Kronecker product. Let $A = (a_{ij})$ and $B = (b_{ij})$ be two matrices of order $m \times n$ and $p \times q$, respectively. Then, $A \otimes B$ is of order $mp \times nq$, which is given by

$$A \otimes B = \begin{pmatrix} a_{11}B & a_{12}B & \ldots & a_{1n}B \\ a_{21}B & a_{22}B & \ldots & a_{2n}B \\ \vdots & \vdots & \vdots & \vdots \\ a_{m1}B & a_{m2}B & \ldots & a_{mn}B \end{pmatrix}.$$

In this appendix, several important notions of linear algebra are introduced. For comprehensive introductions to the scientific, engineering, and physical disciplines that constitute quantum computation (and thereby quantum image processing), readers may refer to [1–4].

References

1. Bouwmeester, D., Ekert, A., Zeilinger, A.E.: The Physics of Quantum Information. Springer, Berlin (2001)
2. Imre, S., Balázs, F.: Quantum Computing and Communications: An Engineering Approach. Wiley, Chichester (2005)
3. Lanzagorta, M., Uhlmann, J.: Quantum Computer Science. Morgan and Claypool, San Rafael (2009)
4. Vedral, V.: Introduction to Quantum Information Science. Oxford University, Oxford (2006)